CH00833324

DOWNSIDE AND THE WAR

Downside & the War

1914—1919

Containing List of Old Gregorians who served in H.M. Forces during the War, together with Memoirs of those Killed in Action or who died on Active Service

COMPILED BY DOM LUCIUS GRAHAM, O.S.B.

Printed for
DOWNSIDE SCHOOL
At Hudson & Kearns, Ltd.
London

MCMXXV

Downside and the War

URING the years 1914-1919, when the Great War was making its heavy toll on the British Armies, it was our custom to give a short obituary notice in the *Downside Review* of Old Gregorians who fell in battle. It was felt, however, that something more permanent and substantial should be done to place on record the splendid deeds of our Old Boys and to show our appreciation and pride in their bravery and sacrifice. With this end in view Dom Lucius Graham was asked to be responsible for producing the proposed work. Dom Lucius was in a position to do this work better than anyone else, as it so happened that practically every Old Gregorian who fell during the War was personally known to him either as a companion when at school or as a boy in the school since he has been on the staff. There can, indeed, be few compilers of War Records who could claim such knowledge of those about whom they were writing. After nearly ten years of most careful work and thought, Dom Lucius gives us this excellent volume, containing as it does a list of all Old Gregorians who served in the armies, with their rank and distinctions and, most important of all, a very comprehensive and accurate record of the lives of those who were killed or died on service. We are much indebted to parents and friends for placing at his disposal letters and records of the greatest value.

We are sure that all Gregorians and the parents, relatives and friends of those whose names are on the Roll of Honour will join together in expressing their gratitude to Dom Lucius for the great work he has done in producing this volume, which will stand as a permanent and worthy record throughout the ages of the splendid achievements and bravery of Old Gregorians who answered their country's call at the hour of her greatest trial.

In the book are included photographs of the War Memorial Cross which stands in front of the main school buildings, and also several photographs of the Nave of the Abbey Church, designed by Sir Giles Gilbert Scott, and built by the generosity of our friends and the Downside community as a memorial of those who fell, and also as a thank-offering for the many who were spared.

We trust that the present and future generations who have the privilege of using the church will from time to time refer to the pages of this book so as to get an insight into the lives and characters of those to whose memory the Nave has been erected, and will thereby be inspired to put their best into their own lives and show themselves worthy of the great sacrifice which was made by their predecessors.

R. S. TRAFFORD
(Headmaster)

July 11th, 1925

Contents

List of Memoirs

THE NAVE

Downside and the War

In Memory of the Old Gregorians who have died for their Country

ALMA MATER, who reignest for ever
    Supreme in each heart,
With a love that the years cannot sever,
    Nor distance can part,

Whose spirit, in days of our boyhood,
    We learnt to obey,
And revere with a trust that will fade not
    Till life pass away;

All honour to those thou hast given
    For Freedom to fight,
Who have offered their young lives to heaven
    For Justice and Right,

Who fulfilled the high mission thou gavest
    Thy children to do,
Facing death 'midst the ranks of the bravest,
    The noble and true.

They have fought the good fight and have conquered
    And gone to their rest,
And their names we will keep in thy annals,
    Loved, honoured, and blest.

And Downside will tell of the story,
    Through ages to be,
Of our heroes who, covered with glory,
    Died worthy of thee.   G. L. G.

Downside in the Services
1914-1919

The following list contains the names of all Old Boys known to have been on Active Service in the Navy or Army during the period covered by the War. For convenience of reference it has been arranged in alphabetical order regardless of rank; the dates after each name indicate the period spent in the School. As this list is concerned only with the services of Old Gregorians during the War, the rank given in each case is the ultimate one held before the close of hostilities; no reference has been made to promotions and other changes which have occurred since the signing of Peace.

AGIUS, ALFRED ALBERT, September, 1900, to July, 1905.
Major, London Regiment. M.C., Despatches, Wounded.

AGIUS, ARTHUR JOSEPH, September, 1903, to December, 1910.
Capt. and Adj., London Regiment. M.C., Despatches.

AGIUS, EDGAR EMMANUEL, September, 1900, to July, 1906.
Capt., London Regiment. Wounded.

AGIUS, RICHARD VICTOR, September, 1907, to July, 1914.
Capt., London Regiment. Killed in Action.

AGIUS, Rev. DOM TANCRED AMBROSE, September, 1900, to July, 1908.
C.F. (4th Class), B.E.F. Despatches, Wounded.

AINSCOUGH, RICHARD, September, 1910, to December, 1915.
Lieut., Royal Field Artillery.

ALLPRESS, HOWARD VINCENT, September, 1906, to July, 1909.
Capt., Royal Garrison Artillery. Wounded.

AMBROSE, CHARLES NAPIER, September, 1886, to July, 1887.
Capt., Royal Engineers.

ARATHOON, JOHN JOSEPH, September, 1890, to December, 1894.
2nd Lieut., Northamptonshire Regiment.

ARBUTHNOTT, JOHN ST. CLAIR, September, 1908, to July, 1909.
2nd Lieut., Indian Army.

AUSTIN, JOHN BYRON FRASER, September, 1911, to April, 1914.
Capt., King's Own Hussars, attached R.A.F.

BANON, FREDERICK L., September to December, 1870.
Brig.-Gen., Assistant Adjutant-Gen. to the Forces. C.B., Despatches (twice).

BARRAUD, CYRIL, June, 1887, to July, 1893.
Lieut., Manitoba Regiment, Canadian Army.

BARRETT, JAMES, January, 1898, to July, 1899.
Surgeon, R.N.V.R., H.M.S. *Imperieuse*. Drowned at Sea.

BARRY, PATRICK REDMOND, September, 1910, to December, 1916.
2nd Lieut., Irish Guards. M.C., Wounded.

BATE, GEORGE BEAUMONT, May, 1909, to December, 1911.
2nd Lieut., Loyal North Lancashire Regiment, attached R.F.C. Killed in Action.

BATES, CYRIL FRANCIS, April, 1901, to July, 1906.
Sergeant, London Regiment. Wounded.

BELLASIS, RICHARD FAUCONBERG, January, 1902, to July, 1903.
Private, B Company, Capetown Highlanders.

BELLOC, LOUIS MARY JOHN, September, 1911, to June, 1915.
Lieut., Royal Engineers, attached R.A.F. Wounded; Killed in Action.

BELLORD, CHARLES EDMUND, September, 1910, to July, 1916.
2nd Lieut., R.A.F. Killed in Action.

BELLORD, CUTHBERT GEORGE, September, 1899, to March, 1904.
Capt., Shropshire Light Infantry, attached R.A.F.

BENSLY, ROBERT HUGH, September, 1910, to June 1917.
2nd Lieut., Royal West Kent Regiment. Wounded.

BERINGTON, JOHN JOSEPH, January, 1896, to July, 1899.
Major, Royal Marine Artillery.

BERKELEY, Rev. DOM OSWALD, September, 1880, to July, 1886.
C.F. (3rd Class), B.E.F. M.C., Despatches.

BERKELEY, ROBERT GEORGE WILMOT, September, 1910, to September, 1913. 2nd Lieut., Machine Gun Corps.

BIRD, CHRISTOPHER ST. JOHN, September, 1902, to July, 1906.
Capt., Royal Engineers. M.C., Despatches.

BIRD, WILFRID JOHN, September, 1902, to July, 1905.
Private, Mounted Rifles (Natal Carabineers).

BLOUNT, CECIL F., September, 1897, to July 1902.
Lieut., Royal Engineers.

BLOUNT, FRANCIS, April, 1901, to July, 1906.
Lieut., Royal Garrison Artillery.

BODENHAM, CONSTANTINE JOSEPH LUBIENSKI, September to December, 1909. 2nd Lieut., Gurkhas.

BODENHAM, HENRY LUBIENSKI, September, 1908, to July, 1914.
2nd Lieut., Black Watch, attached Machine Gun Corps. Killed in Action.

BODENHAM, STANISLAUS JOSEPH LUBIENSKI, September to December, 1909.
2nd Lieut., Irish Guards.

BONAPARTE-WYSE, NAPOLEON ESTELLE, January to July, 1888.
Capt., Royal Garrison Artillery.

BOSHELL, JOHN ABBOT, January, 1901, to March, 1905.
Lieut., Royal Inniskilling Fusiliers.

BOSHELL, WILLIAM DABNEY, January, 1901, to December, 1904.
2nd Lieut., Royal Inniskilling Fusiliers. Invalided.

BOYD, FIELDING H., September, 1892, to December, 1897.
Capt., Royal Engineers. Despatches.

BRANDLING, VINCENT FORD, September, 1888, to March, 1889.
Capt., Protection Company, Royal Defence Corps.

BRIDGER, JOHN CAREY C., September, 1909, to December, 1911.
Capt., Royal Garrison Artillery. Wounded.

BRITTEN, THOMAS XAVIER, September, 1879, to July, 1882.
Lieut.-Col., Mahratta Light Infantry. Despatches, Died of Wounds.

BROOKFIELD, Rev. DOM PETER PAUL, October, 1900, to December, 1905.
C.F. (4th Class), B.E.F.

BROWNE, CHRISTOPHER CORBALLY, January, 1904, to July, 1908.
Gunner, Royal Field Artillery, T.F.

BROWNE, HON. GERALD RALPH, May to December, 1905.
Lieut., Dragoons.

BROWNE, JAMES GERARD, October, 1902, to July, 1906.
Private, Middlesex Regiment. Wounded.

BROWNE, HON. MAURICE DERMOT, May, 1905, to July, 1912.
Lieut., Coldstream Guards. Despatches, Killed in Action.

BRUCE, CHARLES WILLIAM, April, 1910, to July, 1914.
Capt., Gordon Highlanders, attached R.F.C. Wounded; Killed in
Flying Accident.

BRUCE, REGINALD WALTER, April, 1910, to December, 1913.
Capt., Shropshire Light Infantry. M.C., Italian Bronze Medal for
Military Valour, Thrice Wounded.

BULFIN, EDWARD FRANCIS, September, 1911, to December, 1915.
Lieut., Yorkshire Regiment, A.D.C. M.C.

BULLEN, ROBERT H. P., September, 1878, to December, 1880.
Lieut.-Col., Kolar Gold Field Rifle Volunteers.

BURKE, JOHN BERNARD, April, 1907, to July, 1909.
Capt., Grenadier Guards. M.C., Killed in Action.

BURKE, SIR GERALD HOWE, BART., September, 1906, to July, 1910.
Capt., Irish Guards. Twice Wounded.

BURNAND, CYRIL FRANCIS, April, 1904, to July, 1909.
2nd Lieut., Grenadier Guards. Killed in Action.

BUTLER, LEONARD WILLIAM, September, 1909, to July, 1915.
Lieut., Royal Irish Fusiliers. Killed in Action.

BUTLER-BOWDON, BERNARD BASIL JOSEPH, September, 1908, to February,
1915. 2nd Lieut., Lancashire Fusiliers. Killed in Action.

BYRNE, FRANCIS BERNARD, May, 1908, to April, 1913.
Capt., Royal Warwickshire Regiment. Wounded.

BYRNE, FREDERICK W., April, 1902, to July, 1908.
2nd Lieut., Royal Flying Corps. Wounded (twice).

BYRNE, GEORGE ROBERT, April, 1902, to July, 1908.
Lieut., Lancers.

BYRNE, EDMUND GEORGE, September, 1908, to December, 1916.
Gunner, Royal Field Artillery.

BYRNE, THOMAS EDMUND, April, 1910, to April, 1916.
2nd Lieut., Welsh Guards. Killed in Action.

CAFFERATA, BERNARD JOSEPH, April, 1895, to July, 1903.
Lieut., Motor Transport, Army Service Corps.

CAFFERATA, CLEMENT C., April, 1896, to July, 1905.
Corporal, Canadian Forestry Corps. Died of Illness.

CAILLARD, FELIX CLEMENT V. D., January, 1904, to December, 1908.
Capt., Somerset Light Infantry. M.C. and Bar to M.C., Despatches,
Twice Wounded.

CAILLARD, HENRY, April, 1906, to December, 1908.
Private, Eastern Ontario Regiment, Canadian Expeditionary Force.
Wounded.

CAILLARD, PERCY MAURICE BENJAMIN, April, 1907, to December, 1908,
Lieut., Royal Air Force.

CAMPBELL, CHARLES ARTHUR, September, 1901, to December, 1909.
Lieut., Cheshire Regiment. Killed in Action.

CAMPBELL, CYRIL HERBERT, September, 1901, to April, 1910.
Lieut. and Adj., Royal Field Artillery. Wounded.

CAMPDEN, ARTHUR, VISCOUNT, September, 1899, to July, 1902.
Major, Gloucestershire Regiment. O.B.E.

CARY-ELWES, WILFRID GERVASE, September, 1908, to December, 1915.
2nd Lieut., Irish Guards. Killed in Action.

CASE, JOHN A. ASHTON, April, 1904, to October, 1909.
Sub-Lieut., Royal Naval Air Service.

CASTLEROSSE, VALENTINE, VISCOUNT, September, 1905, to July, 1909.
Lieut., Irish Guards. Wounded.

CHARLETON, CUTHBERT S., April, 1906, to April, 1907.
Private, Cyclist Corps, Norfolk Regiment.

CHATTERTON, REV. DOM JOHN STANISLAUS, September, 1895, to July, 1901.
C.F. (Naval).

CHESNEY, ALEXANDER ARTHUR IAN, May, 1911, to March, 1914.
Capt., Intelligence Corps. M.C., Croix de Guerre.

CHISHOLM, ALASTAIR EDWARD, September, 1904, to July, 1908.
Lieut., Royal Scots. Killed in Action.

CLERY, MICHAEL JOHN, September, 1910, to July, 1914.
Lieut., Dragoon Guards. M.C., Wounded.

CLERY, NOEL CAIRNS, September, 1903, to December, 1910.
Capt. and Adj., Royal Field Artillery. M.C., Despatches, Killed in Action.

CLERY, VYVIAN AUGUSTINE CAIRNS, September, 1903, to December, 1909.
Major, Signal Company, Royal Engineers. M.C., Despatches (twice), Wounded.

CLIFFORD, CHARLES OSWALD, September, 1899, to July, 1902.
Sub-Lieut., Royal Naval Volunteer Reserve, *Benbow* Battalion. Interned.

CLIFFORD, HUGH GILBERT, January, 1908, to April, 1913.
Lieut., Lincolnshire Regiment. Killed in Action.

CLUTTON, ARTHUR HENRY, September, 1912, to December, 1916.
2nd Lieut., Royal Field Artillery. M.C. and Bar to M.C.

COATS, JAMES STUART, September, 1908, to February, 1913.
Capt. and Adjutant, Coldstream Guards. M.C., Despatches, Wounded.

COATS, MUIR DUDLEY, January, 1910, to December, 1913.
Capt. and Adjutant, Scots Guards. M.C.

COLEMAN, CECIL MALTWOOD, September, 1912, to July, 1916.
2nd Lieut., Indian Cavalry.

CORBETT, DANIEL M., M.B., September, 1896, to July, 1899.
Major, Royal Army Medical Corps. O.B.E., Despatches (twice), Order of St. Sava.

CORNEY, WULSTAN JOSEPH, October, 1904, to July, 1908.
Lieut., Royal Air Force.

COVENTRY, JOHN, January, 1895, to July, 1899.
Capt., Royal Army Service Corps. Despatches.

COVERDALE, HENRY JOSEPH, September, 1910, to July, 1914.
2nd Lieut., Royal Garrison Artillery.

COX, CHARLES J. BEDE, September, 1902, to July, 1909.
Lance-Corporal, Malay States Volunteer Rifles.

COX, FREDERICK, September, 1910, to July, 1915.
Lieut., Royal West Surrey Regiment. Wounded.

COXON, RAYMOND ERNEST, September, 1906, to July, 1908.
Lieut., Irish Guards.

CRYAN, ROBERT WILLIAM WHITTY, September, 1904, to July, 1911.
Capt., North Staffordshire Regiment. Despatches.

CUBITT, CHARLES CYRIL, September, 1907, to April, 1913.
Lieut., Grenadier Guards. M.C., Wounded.

CUMING, ARTHUR ERIC M., January, 1912, to June, 1915.
Capt., Royal Irish Fusiliers (Reserve). M.C. and Bar to M.C., Died of Wounds.

DALY, AUGUSTINE, September, 1900, to December, 1906.
Lieut., Royal Field Artillery. M.C., Despatches.

DALY, DENIS WILLIAM, May, 1908, to July, 1913.
Lieut., Hussars. Wounded.

DALY, JAMES HENRY, May, 1912, to July, 1917.
2nd Lieut., Lancers.

DALY, JAMES M., September, 1903, to December, 1908.
2nd Lieut., Leinster Regiment.

DALY, LOUIS D., September, 1896, to July, 1902.
Major, Leinster Regiment. D.S.O., Despatches (four times), Wounded.

DALY, CECIL WILLIAM, September, 1910, to December, 1914.
2nd Lieut., Rifle Brigade. Killed in Action.

DAME, JOHN WILLIAM, May, 1909, to July, 1916.
2nd Lieut., Irish Guards. Killed in Action.

DEASE, ARTHUR J., April, 1884, to December, 1886.
Lieut., Red Cross, Section Sanitaire Anglaise No.3.   Croix de Guerre.

DEASE, RICHARD EDMUND, September, 1908, to July, 1915.
Capt., South Irish Horse.

DEASE, WILLIAM G., September, 1878, to July, 1884.
Major, Remount Department.

DE ARTIMÉ, PAUL, February, 1892, to April, 1895.
Capt., Royal Army Service Corps. Despatches.

DE BLESS, GERVASE ANTHONY H., May, 1908, to January, 1915.
Midshipman, H.M.S. *Revenge*. Died at Sea.

DE BURLET, PIERRE, February to July, 1893.
Lieut., Belgian Transport Service.

D'ERLANGER, LEO ALFRED, April to July, 1910.
2nd Lieut., Grenadier Guards.

DE LA HOYDE, WALTER, September, 1895, to July, 1897.
Rifleman, Ceylon Planters Rifle Corps.

DE LA PASTURE, CHARLES EDWARD M., September, 1892, to December,
1895. Capt., Scots Guards. Despatches, Killed in Action.

DE LA PASTURE, GERARD HUBERT, MARQUIS, September, 1899, to July,
1903. Major, King's African Rifles, British East Africa. M.C. and
Bar to M.C., Wounded.

DE LISLE, RUDOLPH H. E. MARCH PHILLIPPS, September to December,
1903. Lieut., R.N., H.M.S. *Invincible*. Invalided.

DE NAVARRO, ALMA JOSE, September, 1909, to February, 1913.
Attached Sanitary Corps, U.S. Army.

DE SALIS, ANTHONY D. R., September, 1909, to April, 1913.
Lieut., Irish Guards. Wounded.

DE STACPOOLE, EDWARD HUBERT, September, 1901, to December, 1906.
Capt. and Brigade Major, Leinster Regiment. M.C., Despatches
(twice), Croix de Guerre, Wounded.

DE STACPOOLE, FRANCIS, January, 1901, to December, 1906.
2nd Lieut., Irish Guards. Wounded.

DE STACPOOLE, GEORGE M. E., J.P., September, 1901, to July, 1904.
Staff Capt., Connaught Rangers.

DE STACPOOLE, ROBERT, September, 1902, to October, 1909.
Lieut., Connaught Rangers. Killed in Action.

DE STACPOOLE, RODERIC ALGERNON, January, 1905, to December, 1911.
2nd Lieut., Royal Field Artillery. Despatches, Killed in Action.

DE TRAFFORD, CUTHBERT HENRY, September, 1909, to July, 1915.
Lieut., London Regiment.

DE TRAFFORD, HUBERT E. F., May, 1908, to July, 1910.
Capt., Dragoons. Wounded.

DE TRAFFORD, RAYMUND V., January, 1908, to March, 1910.
2nd Lieut., Coldstream Guards.

DE TRAFFORD, RUDOLPH, September, 1907, to July, 1911.
Capt., Intelligence Corps. O.B.E., Despatches (twice), Order of the
Crown of Roumania.

DE TRAFFORD, SICELL NOEL, January, 1904, to July, 1906.
2nd Lieut., Royal West Surrey Regiment.

DENMAN, FRANCIS WOODCOCK, January, 1901, to January, 1903.
Private, Royal Army Medical Corps.

DE WITTE, BARON ERIC ALPHONSUS BENEDICT, October, 1894, to July,
1896. N.C.O., Belgian Transport Service.

DILLON, GERALD ALOYSIUS, September, 1909, to July, 1914.
2nd Lieut., Inniskilling Dragoons.

DILLON, JOHN JOSEPH, September, 1909, to April, 1914.
Lieut., Connaught Rangers. M.C., Despatches, Wounded.

DILLON, THEOBALD AUGUSTUS, January, 1909, to July, 1913.
Capt., Connaught Rangers.

D'OILLIAMSON, THOMAS ELIE, January, 1901, to November, 1902.
Lieut., 46th Artillery Regiment (French Army). Legion of Honour,
Croix de Guerre, Wounded.

DOLAN, HENRY ERIC, September, 1909, to July, 1913.
Lieut., Royal Field Artillery, attached R.A.F. M.C., twice Wounded ;
Killed in Action.

DOWNING, FRANCIS GEOFFREY, January, 1909, to September, 1914.
Lieut., Middlesex Regiment. Died of Illness.

DRUITT, EVERARD JOSEPH, January, 1906, to July, 1913.
2nd Lieut., Royal Berkshire Regiment. Killed in Action.

DUNBAR, JOSEPH CAMERON, September, 1891, to July, 1896.
Major, Royal Horse Artillery. D.S.O., Despatches (three times),
Order of the Crown of Italy.

DUNCAN, JOHN DOUGLAS, June, 1912, to March, 1917.
2nd Lieut., Irish Guards.

DUNN, JOHN HAROLD, October, 1900, to October, 1902.
Capt., South African Police.

DWYER, R. FRANCIS, April, 1901, to December, 1903.
Lieut., Royal Army Service Corps.

DWYER, WALTER JOSEPH, September, 1898, to December, 1900.
Lieut., South Irish Horse.

ELLISON, ALFRED JOSEPH, September, 1908, to July, 1914.
Capt., York and Lancaster Regiment. Wounded.

ELWES, FRANCIS GUY, September, 1907, to July, 1910.
Capt., Gloucestershire Regiment. O.B.E.

ELWES, RUDOLPH PHILIP, April, 1907, to July, 1910.
Capt., Coldstream Guards. M.C., Wounded, Prisoner of War.

ELWES, VALENTINE, May, 1908, to July, 1910.
Midshipman, H.M.S. *Shannon*.

EMMET, JAMES ALBERT GARLAND, September, 1912, to July, 1915.
Lieut., Life Guards.

EMMET, ROBERT, September, 1911, to October, 1914.
2nd Lieut., Life Guards. Died of Illness.

ENGLISH, GEORGE E., September, 1891, to December, 1898.
Sergeant, Rifle Brigade.

ENGLISH, REGINALD R., January, 1893, to July, 1901.
Lance-Corporal, Hereford Regiment, attached R.E.

ESMONDE, JOHN HENRY GRATTAN, January, 1910, to December, 1911.
Midshipman, H.M.S. *Invincible*. Killed in Action.

EVERETT, WILLIAM HANMER, April, 1910, to December, 1911.
2nd Lieut., Central India Horse.

EYSTON, CHARLES JOHN, April, 1907, to July, 1908.
Lieut., Rifle Brigade.

FAIRLIE, FRANCIS JOSEPH, May, 1911, to December, 1917.
2nd Lieut., Scots Guards.

FARRELL, CECIL JOSEPH, September, 1895, to July, 1904.
Capt. and Adjutant, Leinster Regiment.

FENDALL, CHARLES MAGRATH, September, 1905, to July, 1908.
2nd Lieut., Royal Field Artillery. Killed in Action.

FERRERS, CECIL RALPH, September, 1898, to July, 1905.
Sergeant, Malay States Volunteer Rifles.

FETHERSTONHAUGH, GEORGE, September, 1891, to July, 1894.
Lieut., Royal Army Service Corps.

FFRENCH-MULLEN, DOUGLAS R. ST. J., April, 1906, to July, 1910.
Major, Royal Engineers. Despatches (twice), Croix de Guerre.

FINDLAY, GEORGE SWAINSTON ADAMSON, April, 1904, to July, 1909.
Capt., Royal Field Artillery.

FINDLAY, JOHN ADAMSON, April, 1904, to July, 1910.
Lieut., Railway Transport Dept.

FITZGERALD, ARTHUR PATRICK, April, 1898, to July, 1902.
Private, Vancouver Battalion, Canadian Exped. Force.

FITZGERALD, HON. ARTHUR SOUTHWELL, September, 1874, to March, 1875.
Major, Royal Irish Regiment.

FITZGERALD, JOHN DAVID, September, 1903, to April, 1908.
Capt., Railway Transport Dept.

FLEMING, HUGH JOSEPH, May, 1909, to July, 1913.
2nd Lieut., Dorsetshire Regiment. Killed in Action.

FODEN-PATTINSON, HUBERT LAWRENCE, September, 1909, to July, 1917.
2nd Lieut., Royal Air Force.

FORSTER, JOHN JOSEPH, September, 1905, to July, 1911.
Lieut., Northumbrian Brigade, R.F.A.

FORSTER, THOMAS, September, 1904, to July, 1910.
Lieut., Royal Engineers, T.F. M.C., Twice Wounded.

FORSTER, WILLIAM, September, 1904, to July, 1910.
Private, Royal Fusiliers. Killed in Action.

FOTTRELL, BRENDAN JOSEPH, January, 1899, to April, 1902.
2nd Lieut., Royal Irish Regiment. Killed in Action.

FOX, ANTHONY, September, 1864, to July, 1868.
Private, National Guard. Killed in accident.

FOX, WALTER BASIL, May, 1908, to July, 1910.
Lieut., Gurkha Rifles. Wounded.

FRENCH, CHARLES HENRY, September, 1902, to October, 1909.
2nd Lieut., Royal Warwickshire Regiment. Wounded.

FRENCH, HON. ROBERT, February, 1869, to December, 1875.
Lieut.-Col., Gloucestershire Regiment, Commanding Depot,
Horfield Barracks, Bristol.

FRIEND, CHARLES PHILIP, October, 1902, to July, 1910.
Lieut., Royal Field Artillery. Wounded; Died of Illness.

FRIEND, DOM FRANCIS FERDINAND, October, 1902, to July, 1909.
C.F. (4th Class).

GALBRAITH, EDGAR DAVID, September, 1894, to July, 1899.
Brevet Major, Indian Army. D.S.O., Despatches (twice), Legion of
Honour.

GALLINI, THEODORE C. S., September, 1893, to July, 1897.
Petty Officer, R.N. Armoured Cars.

GARTLAN, GERALD JOHN, September, 1902, to April, 1907.
Major, Royal Irish Rifles. D.S.O., M.C., Despatches (three times),
Twice Wounded.

GERARD, GILBERT MEADE, April, 1904, to July, 1906.
Capt., Highland Light Infantry. Twice Wounded; Died of Illness.

GHEWY, GILBERT WILLIAM, September, 1903, to July, 1908.
Capt., Canadian Engineers.

GILES, BASIL FRANCIS, September, 1907, to March, 1917.
2nd Lieut., Queen's Royal West Surrey Regiment.

GOULDSBURY, HENRY CULLEN, January, 1894, to December, 1896.
Capt., Royal Berkshire Regiment, attached King's African Rifles.
Despatches, Died on Active Service.

GRACE, CLEVELAND RAPHAEL, September, 1898, to April, 1899.
Lieut., Lovat's Scouts.

GRAHAM, LIONEL AUGUSTINE, September, 1899, to July, 1906.
Capt., Royal Army Medical Corps, Metras Camp, Alexandria.

GRATTAN-BELLEW, WILLIAM ARTHUR, January, 1906, to July, 1911.
Major, Royal Flying Corps. M.C., Despatches, Killed in Action.

GREEN, DEMETRIUS FREDERICK, September, 1897, to July, 1900.
Capt., Northumberland Fusiliers. Died on Active Service.

GREEN, JOHN AUGUSTINE, April, 1893, to December, 1894.
Lieut., Royal Field Artillery.

GREGORY, BRIAN O'FARRELL, January, 1910, to July, 1913.
Assistant Paymaster, H.M.S. *Prince of Wales*.

GREGORY, HENRY JAMES MAURICE, September, 1899, to July, 1902.
Lieut., Royal Field Artillery.

GREGORY, RICHARD DOUGLAS, September, 1874, to December, 1878.
Private, Canadian A.S.C.

GREIG, HUGH IRWIN, April, 1888, to March, 1891.
Major, Royal Garrison Artillery. Order of Leopold, Killed in
Action.

GREIG, JOHN GLENNIE, C.I.E., April, 1888, to April, 1889.
Major, Pioneers, Egyptian Expeditionary Force.

GRISEWOOD, HARMAN J. M., October, 1892, to July, 1897.
Lieut.-Col., Royal Sussex Regiment.

GROVE, WALTER ASHTON, September, 1909, to November, 1913.
Lieut., Royal Berkshire Regiment.

GUISE-BROWN, HAROLD, May, 1905, to July, 1909.
Lieut., Irish Guards. M.C., Despatches, Wounded.

HALLINAN, EDWARD VICTOR, September, 1908, to December, 1914.
Lieut., Royal Field Artillery. M.C., Wounded.

HALLINAN, FRANCIS, September, 1909, to December, 1915.
Lieut., Royal Army Service Corps.

HANLEY, HUBERT ARTHUR OLDFIELD, April, 1894, to March, 1900.
Major, Middlesex Regiment. D.S.O., M.C., Despatches (three times).

HANNAN, CORNELIUS JOSEPH, September, 1906, to July, 1907.
Lieut., North Somerset Yeomanry, T.F.

HARFORD, ERNEST W., September, 1894, to July, 1898.
Lieut., Royal Garrison Artillery.

HARRINGTON, CYRIL ASHLIN, January, 1901, to April, 1904.
Private, Victoria Rifles of Canada, Canadian Contingent.

HARRIS, WILLIAM ANDERSON, September to December, 1904.

HARTLEY, D'ARCY JOHN J., September, 1901, to December, 1902.
Lieut., Dragoon Guards. Killed in Action.

HARVEY, JOHN DOUGLAS, September, 1902, to April, 1904.
Lieut., R.N., H.M.S. *Oriole*.

HASKETT-SMITH, CARLOS EDGAR, September, 1897, to December, 1898.
Lieut., R.N.V.R., H.M.S. *Tarlair*.

HASKETT-SMITH, ERNEST ARTHUR, September, 1897, to December, 1898.
Capt., Worcestershire Regiment, A.D.C. to the Governor of Bengal. Wounded.

HAWKINS, ALEXANDER EDWARD, September, 1907, to April, 1910.
Major, Royal Field Artillery. Despatches, Died of Wounds.

HAWKINS, CLAUDE SOMERFIELD, May, 1899, to December, 1904.
2nd Lieut., Royal Army Service Corps.

HAWKINS, JOHN DENIS, May, 1899, to December, 1904.
Capt., Royal Field Artillery.

HAY, LINDSAY FITZGERALD, September, 1902, to July, 1910.
Capt., Black Watch. Despatches, Twice Wounded.

HAYDON, JOSEPH CHARLES, January, 1912, to December, 1916.
Lieut., Irish Guards. Despatches.

HERBERT, EDWARD BLEIDDIAN, September, 1866, to December, 1869.
Lieut.-Col., Commandant, Monmouthshire Volunteer Regiment.

HERRICK, HARRY EUSTACE, September, 1903, to July, 1908.
Capt., Royal Irish Fusiliers. Killed in Action.

HEWETT, STEPHEN HENRY, September, 1905, to August, 1911.
2nd Lieut., Royal Warwickshire Regiment. Killed in Action.

HEYDON, GEORGE, April, 1894, to August, 1899.
Major, A.A.M.C., Australian Expeditionary Force. M.C., Wounded.

HEYWOOD-JONES, RICHARD P., September, 1909, to July, 1912.
Private, Lancers.

HILLIER, MAURICE, September, 1911, to June, 1915.
2nd Lieut., King's Own Scottish Borderers. Killed in Action.

HOBDELL, ARTHUR BIRT, April, 1903, to July, 1911.
Capt., Wiltshire Regiment. Thrice Wounded ; Died of Wounds.

HOGHTON, HUBERT, September, 1902, to July, 1905.
Lieut., Royal Field Artillery.

HOMERSHAM, JOHN HENRY, September, 1910, to December, 1915.
Driver, Res. Batt. Royal Horse Artillery, H.A.C.

HONYWOOD, WILLIAM WYNN, January, 1907, to July, 1909.
Lieut., Lancers, attached R.A.F. M.C., Despatches (thrice), Thrice Wounded.

HOUGHTON, MURTAUGH J., September, 1883, to April, 1885.
Capt., Royal Army Medical Corps.

HOUNSELL, RANDAL HENRY, September, 1901, to December, 1908.
Capt., Royal Engineers. Despatches.

HOWARD, SIR FRANCIS, K.C.B., D.S.O., January to December, 1860.
Major-Gen., Inspector of Infantry to the New Army. K.C.M.G., Despatches.

HUMFREY, HENRY BRABAZON, September, 1909, to July, 1915.
Lieut., Deccan Horse.

HUNNYBUN, NIGEL MARTIN, September, 1879, to January, 1885.
Capt., East Lancashire Regiment.

HUTH, NOEL, April, 1899, to April, 1904.
Capt., Royal Garrison Artillery.

JACKSON, BASIL RAWDON, September, 1905, to July, 1910.
Lieut., Royal Garrison Artillery.

JACKSON, ROBERT HUGH HOLMES, September, 1903, to July, 1909.
Major, East Surrey Regiment, attached Machine Gun Company.
O.B.E., M.C., Despatches (twice), Russian Order of St. Anne,
Wounded.

JAMES, FRANCIS RAYMUND, September, 1903, to July, 1912.
Capt., Royal Field Artillery, attached R.E. M.C.

JEFFRIES, WILLIAM FRANCIS, January, 1902, to July, 1909.
Major, Royal Dublin Fusiliers. D.S.O., Despatches (twice), Twice
Wounded.

JOHNSON, WALTER GUY, April, 1906, to December, 1911.
Private, Hussars.

JUMP, HENRY, April, 1893, to April, 1900.
Capt., Dragoons. Prisoner of War, Wounded.

KAVANAGH, V. HUBERT, April to July, 1889.
Capt., Royal Irish Fusiliers. Wounded.

KEATINGE, RT. REV. BISHOP WILLIAM L., September, 1883, to July, 1887,
C.F. (1st Class), Principal Catholic Chaplain. C.M.G., C.B.E.,
Despatches (five times), Legion of Honour.

KEENAN, JAMES BROWNE, September, 1908, to July, 1914.
Capt. and Adjutant, Irish Guards. Wounded (twice).

KEENAN, NORBERT MICHAEL, September, 1880, to December, 1881.

KELLY, JOHN VINCENT, April, 1912, to December, 1915.
Lieut., Royal Field Artillery.

KENDAL, RICHARD PETER JOSEPH, September, 1888, to April, 1895.
Private, East Yorkshire Regiment. Wounded.

KENYON, JOSEPH ROBERT, September, 1892, to July, 1900.
Major, Royal Field Artillery. M.C., Despatches.

KILKELLY, CHARLES RANDOLPH, C.M.G., M.V.O., February, 1873, to
July, 1878.
Surgeon Lieut.-Col., Grenadier Guards.

KILKELLY, PATRICK PERCY, September, 1878, to July, 1885.
Surgeon Lieut.-Col., Indian Medical Service.

KILLEEN, OLIVER J. H., LORD, January, 1910, to June, 1914.
Lieut., Lancers. M.C.

KING, EDWARD THOMAS, September, 1894, to April, 1896.
Capt., Royal Garrison Artillery, T.F.

KING, HAROLD F. SHERWOOD, September, 1886, to July, 1888.
Capt., Divisional Ammunition Column, Royal Field Artillery.

KING, WILLIAM, September, 1891, to July, 1895.
Lieut., Royal Flying Corps.

KIRKPATRICK, FREDERICK ARTHUR I., September, 1907, to December, 1910.
Midshipman, H.M.S. *St. Vincent*.

KIRKPATRICK, IVONE AUGUSTINE, April, 1907, to November, 1914.
Lieut., Royal Inniskilling Fusiliers. Despatches (twice), Croix
de Guerre (Belge), Wounded.

KOCH DE GOOREYND, ALEXANDER, May, 1908, to July, 1912.
Lieut., Irish Guards.

KOE, PHILIP STEPHEN, September, 1909, to December, 1914.
2nd Lieut., York and Lancaster Regiment. Killed in Action.

KYNASTON, HUBERT, May, 1896, to July, 1902.
2nd Lieut., Machine Gun Corps.

LAMBERT, CECIL, March to July, 1894.
Lieut., London Regiment. Despatches.

LANE-JOYNT, WILLIAM S. R., April, 1899, to April, 1904.
Capt., Royal Army Service Corps. Wounded.

LANGDALE, REV. DOM ODO GRATTAN, May, 1877, to May, 1880.
C.F. (4th Class), B.E.F.

LANGRAN, WILLIAM HENRY, September, 1903, to July, 1912.
Capt., West Yorkshire Regiment. M.C., Prisoner of War.

LANGTON, THEOBALD MICHAEL, September, 1880, to December, 1883.
Major, Inspector of Administrative Services.

LAWDER, NOEL WILFRID, January, 1898, to April, 1901.
Major, Bedfordshire Regiment, attached Nigeria Regiment. Killed in Action.

LEAHY, JOHN HAROLD, January, 1913, to July, 1915.
Capt., Royal Field Artillery. M.C.

LEAHY, NOEL EDWARD, September, 1912, to July, 1915.
Lieut., Royal Field Artillery. Killed in Action.

LEARY, SIDNEY A. D., February, 1897, to July, 1900.
Trooper, Australian Light Horse.

LEE, FRANCIS, September, 1880, to July, 1882.
Brig.-Gen., Cyclists' Brigade. C.B.E.

LESCHER, ROBERT JOSEPH, January, 1900, to July, 1904.
2nd Lieut., Sikhs (Frontier Force).

LE SUEUR, JOHN HENRY RONDEL, January, 1907, to July, 1915.
Lieut., Royal Engineers.

LETEUX, FRANCIS, December, 1879, to July, 1883.
Private, Canadian Machine Gun Corps. Killed in Action.

LEVELIS-MARKE, PHILIP, September, 1910, to July, 1916.
Lieut., Royal West Kent Regiment. M.C., Wounded.

LITTLEWOOD, CHARLES WILLIAM, January, 1910, to July, 1915.
2nd Lieut., Royal Engineers. M.C., Killed in Action.

LIVESEY, REGINALD, May, 1902, to April, 1904.
2nd Lieut., Royal Lancaster Regiment.

LONGSTAFF, EADBERT RALPH, September, 1894, to July, 1897.
Capt., Royal Army Medical Corps.

LORD, ARTHUR FRANCIS, October, 1883, to July, 1887.
Capt., Royal Engineers.

LORD, EUSTACE CHARLES, May, 1908, to March, 1917.
2nd Lieut., Irish Guards. Killed in Action.

LOUGHREY, EDWARD JOSEPH, September, 1906, to July, 1908.
Lieut., Royal Garrison Artillery.

LOUTIT, AUSTIN SINCLAIR, April, 1895, to July, 1898.
Surgeon, R.N.V.R., H.M.S. *Irresistible*.

LOWE, PRESCOTT WILLOUGHBY, September, 1908, to December, 1914.
2nd Lieut., Duke of Cornwall's Light Infantry.

LYNCH-STAUNTON, GEOFFREY, February, 1911, to June, 1914.
2nd Lieut., Hussars. Killed in Action.

LYONS, JOHN CROMIE, September, 1898, to July, 1900.
Trooper, Australian Light Horse.

LYONS, JOHN LOUIS, September, 1893, to July, 1896.
Lieut., Royal Army Service Corps.

MACARDLE, JOHN ROSS, September, 1901, to July, 1902.
Capt., Royal Field Artillery. M.C.

MACARDLE, KENNETH CALLAN, September, 1901, to July, 1902.
2nd Lieut., Manchester Regiment. Killed in Action.

MACDERMOT, EDWARD T., September, 1883, to July, 1888.
Major, Assistant Inspector Q.M.G. Services S.C. Despatches.

MACDERMOT, FRANCIS CHARLES, September, 1898, to July, 1905.
Major, Royal Army Service Corps. Despatches (four times).

MACDERMOT, HUGH MAURICE, April, 1906, to December, 1908.
2nd Lieut., Royal Irish Fusiliers. Killed in Action.

MACDONNELL, FRANCIS W. J., September, 1881, to July, 1887.
Major, West Yorkshire Regiment. Died of Illness.

MCGEE, EUSTACE JOSEPH, September, 1907, to July, 1910.
Lieut., Royal Air Force. Killed in Aeroplane Accident.

MCGRATH, GEORGE NOEL, September, 1898, to July, 1899.
Lieut., Dragoon Guards. Died of Wounds.

MacLachlan, Geoffrey Cheasty, September, 1910, to December, 1917.
2nd Lieut., Irish Guards.

MacLachlan, James Graham, September, 1910, to December, 1916.
2nd Lieut., Irish Guards. Wounded.

McLoughlin, Eugene Joseph, September, 1910, to July, 1912.
Lieut., Royal Air Force.

McLoughlin, Francis James, April, 1912, to June, 1913.
Private, Artists Rifles.

McLoughlin, John Henry, September, 1910, to July, 1913.
2nd Lieut., Royal Irish Regiment. Prisoner of War.

McManus, Terence Joseph, September, 1910, to April, 1915.
Lieut., Middlesex Regiment. Died of Wounds.

Macmullen, Jack Francis, September, 1905, to April, 1911.
Capt. and Adjutant, Royal Army Service Corps. Wounded.

Macnamara, John Philip, April, 1906, to July, 1911.
Capt., Royal Army Medical Corps.

McShane, Basil Augustine, September, 1912, to June, 1915.
2nd Lieut., Rifle Brigade.

Madden, Richard More, September, 1881, to July, 1886.
Capt., Royal Army Medical Corps.

Madden, Thomas E. McDonnell, January, 1882, to July, 1886.
Major, Royal Garrison Artillery.

Mahony, Daniel James, September, 1890, to March, 1893.
Capt. and Adjutant, Royal Garrison Artillery.

Mahony, Martin F. J. R., September, 1908, to July, 1912.
Lieut., Royal Irish Fusiliers, attached R.A.F. Wounded.

Manby-Colegrave, Gerard T., October to December, 1897.
Lieut., Royal Garrison Artillery. Died of Wounds.

Mansfield, Eustace Lattin, September, 1895, to July, 1896.
Major, Northamptonshire Regiment. Wounded.

MANSFIELD, TIRSO LATTIN M. L., September, 1901, to April, 1904.
Capt., Nigeria Regiment.

MARCH, BERNARD OSWALD, January, 1895, to December, 1899.
Major, Royal Field Artillery. D.S.O., M.C., Despatches, Wounded.

MARLEY, VERNON DOUGLAS KENNETH, September, 1909, to July, 1914.
Lieut., Manchester Regiment. Twice Wounded.

MARSHALL, ALBERT WILFRID C., May, 1910, to April, 1911.
Lieut., Labour Corps.

MARTIN, CHARLES ANDREW, January, 1906, to April, 1912.
Lieut., Royal Dublin Fusiliers. Despatches, Serbian Order of the White Eagle, Died of Wounds.

MARTIN, LAURENCE JOHN, September, 1909, to March, 1917.
Cavalry Reserve.

MARTIN, RICHARD ROSS, January, 1908, to April, 1913.
Major, Royal Irish Rifles. Despatches (twice).

MARTIN, THOMAS FITZGERALD, September, 1910, to July, 1914.
Capt. and Adjutant, Royal Field Artillery. M.C.

MARTIN, THOMAS SHANNON, September, 1904, to July, 1908.
Capt., Connaught Rangers. Wounded.

MASKELL, WILLIAM E., September, 1884, to May, 1890.
Major, Devonshire Regiment. O.B.E.

MATHEW, THEOBALD, September, 1909, to December, 1916.
Lieut., Welsh Guards. Wounded.

MAUDE, AYLMER A. J. P., September, 1904, to July, 1910.
Lieut., Rifle Brigade.

MAXWELL, GERALD CONSTABLE, September, 1905, to June, 1913.
Capt., Royal Air Force. M.C., D.F.C., A.F.C.

MAXWELL, IAN CONSTABLE, September, 1903, to July, 1909.
Capt., Cameron Highlanders, attached R.A.F. Wounded.

MAXWELL, RONALD CONSTABLE, September, 1903, to July, 1910.
Lieut., Royal Naval Air Service.

MAXWELL-SCOTT, MALCOLM J. R., September, 1895, to July, 1897.
Lieut.-Com. R.N., H.M.S. *Angora*. D.S.O.

MIERS, DOUGLAS N. C. CAPEL, May to December, 1890.
Capt., Cameron Highlanders. Killed in Action.

MILLER, ERNEST ALFRED, September, 1889, to July, 1893.
Capt., Royal Army Medical Corps.

MITCHELL, JOHN, September, 1902, to July, 1905.
Sergeant, Mounted Rifles (Natal Carabineers).

MOLYNEUX-SEEL, LOUIS E. H., January, 1885, to July, 1891.
Capt., Border Regiment. Killed in Action.

MOORE, MAURICE STOREY, January, 1908, to April, 1911.
Lieut., Scottish Horse, T.F.

MORRALL, JOHN BERNARD, September, 1892, to July, 1898.
2nd Lieut., Royal Warwickshire Regiment. Died of Wounds.

MORRISS, JACK SEPTIMUS, January, 1912, to February, 1915.
2nd Lieut., Royal Warwickshire Regiment. Killed in Action.

MORROGH, EDWARD AUGUSTINE, September, 1891, to July, 1894.
Lieut., Special Reserve.

MOSTYN, REV. EDWARD, October, 1880, to December, 1888.
C.F., Lieut.-Col. (2nd Class), D.A.P.C., XVIII Army Corps.

MOSTYN, GEORGE A., September, 1910, to July, 1916.
2nd Lieut., King's Royal Rifles.

MOSTYN, JOSEPH CECIL M., September, 1903, to December, 1909.
Capt., Royal Field Artillery. M.C., Despatches.

MOSTYN, J. EDWARD HUBERT, April, 1899, to July, 1906.
Capt., Royal Sussex Regiment. Wounded.

MOSTYN, JOSEPH PHILIP, April, 1906, to July, 1912.
Lieut., Royal Sussex Regiment, attached R.A.F. Despatches,
Wounded.

MOYSEY, FRANCIS, September, 1900, to December, 1907.
Capt., Suffolk Regiment. Despatches, Prisoner of War.

MUIRHEAD-GOULD, GERARD C., January, 1901, to December, 1902.
Lieut.-Commander, R.N., H.M.S. *Emperor of India*. D.S.C.,
Despatches, Legion of Honour, Greek Order of the Redeemer.

MURPHY, ALFRED DURHAM, April, 1902, to December, 1906.
Lieut.-Col., Leinster Regiment. D.S.O., M.C., Despatches (four
times), Killed in Action.

MURPHY, EDWIN MIDLETON HALE, September, 1895, to July, 1899.
Capt., Leinster Regiment. Died of Wounds.

MURPHY, HARVEY JOHN JOSEPH, September, 1912, to July, 1917,
Private, West Yorks Regiment.

MURRAY, EVERITT GEORGE, April, 1906, to July, 1908.
Capt., Royal Army Medical Corps. O.B.E.

MURRAY, ROGER E., May, 1908, to July, 1911.
2nd Lieut., Royal Field Artillery.

MURRAY, THORKELE H. E., April, 1906, to July, 1909.
Lieut., Royal Field Artillery. Wounded.

MURROW, HENRY LLOYD, September, 1891, to April, 1895.
Lieut.-Col., Royal Garrison Artillery. D.S.O., Despatches, Order of
the Star of Roumania.

NASH, JAMES HARAN, September, 1908, to July, 1915.
Lieut., Irish Guards. Killed in Action.

NASH, VINCENT HAROLD, September, 1908, to July, 1916.
2nd Lieut., Irish Guards.

NELSON, ALBERT F. J. H., September, 1903, to July, 1905.
Private, Australian Infantry. Twice Wounded.

NEVILE, BERNARD PHILIP, April, 1902, to July, 1905.
Capt., Lincolnshire Regiment. Killed in Action.

NIALL, FRANCIS, September, 1893, to July, 1896.
Lieut., Wiltshire Regiment, attached Devon Regiment. Wounded.

NICHOLSON, EDWARD FRANCIS DALE, September, 1895, to December, 1899.
Major, South Lancashire Regiment. Died of Wounds.

NOEL, HON. ROBERT E. T. M., April, 1901, to July, 1907.
Capt., Royal Fusiliers, Assistant Commissioner of Police, S. Province, Nigeria. Died of Illness.

NUGENT, JOHN FAGAN H., September, 1902, December, 1907.
Capt., Punjabis, A.D.C. to H.E. Governor of Ceylon. D.S.O. Despatches (twice), Wounded.

O'CONNOR, DESMOND MAURICE MAX, June, 1906, to December, 1907.
Trooper, Australian Light Horse. Wounded.

O'CONNOR, RODERICK ALAN EDWARD, June, 1906, to December, 1907.
2nd Lieut., Leinster Regiment. Killed in Action.

O'DRISCOLL, PATRICK FINBARRE, September, 1909, to July, 1914.
Lieut., Irish Guards. Twice Wounded.

O'FARRELL, HUGH ARCHIBALD, September, 1908, to July, 1917.
2nd Lieut., Irish Guards. Killed in Action.

O'GORMAN, BERNARDINE, January, 1885, to July, 1886.
Major, General List. D.S.O., Despatches, Chinese Order of Wen-Hu.

O'GORMAN, MERVYN J. P., C.B., January, 1885, to July, 1886.
Lieut.-Col., Royal Field Artillery. Despatches.

O'HARA, PATRICK GILBERT W., May, 1909, to July, 1914.
2nd Lieut., East Surrey Regiment. Killed in Action.

OVERTON, ARTHUR GOE, September, 1912, to December, 1916.
2nd Lieut., Lancers.

PAGE, WILLIAM SIDNEY, September, 1891, to July, 1894.
Major, A.A.M.C.

PARKES, FRANCIS JOSEPH, September, 1887, to December, 1888.
Capt., Cambridgeshire Regiment.

PARNELL, RODERIC JOSEPH G., September, 1896, to July, 1901.
Surgeon, Royal Naval Hospital, Haslar.

PARSONS, RICHARD ALFRED, September, 1898, to December, 1902.
Capt., Royal Army Medical Corps.

PAULING, GEORGE FRANCIS, September, 1906, to December, 1907.
Lieut., Grenadier Guards. M.C., Killed in Action.

PAYEN-PAYNE, CECIL MARRIOT, May, 1908, to June, 1915.
Lieut., Royal Scots Fusiliers, attached Machine Gun Cavalry.

PETRE, LIONEL GEORGE, LORD, September, 1902, to July, 1905.
Capt., Coldstream Guards. Died of Wounds.

PETRE, RODERIC LORAINE, April, 1900, to December, 1905.
Brevet-Major, South Wales Borderers. D.S.O., M.C., Despatches
(seven times), Twice Wounded.

PLUNKETT, HON. GERALD WILLIAM DESMOND, September, 1912, to July, 1913.
Private, Royal Army Service Corps, M.T.

POTOCKI, COUNT JOSEPH, September, 1905, to July, 1911.
Lieut., Lancers, Guards (Russian Army).

POTOCKI, COUNT ROMAN, September, 1905, to July, 1910.
Lieut., Lancers, Guards (Russian Army).

POWER, FREDERICK THOMAS ALFRED, September, 1908, to July, 1913.
Lieut., Royal Dublin Fusiliers. M.C.

PRIOR, EDWARD R. SEYMOUR, September, 1905, to July, 1908.
Lieut.-Col., South Lancashire Regiment, attached Cheshire Regiment.
D.S.O., M.C., and Bar to M.C., Despatches, Died of Wounds.

PRIOR, HORACE F. SEYMOUR, September, 1905, to July, 1906.
Major, Hampshire Regiment.

PURCELL-GILPIN, GEOFFREY RICHARD, September, 1896, to April, 1899.
Lieut., R.N.V.R., H.M.S. *Osiris II.* D.S.C.

PURCELL-GILPIN, PETER R., September, 1896, to December, 1901.
Capt., Scots Guards. M.C., and Bar to M.C., Wounded.

PURCELL-GILPIN, VICTOR ST. JOHN, September, 1899, to April, 1906.
Lieut., London Regiment.

QUINN, AUSTIN TALBOT, September, 1896, to July, 1898.
C.P.O., Royal Naval Air Service. Wounded.

QUINN, HERBERT OVERTON, September, 1896, to July, 1898.
Corporal, Motor Cyclist Despatch Rider, Reserve Special Corps, Royal Engineers. Royal Victoria Medal, Wounded.

RADCLIFFE, EVERARD J. R. H., May, 1894, to July, 1901.
Capt., Yorkshire Hussars, T.F.

RADCLIFFE, JOSEPH F. E., April, 1902, to July, 1908.
Lieut., Northumberland Fusiliers. Wounded.

RADCLIFFE, ROBERT JOHN, April, 1910, to July, 1915.
2nd Lieut., Hussars.

RANSLEY, WILLIAM CYRIL, September, 1883, to July, 1884.
Lieut., Assistant Inspector of R.E. Machinery.

RAWLINSON, REV. DOM BERNARD STEPHEN, April, 1876, to December, 1882.
C.F. (1st Class), Colonel, Senior Roman Catholic Chaplain in France and Assistant to Principal Chaplain, B.E.F., C.M.G., O.B.E., Despatches (five times), Legion of Honour, Order of Christ.

REYNOLDS, JOHN ROSKELL, September, 1910, to July, 1917.
2nd Lieut., Irish Guards.

REYNOLDS, W. C. NOEL, September, 1901, to July, 1908.
Capt. and Adjutant, Irish Guards. O.B.E., Wounded.

RIDDELL, EDWARD P. A., January to December, 1888.
Lieut.-Col., Temp. Brigadier-Gen., Rifle Brigade. C.M.G., D.S.O., Bar to D.S.O., and Second Bar to D.S.O., Despatches (four times), Wounded (five times).

ROBERTSON, JOHN FRANCIS MORTIMER, January, 1913, to December, 1914.
Midshipman, H.M.S. *Renown*.

ROCHE, PATRICK J., September, 1889, to July, 1895.
Lieut., Royal Inniskilling Fusiliers.

ROCHE-KELLY, EDMUND JOHN, September, 1894, to July, 1899.
Lieut.-Col., Royal Irish Regiment. D.S.O., Despatches (twice), Legion of Honour.

ROCHE-KELLY, JAMES, September, 1893, to July, 1898.
Lieut.-Col., South Irish Horse. M.C., Despatches.

ROPER, CECIL ALFRED, October, 1898, to July, 1901.
Lieut., Royal Naval Reserve.

ROSE, CECIL GUY, September, 1888, to December, 1893.
Major, Royal Engineers.

ROSKELL, WILLIAM J., October, 1888, to June, 1892.
Lieut.-Col., North Staffordshire Regiment. Despatches.

ROSS, CONRAD, September, 1896, to July, 1897.
Major, Royal Artillery, Assistant Proof and Experimental Officer, O.B.E.

ROSS, JOSEPH FRANCIS, September, 1911, to December, 1917.
2nd Lieut., Irish Guards.

ROWLAND, PERCY JOHN, April, 1904, to December, 1907.
Lieut., Motor Transport.

ROWLEY, CHARLES, September, 1908, to July, 1910.
2nd Lieut., Life Guards.

RYAN, JAMES EDMUND, September, 1913, to July, 1917.
2nd Lieut., Royal Garrison Artillery.

RYAN, JAMES HENRY A., September, 1905, to December, 1910.
Capt., King's Liverpool Regiment. M.C., Despatches, Killed in Action.

RYAN, THADDEUS WALTER, September, 1894, to December, 1902.
Major, Royal Army Service Corps.

SAMPSON, FRANCIS, September, 1896, to July, 1897.

SAUNDERS, HILARY ST. GEORGE, September, 1910, to December, 1915.
Lieut., Welsh Guards. M.C.

SAUNDERS, PATRICK CORNELIUS, January, 1891, to December, 1894.
Major, Ludianah Sikhs. Prisoner of War, Despatches.

SEGAR, GEORGE BERNARD, September, 1900, to July, 1902.

SHARPE, GERALD MEREDITH, April, 1897, to July, 1900.
Capt. and Brigade Major, Berkshire Regiment. D.S.O., O.B.E., Despatches (three times), Belgian Order of the Crown, with War Cross, Croix de Guerre (French).

SHERLOCK, THOMAS DAVID, September, 1895, to January, 1897.
Capt., Royal Irish Regiment. M.B.E.

SHINE, HUGH PATRICK, September, 1905, to December, 1913.
2nd Lieut., Royal Irish Fusiliers. Wounded; Killed in Action.

SHINE, JAMES OWEN WILLIAMS, September, 1902, to July, 1909.
Capt., Royal Dublin Fusiliers. Killed in Action.

SHINE, JOHN DENIS, September, 1905, to July, 1912.
2nd Lieut., Royal Irish Regiment. Killed in Action.

SIMPSON, PHILIP WITHAM, September, 1908, to July, 1913.
Capt., East Surrey Regiment, attached Royal Warwickshire Regiment.

SMITH, W. RAYMOND, January, 1888, to December, 1890.
Company Sergt.-Major, Machine Gun Corps.

SMITH-GRANT, WILLIAM HENRY, May, 1909, to July, 1914.
Capt., Gordon Highlanders. M.C., Wounded (twice).

SMITH-SLIGO, ARCHIBALD GEORGE R. J., September, 1903, to July, 1907.
Lieut., Cameron Highlanders. Killed in Action.

SMITH-SLIGO, RONALD WILLIAM M. G., September, 1903, to July, 1907.
Capt., Highland Light Infantry.

SNEAD-COX, GEOFFREY PHILIP J., September, 1909, to July, 1912.
2nd Lieut., Royal Welch Fusiliers. Killed in Action.

SNEAD-COX, RICHARD, September, 1906, to July, 1911.
2nd Lieut., Royal Scots. Killed in Action.

SPALLETTI, FRANCO, April to July, 1903.
Italian Cavalry.

SPRING, RICHARD FREDERICK M., September, 1900, to April, 1904.
Lieut., Royal Irish Regiment. Wounded (twice).

SPRUYT, CARLO LEON G. M., September, 1891, to May, 1892.
Belgian Field Artillery.

STANTON, JAMES BASIL M., April, 1910, to June, 1914.
Lieut., King's Own Scottish Borderers, A.D.C. to G.O.C. Harwich
Garrison. Wounded.

STAPLETON, GREGORY, September, 1875, to July, 1878.
Commander, R.N. Order of Avis.

STAPLETON-BRETHERTON, OSMUND F. J. H., May, 1908, to July, 1915.
Lieut., Lancers. Killed in Action.

STOKES, ANTONY SCOTT, September, 1908, to March, 1917.
2nd Lieut., Irish Guards. Wounded.

STOKES, ADRIAN EDWARD, May, 1908, to July, 1914.
Lieut., King's Royal Rifles.

STOKES, RICHARD RAPIER, April, 1907, to July, 1915.
Major, Royal Field Artillery. M.C., Bar to M.C., Croix de Guerre.

STONOR, CUTHBERT, May, 1901, to July, 1905.
2nd Lieut., Royal Inniskilling Fusiliers. Killed in Action.

STOURTON, HON. ALFRED E. C. J., September, 1884, to July, 1888.
Major, King's Own Royal Lancaster Regiment.

STOURTON, HON. JOHN JOSEPH, May, 1912, to July, 1917.
2nd Lieut., Hussars.

STOURTON, HON. WILLIAM MARMADUKE, January, 1907, to June, 1914.
Lieut., Grenadier Guards. M.C.

STRICKLAND, EDWARD GEORGE, September, 1894, to December, 1895.
Corporal, Ceylon Planters' Rifle Corps.

SUMNER, ERNEST, September, 1889, to July, 1892.
2nd Lieut., Cheshire Yeomanry.

SUMNER, GEORGE J., September, 1889, to July, 1891.
Lieut., Remount Department. Despatches.

SWAYNE, FRANCIS GERALD, September, 1892, to July, 1893.
Major, Indian Army.

SWEENY, THURSTON HUMPHRYS, September, 1908, to July, 1912.
Lieut., Royal Engineers. Wounded.

SWEETMAN, MICHAEL JAMES, September, 1876, to October, 1885.
Lieut.-Col., East Yorks Regiment. O.B.E., Order of St. Stanislas, Despatches (twice).

SWEETMAN, MICHAEL J. J. (HAMISH), September, 1877, to December, 1884.
Major, Worcestershire Regiment. Despatches, Died of Wounds.

TAAFFE, GEORGE RANDALL JOSEPH, September, 1907, to July, 1914.
Lieut., Royal West Kents, attached 1st Garrison Hampshire Regiment.

TALBOT, FRANCIS JOHN REGINALD, May, 1903, to July, 1905.
2nd Lieut., South Staffordshire Regiment.

TALBOT, REGINALD A., September, 1882, to December, 1883.
Lieut., Territorial Force Reserve.

TAYLOR, CHARLES JOSEPH G., September, 1897, to December, 1903.
Medical Officer, attached Royal Naval Air Service.

THOMPSON, EDWARD J. V. C., September to December, 1904.
2nd Lieut., Royal Welch Fusiliers. Died of Wounds.

THOMPSON, PHILIP GORDON G., January, 1882, to July, 1885.
Lieut., Royal Army Medical Corps, attached Royal Field Artillery.

TIDMARSH, DAVID M., September, 1905, to December, 1909.
Capt., Royal Irish Regiment, attached R.A.F. M.C., Despatches, Prisoner of War.

TIDMARSH, JOHN M., September, 1905, to April, 1910.
Lieut., West Riding Regiment, attached R.A.F. Killed in Accident.

TOPHAM, ARTHUR RONALD, September, 1898, to July, 1903.
2nd Lieut.

TREVOR-JONES, EDWARD EVAN, September, 1906, to July, 1914.
2nd Lieut., Rifle Brigade. Killed in Action.

TREVOR-JONES, JOHN ERIC, September, 1906, to July, 1914.
Capt. and Adjutant, Rifle Brigade. M.C., Killed in Action.

TURNBULL, BERTRAND, April, 1900, to July, 1904.
Lieut., Royal Garrison Artillery. Despatches.

TURNBULL, ERIC, September, 1901, to July, 1909.
Lieut., Royal Garrison Artillery.

TURNBULL, REV. DOM GEORGE ROBERT, May, 1905, to December, 1909.
Lance-Corporal, Royal Army Medical Corps.

TURNBULL, GERARD ILTYD, January, 1899, to July, 1904.
Lieut., Welch Regiment. M.C., Died of Wounds.

TURNBULL, JOHN OSWIN, April, 1901, to July, 1907.
Capt., Welch Regiment. Wounded; Killed in Action.

TURNBULL, PAUL S., September, 1894, to July, 1900.
Lieut., Welch Regiment. Wounded.

TURNBULL, WILFRID, September, 1912, to December, 1917.
2nd Lieut., Royal West Surrey Regiment.

TURNER, BASIL RONALD, September, 1909, to June, 1915.
2nd Lieut., Dragoon Guards.

TURNER, GILBERT AUSTIN, September, 1909, to July, 1915.
2nd Lieut., Royal West Kents, attached Loyal North Lancashire
Regiment. Killed in Action.

TYRRELL, FRANCIS C. V., May, 1904, to July, 1911.
2nd Lieut., Coldstream Guards. Died of Wounds.

VAN CUTSEM, EDWARD C. L., October, 1887, to July, 1888.
Major, Shropshire Light Infantry, attached K.R.R.C. M.C.,
Order of Leopold, Croix de Guerre (Belge). Wounded.

VAN CUTSEM, RICHARD E. G., April, 1887, to July, 1894.
Capt., Leinster Regiment.

VAVASOUR, SIR LEONARD PIUS, Bart., April, 1890, to December, 1894.
Lieut.-Com. R.N., H.M.S. *Endymion*.

VIAN, CHRISTOPHER ARTHUR, January, 1911, to July, 1914.
Lieut., Coldstream Guards. Despatches. Wounded.

WALKER, RICHARD, April, 1894, to July, 1902.
2nd Lieut., Lancashire Fusiliers. Killed in Action.

WALMSLEY, HOWARD JOSEPH, September, 1907, to April, 1914.
Private, Royal Army Service Corps, Motor Transport.

WARDROPER, JOHN B., May, 1899, to December, 1904.
Sergeant, Inns of Court O.T.C.

WARE, EDGAR FELIX, September, 1885, to July, 1888.
Capt., V.B. Devonshire Regiment.

WARING, DENIS ANTHONY, September, 1911, to December, 1914.
Private, Honourable Artillery Company.

WARRINGTON, JOSEPH, September, 1889, to July, 1895.
Capt., Royal Field Artillery. Wounded.

WATERS, CHARLES LOUIS, September, 1896, to July, 1901.
Capt., Royal Berkshire Regiment, attached Nigeria Regiment. M.C.,
and Bar to M.C. Died of Wounds.

WATKINS, ILTYD EDWIN MAITLAND, September, 1904, to July, 1908.
Capt., Monmouthshire Regiment. Killed in Action.

WATKINS, SIEGFRIED RICKARDS, September, 1899, to December, 1900.
Flight-Lieut., Royal Naval Air Service.

WATNEY, GUY FELIX P., April to December, 1904.
2nd Lieut., Royal Field Artillery.

WATSON, JOHN AUGUSTUS, May, 1909, to May, 1917.
2nd Lieut., Royal Garrison Artillery.

WATTS, REGINALD CUTHBERT, January, 1904, to July, 1911.
Major, Royal Warwickshire Regiment. M.C., Despatches.

WEGG-PROSSER, CHARLES E., September, 1875, to July, 1876.
Major, Rifle Brigade.

WELD-BLUNDELL, REV. DOM ALFRED ADRIAN, October, 1877, to July, 1878.
C.F. (4th Class), B.E.F.

WELD-BLUNDELL, LOUIS JOSEPH S., September, 1902, to April, 1905.
Private, Queen's Westminster Rifles. Died of Illness.

WELD-BLUNDELL, RICHARD SHIRBURNE, September, 1902, to April, 1905.
2nd Lieut., Liverpool Regiment. Died from Accident.

WESTLAKE, AUSTIN M., September, 1900, to December, 1901.
Private, Artists' Rifles. Despatches.

WESTLAKE, PHILIP M. J., May, 1889, to July, 1894.
Sergeant, Northumberland Fusiliers.

WILCOCKS, OSMUND, April, 1881, to December, 1885.
Capt., V.B. Devonshire Regiment.

WILKINSON, SIDNEY JOHN, April, 1903, to July, 1905.
Capt., Royal Army Service Corps. Despatches.

WILKINSON, VALENTINE, April, 1903, to July, 1904.
Capt. and Adjutant, Border Regiment. M.C., Despatches.

WILLETT, EDWARD ARCHIBALD, September, 1891, to July, 1897.
Private, Sportsman's Battalion, Royal Fusiliers. Died of Illness.

WILLETT, JOHN WICKHAM, April, 1901, to April, 1908.
Lieut., London Regiment. Wounded.

WILLIAMS, GEORGE VALENTINE, April, 1895, to July, 1900.
Capt., Irish Guards. M.C., Despatches, Belgian Order of the Crown, Wounded.

WILSON, CYRIL HERBERT, May, 1909, to December, 1915.
Cadet, Indian Army. Invalided.

WILSON, CYRIL J. N. W., March to December, 1904.
Capt., East Kent Regiment. Despatches, Wounded.

WILSON, HERBERT VAUGHAN, April, 1907, to April, 1912.
Capt., Graves Registration Units.

WINSTANLEY, HUBERT J., September, 1902, to July, 1907.
Private, London Regiment (Artists' Rifles O.T.C.).

WOOD, FRANCIS M., February, 1888, to December, 1889.
Private, Otago Regiment, New Zealand Contingent. Wounded.

WOOD, JOHN PATRICK HAMILTON, January, 1893, to December, 1896.
Capt., Manchester Regiment. Killed in Action.

WOOLLETT, JOHN CHARLES, September, 1901, to July, 1905.
Capt., Royal Air Force. Died of Illness.

WOOLLETT, JOHN SYDNEY, September, 1909, to July, 1912.
2nd Lieut., South Lancashire Regiment.

WORSLEY-WORSWICK, BASIL HENRY, May, 1894, to July, 1899.
2nd Lieut., King Edward's Horse. Killed in Action.

WORSLEY-WORSWICK, CHRISTOPHER FRANCIS, April, 1895, to July, 1903.
Lieut., Leicestershire Regiment. Wounded.

WYNN, JOHN, April, 1912, to July, 1914.
2nd Lieut., Royal Air Force.

WYNTER, FRANCIS A., D.S.O., February, 1883, to December, 1886.
Lieut.-Col., Temp. Brigadier-General, Royal Garrison Artillery.
C.M.G., Despatches (four times), Croix de Guerre. Wounded.

YOUNG, REV. DOM STANISLAUS DOMINIC, October, 1896, to July, 1900.
C.F. (3rd Class), Major, Assistant to Principal Chaplain, B.E.F.
D.S.O., O.B.E., Despatches (three times).

YOURELL, JAMES RUSSELL, M.B., September, 1898, to July, 1901.
Capt., Royal Army Medical Corps. Despatches.

DE SKRZYNSKI, ANTHONY, September, 1906, to July, 1907.
Killed in Action.

SAPIEHA, PRINCE ALFRED MARIA, January, 1908, to July, 1913.
Killed in Action.

INTERIOR OF THE NAVE
(looking North-West)

Chaplains to the Forces

MEMBERS OF THE DOWNSIDE COMMUNITY.

AGIUS, REV. DOM TANCRED AMBROSE, September, 1900.
C.F. (4th Class), B.E.F. Despatches. Wounded.

BERKELEY, REV. DOM OSWALD, September, 1880.
C.F. (3rd Class), B.E.F. M.C. Despatches.

BIRT, REV. DOM HENRY NORBERT, September, 1880.
C.F. (4th Class). Military Hospital, Netley. Despatches.

BROOKFIELD, REV. DOM PETER PAUL, October, 1900.
C.F. (4th Class), B.E.F.

BUTLER, REV. DOM RICHARD URBAN, September, 1902.
C.F. (2nd Class), D.A.P.C. and Senior Catholic Chaplain with British Army in Italy. O.B.E., Despatches.

CAMM, REV. DOM REGINALD BEDE, September, 1913.
C.F. (4th Class), Cairo, Egypt.

CHAPMAN, REV. DOM HENRY JOHN.
C.F. (4th Class), B.E.F.

CHATTERTON, REV. DOM JOHN STANISLAUS, September, 1895.
C.F. (Naval).

DAVEY, REV. DOM JOSEPH RICHARD, September, 1907.
C.F. (4th Class), B.E.F. Wounded.

FRIEND, REV. DOM FRANCIS FERDINAND, October, 1902.
C.F. (4th Class), B.E.F.

HUDLESTON, REV. DOM GILBERT ROGER, September, 1898.
C.F. (4th Class), Tiflis.

LANGDALE, REV. DOM ODO GRATTAN, May, 1877.
C.F. (4th Class), B.E.F.

RAWLINSON, REV. DOM BERNARD STEPHEN, April, 1876.
C.F. (1st Class), Senior Catholic Chaplain in France, and Assistant to Principal Chaplain, B.E.F. C.M.G., O.B.E., Despatches (five times), Legion of Honour, Order of Christ.

WEBSTER, REV. DOM DOUGLAS RAYMUND, September, 1902.
C.F. (4th Class), B.E.F.

YOUNG, REV. DOM STANISLAUS DOMINIC, October, 1896.
C.F. (3rd Class), Assistant to Principal Chaplain, B.E.F. D.S.O., O.B.E., Despatches (three times).

OTHER OLD GREGORIANS.

KEATINGE, RT. REV. BISHOP WILLIAM LEWIS, September, 1883, to July, 1887.
C.F. (1st Class), Principal Catholic Chaplain. C.M.G., C.B.E., Despatches (five times), Legion of Honour.

MOSTYN, REV. EDWARD, October, 1880, to December, 1888.
C.F. (2nd Class), Deputy Assistant to Principal Chaplain, XVIII Army Corps.

WELD-BLUNDELL, REV. DOM ALFRED ADRIAN, October, 1877, to July, 1878.
C.F. (4th Class), B.E.F.

Cadets

AT R.N.C., OSBORNE.

BETHELL, PETER PAUL, September, 1915, to March, 1918.

AT R.N.C., KEYHAM.

DOLAN, GERALD ROBERT, April, 1910, to December, 1913.

EMMET, THOMAS ADDIS, May, 1914, to July, 1917.

AT R.M.A., WOOLWICH.

FOWLER, MAURICE ALBAN JAMES, April, 1913, to July, 1916.

GAFFNEY, EDWARD SEBASTIAN BURKE, September, 1911, to December, 1918.

AT R.M.C., SANDHURST.

COOPE, EDWARD FRANCIS, January, 1914, to December, 1918.

HARVEY, CHARLES BASSETT, September, 1910, to December, 1918.

KILKELLY, GERALD, May, 1914, to March, 1917.

LYTTON, HON. NOEL ANTHONY, September, 1913, to July, 1918.

MALET, GUY SEYMOUR, May, 1911, to March, 1917.

MARTIN, ERNEST OWEN, September, 1912, to March, 1917.

PAYEN-PAYNE, LOVELL VYVIAN, May, 1909, to December, 1918.

WEBER, HENRY NICHOLAS, September, 1910, to July, 1918.

WOULFE-FLANAGAN, STEPHEN HUGH JAMES, January, 1911, to July, 1918.

AT OFFICER CADET BATTALIONS.

CHAMBERS, JOHN COLPOYS, May, 1909, to June, 1918.

WALSH, JOHN SAVILLE, September, 1912, to July, 1918.

Roll of Honour

KILLED IN ACTION, OR DIED ON SERVICE.

AGIUS, CAPT. R. V., London Regiment.

BARRETT, SURGEON J., R.N.V.R., H.M.S. *Imperieuse.*

BATE, 2ND LIEUT. G. B., Loyal North Lancashire Regiment.

BELLOC, LIEUT. L. M. J., Royal Engineers, attached R.A.F.

BELLORD, 2ND LIEUT. C. E., Royal Air Force.

BODENHAM, 2ND LIEUT. H. L., Black Watch, attached Machine Gun Corps.

BRITTEN, LIEUT.-COL. T. X., Mahratta Light Infantry.

BROWNE, LIEUT. HON. M. D., Coldstream Guards.

BRUCE, CAPT. C. W., Gordon Highlanders, attached Royal Flying Corps.

BURKE, CAPT. J. B., M.C., Grenadier Guards.

BURNAND, 2ND LIEUT. C. F., Grenadier Guards.

BUTLER, LIEUT. L. W., Royal Irish Fusiliers.

BUTLER-BOWDON, 2ND LIEUT. B. B., Lancashire Fusiliers.

BYRNE, 2ND LIEUT. T. E., Welsh Guards.

CAFFERATA, CORPORAL C. C., Canadian Forestry Corps.

CAMPBELL, LIEUT. C. A., Cheshire Regiment.

CARY-ELWES, 2nd LIEUT. W. G., Irish Guards.

CHISHOLM, LIEUT. A. E., Royal Scots.

CLERY, CAPT. and ADJ. N. C., M.C., Royal Field Artillery.

CLIFFORD, LIEUT. H. G., Lincolnshire Regiment.

CUMING, CAPT. A. E. M., M.C., Royal Irish Fusiliers.

DALY, 2nd LIEUT. C. W., Rifle Brigade.

DAME, 2nd LIEUT. J. W., Irish Guards.

DE BLESS, MIDSHIPMAN G. A. H., H.M.S. *Revenge.*

DE LA PASTURE, CAPT. C. E. M., Scots Guards.

DE STACPOOLE, LIEUT. R., Connaught Rangers.

DE STACPOOLE, 2nd LIEUT. R. A. A., Royal Field Artillery.

DOLAN, LIEUT. H. E., Royal Air Force.

DOWNING, LIEUT. F. G., Middlesex Regiment.

DRUITT, 2nd LIEUT. E. J., Royal Berkshire Regiment.

EMMET, 2nd LIEUT. R., Life Guards.

ESMONDE, MIDSHIPMAN J. H. G., H.M.S. *Invincible.*

FENDALL, 2nd LIEUT. C. M., Royal Field Artillery.

FLEMING, 2nd LIEUT. H. J., Dorsetshire Regiment.

FORSTER, PRIVATE W., Royal Fusiliers.

FOTTRELL, 2nd LIEUT. B. J., Royal Irish Regiment.

FOX, A., National Guard.

FRIEND, LIEUT. C. P., Royal Field Artillery.

GERARD, CAPT. G. M., Highland Light Infantry.

GOULDSBURY, CAPT. H. C., King's African Rifles.

GRATTAN-BELLEW, MAJOR W. A., M.C., Royal Flying Corps.

GREEN, CAPT. D. F., Northumberland Fusiliers.

GREIG, MAJOR H. I., Royal Garrison Artillery.

HARTLEY, LIEUT. D. J., Dragoon Guards.

HAWKINS, MAJOR A. E., Royal Field Artillery.

HERRICK, CAPT. H. E., Royal Irish Fusiliers.

HEWETT, 2nd LIEUT. S. H., Royal Warwickshire Regiment.

HILLIER, 2nd LIEUT. M., King's Own Scottish Borderers.

HOBDELL, CAPT. A. B., Wiltshire Regiment.

KOE, 2ND LIEUT. P. S., York and Lancaster Regiment.

LAWDER, CAPT. N. W., Bedfordshire Regiment, attached Nigeria
Regiment.

LEAHY, LIEUT. N. E., Royal Field Artillery.

LETEUX, PRIVATE F., Canadian Machine Gun Corps.

LITTLEWOOD, 2nd LIEUT. C. W., M.C., Royal Engineers.

LORD, 2nd LIEUT. E. C., Irish Guards.

LYNCH-STAUNTON, 2nd LIEUT. G., Hussars.

MACARDLE, 2nd LIEUT. K. C., Manchester Regiment.

MACDERMOT, 2nd LIEUT. H. M., Royal Irish Fusiliers.

MACDONNELL, MAJOR F. W. J., West Yorkshire Regiment.

MANBY-COLEGRAVE, LIEUT. G. T., A.S.C., R.G.A.

MARTIN, LIEUT. C. A., Royal Dublin Fusiliers.

McGEE, LIEUT. E. J., Royal Air Force.

McGRATH, LIEUT. G. N., Dragoon Guards.

McMANUS, LIEUT. T. J., Middlesex Regiment.

MIERS, CAPT. D. N. C. C., Cameron Highlanders.

MOLYNEUX-SEEL, CAPT. L. E. H., Border Regiment.

MORRALL, 2nd LIEUT. J. B., Royal Warwickshire Regiment.

MORRISS, 2nd LIEUT. J. S., Royal Warwickshire Regiment.

MURPHY, LT.-COL. A. D., D.S.O., M.C., Leinster Regiment.

MURPHY, CAPT. E. M. H., Leinster Regiment.

NASH, LIEUT. J. H., Irish Guards.

NEVILE, CAPT. B. P., Lincolnshire Regiment.

NICHOLSON, MAJOR E. F. D., South Lancashire Regiment.

NOEL, CAPT. HON. R. E. T. M., Royal Fusiliers.

O'CONNOR, 2nd LIEUT. R. A., Leinster Regiment.

O'FARRELL, 2nd LIEUT. H. A., Irish Guards.

O'HARA, 2nd LIEUT. P. G., East Surrey Regiment.

PAULING, LIEUT. G. F., M.C., Grenadier Guards.

PETRE, CAPT. L. G. LORD, Coldstream Guards.

PRIOR, LIEUT.-COL., E. R. S., D.S.O., M.C., South Lancashire Regiment.

RYAN, CAPT. J. H. A., M.C., King's Liverpool Regiment.

SHINE, 2nd LIEUT. H. P., Royal Irish Fusiliers.

SHINE, 2nd LIEUT. J. D., Royal Irish Regiment.

SHINE, CAPT. J. O., Royal Dublin Fusiliers.

SMITH-SLIGO, LIEUT. A. G. R. J., Cameron Highlanders.

SNEAD-COX, 2nd LIEUT. G. P. J., Royal Welch Fusiliers.

SNEAD-COX, 2nd LIEUT. R., Royal Scots.

STAPLETON-BRETHERTON, LIEUT. O. F. J. H., Lancers.

STONOR, 2nd LIEUT. C., Royal Inniskilling Fusiliers.

SWEETMAN, MAJOR M. J. J. (Hamish), Worcestershire Regiment.

THOMPSON, 2nd LIEUT. E. J. V. C., Royal Welch Fusiliers.

TIDMARSH, LIEUT. J. M., West Riding Regiment, attached R.A.F.

TREVOR-JONES, 2nd LIEUT. E. E., Rifle Brigade.

TREVOR-JONES, CAPT. J. E., M.C., Rifle Brigade.

TURNBULL, LIEUT. G. I., M.C., Welch Regiment.

TURNBULL, CAPT. J. O., Welch Regiment.

TURNER, 2nd LIEUT. G. A., Royal West Kent Regiment.

TYRRELL, 2nd LIEUT. F. C. V., Coldstream Guards.

WALKER, 2nd LIEUT. R., Lancashire Fusiliers.

WATERS, CAPT. C. L., M.C., Royal Berkshire Regiment.

WATKINS, CAPT. I. E. M., Monmouthshire Regiment.

WELD-BLUNDELL, PRIVATE L. J. S., Queen's Westminster Rifles.

WELD-BLUNDELL, 2nd LIEUT. R. S., King's Liverpool Regiment.

WILLETT, E. A., Sportsman's Battalion, Royal Fusiliers.

WOOD, CAPT. J. P. H., Manchester Regiment.

WOOLLETT, CAPT. J. C., Royal Air Force.

WORSLEY-WORSWICK, 2nd LIEUT. B. H., King Edward's Horse.

WOUNDED.

AGIUS, MAJOR A. A., M.C., London Regiment.

AGIUS, CAPT. E. E., Royal Fusiliers.

AGIUS, REV. DOM T. A., C.F. (4th class).

ALLPRESS, CAPT. H. V., Royal Garrison Artillery.

BARRY, 2nd LIEUT. P. R., M.C., Irish Guards.

BARRAUD, LIEUT. C., Manitoba Regiment.

BATES, SERGT. C. F., London Regiment.

BELLOC, LIEUT. L. M. J., Royal Engineers, attached R.A.F. (since killed in action).

BENSLY, 2nd LIEUT. R. H., Royal West Kent Regiment.

BRIDGER, CAPT. J. C., Royal Garrison Artillery.

BROWNE, PRIVATE J. G., Middlesex Regiment.

BROWNE, LIEUT. HON. M. D., Coldstream Guards (since killed in action).

BRUCE, CAPT. C. W., Gordon Highlanders (twice—since killed in accident).

BRUCE, CAPT. R. W., Shropshire Light Infantry (three times).

BURKE, CAPT. SIR G. H., Bart., Irish Guards (twice).

BYRNE, CAPT. F. B., Royal Warwickshire Regiment.

BYRNE, 2nd LIEUT. F. W., Royal Air Force (twice).

CAILLARD, CAPT. F. C. V. D., M.C., Somerset Light Infantry (twice).

CAILLARD, PRIVATE H., E. Ontario Regiment, Canadian Exped. Force.

CAMPBELL, LIEUT. C. H., Royal Field Artillery.

CASTLEROSSE, LIEUT. VISCOUNT, Irish Guards.

CLERY, LIEUT. M. J., M.C., Dragoon Guards.

CLERY, MAJOR V. A. C., M.C., Signal Company, Royal Engineers.

CLIFFORD, LIEUT. H. G., Lincolnshire Regiment (since killed in action).

COATS, CAPT. and ADJ. J. S., M.C., Coldstream Guards.

COX, LIEUT. F., Royal West Surrey Regiment.

CUBITT, LIEUT. C. C., Grenadier Guards (twice).

DALY, LIEUT. D. W., Hussars.

DALY, MAJOR L. D., D.S.O., Leinster Regiment.

DAVEY, REV. DOM J. R., C.F. (4th Class).

DE LA PASTURE, MAJOR, MARQUIS, M.C., King's African Rifles.

DE SALIS, LIEUT. A. D. R., Irish Guards.

DE STACPOOLE, CAPT. E. H. M., Leinster Regiment.

DE STACPOOLE, 2nd LIEUT. F., Irish Guards.

DE TRAFFORD, CAPT. H. E. F., Dragoons.

DILLON, LIEUT. J. J., M.C., Connaught Rangers.

D'OILLIAMSON, LIEUT. T. E., French Artillery Regiment.

DOLAN, LIEUT. H. E., M.C., Royal Air Force (twice—since killed in action).

ELLISON, CAPT. A. J., York and Lancaster Regiment.

ELWES, CAPT. R. P., M.C., Coldstream Guards (Prisoner of War).

FORSTER, LIEUT. T., Royal Engineers, T.F. (twice).

FOX, LIEUT. W. B., Gurkha Rifles.

FRENCH, LIEUT. C. H., Royal Warwickshire Regiment.

FRIEND, LIEUT. C. P., Royal Field Artillery (since died of illness).

GARTLAN, MAJOR G. J., D.S.O., M.C., Royal Irish Rifles (twice).

GERARD, CAPT. G. M., Highland Light Infantry (twice—since died of illness).

HALLINAN, LIEUT. E. V., M.C., Royal Field Artillery.

HASKETT-SMITH, CAPT. E. A., Worcestershire Regiment.

HAY, CAPT. L. F., Black Watch (twice).

HERRICK, CAPT. H. E., Royal Irish Fusiliers (since killed in action).

HEYDON, MAJOR G., M.C., A.M.C., A.E.F.

HOBDELL, CAPT. A. B., Wiltshire Regiment (three times—since died of wounds).

HONYWOOD, LIEUT. W. W., M.C., Lancers (three times).

JACKSON, MAJOR R. H. H., Machine Gun Corps.

JEFFRIES, MAJOR W. F. C., D.S.O., Royal Dublin Fusiliers (twice).

JUMP, CAPT. H., Dragoons (Prisoner of War).

KAVANAGH, CAPT. V. H., Royal Irish Fusiliers.

KEENAN, CAPT. J. B., Irish Guards (twice).

KENDAL, PRIVATE R. P. J., East Yorkshire Regiment.

KIRKPATRICK, LIEUT. I. A., Royal Inniskilling Fusiliers.

LANE-JOYNT, CAPT. W. S. R., Royal Army Service Corps.

LEVELIS-MARKE, LIEUT. P. L., M.C., Royal West Kent Regiment.

MacLACHLAN, 2nd LIEUT. J. G., Irish Guards.

MACMULLEN, 2nd LIEUT. J. F., South Wales Borderers.

McMANUS, LIEUT. T. J., Middlesex Regiment.

MAHONY, LIEUT. M. F. J. R., Royal Air Force (Prisoner of War).

MANSFIELD, MAJOR E. L., Northamptonshire Regiment.

MARCH, MAJOR B. O., D.S.O., M.C., Royal Field Artillery.

MARLEY, LIEUT. V. D. K., Manchester Regiment (twice).

MARTIN, LIEUT. C. A., Royal Dublin Fusiliers (twice—since died of wounds).

MARTIN, CAPT. T. S., Connaught Rangers.

MATHEW, LIEUT. T., Welsh Guards.

MAXWELL, CAPT. I. C., Cameron Highlanders, attached R.A.F.

MORRALL, 2nd LIEUT. J. B., Royal Warwickshire Regiment (since died of wounds).

MOSTYN, CAPT. J. E. H., Royal Sussex Regiment.

MOSTYN, LIEUT. J. P., Royal Sussex Regiment.

MURRAY, 2nd LIEUT. T. H. E., Royal Field Artillery.

NELSON, PRIVATE A. H., Australian Infantry (twice).

NIALL, 2nd LIEUT. F., Wiltshire Regiment.

NUGENT, CAPT. J. F. H., D.S.O., Punjabis.

O'CONNOR, TROOPER D. M. M., Australian Light Horse.

O'DRISCOLL, LIEUT. P. F., Irish Guards (twice).

PAULING, LIEUT. G. F., M.C., Grenadier Guards (since killed in action).

PETRE, MAJOR R. L., D.S.O., M.C., South Wales Borderers (twice).

PURCELL-GILPIN, CAPT. P. R., M.C., Scots Guards.

QUINN, C.P.O. A. T., Naval Flying Service.

QUINN, CORPORAL H. O., Motor Cyclist Despatch Rider.

RADCLIFFE, LIEUT. J. F. E., Northumberland Fusiliers.

REYNOLDS, CAPT. N. C., Irish Guards.

RIDDELL, BRIG.-GEN. E. P. A., C.M.G., D.S.O., Rifle Brigade (five times).

ROCHE-KELLY, LIEUT.-COL. J., M.C., South Irish Horse (twice).

SHINE, 2nd LIEUT. H. P., Royal Irish Fusiliers (since killed in action).

SHINE, CAPT. J. O. W., Royal Dublin Fusiliers (since killed in action).

SMITH-GRANT, CAPT. W. H., M.C., Gordon Highlanders (twice).

SPRING, LIEUT. R. F. M., Royal Irish Regiment (twice).

STANTON, LIEUT. J. B. M., King's Own Scottish Borderers.

STOKES, 2nd LIEUT. A. S., Irish Guards.

SWEENY, LIEUT. T. H., Royal Engineers.

SWEETMAN, MAJOR M. J. J. (Hamish), Worcestershire Regiment (since died of wounds).

TURNBULL, LIEUT. G. I., M.C., Welch Regiment (since died of wounds).

TURNBULL, CAPT. J. O., Welch Regiment (since killed in action).

VAN CUTSEM, MAJOR E. C. L., M.C., Shropshire Light Infantry.

VIAN, LIEUT. C. A., Coldstream Guards.

WARRINGTON, CAPT. J., Royal Field Artillery.

WILLETT, 2nd LIEUT. J. W., London Regiment.

WILLIAMS, CAPT. G. V., M.C., Irish Guards.

WILSON, CAPT. C. J. N. W., East Kent Regiment.

WOOD, PRIVATE F. M., Otago Regiment, New Zealand Contingent.

WOOD, CAPT. J. P. H., Manchester Regiment (since killed in action).

WORSLEY-WORSWICK, LIEUT. C. F., Leicestershire Regiment.

WYNTER, LT.-COL. F. A., C.M.G., D.S.O., Royal Garrison Artillery.

PRISONERS OF WAR.

ELWES, CAPT. R. P., M.C., Coldstream Guards.

JUMP, CAPT. H., Dragoons (wounded).

LANGRAN, CAPT. W. H., M.C., West Yorkshire Regiment.

MAHONY, LIEUT. M. F. J. R., Royal Irish Fusiliers, attached Royal Air Force.

MARTIN, LIEUT. C. A., Royal Dublin Fusiliers (died of wounds).

McLOUGHLIN, 2nd LIEUT. J. H., Royal Irish Regiment.

MORRALL, 2nd LIEUT. J. B., Royal Warwickshire Regiment (died of wounds).

MOYSEY, CAPT. F., Suffolk Regiment.

SAUNDERS, MAJOR P. C., Ludianah Sikhs.

TIDMARSH, CAPT. D. M., M.C., Royal Irish Regiment, attached Royal Air Force.

TURNBULL, LIEUT. G. I., M.C., Welch Regiment (died of wounds).

ORDER OF THE BATH.

BANON, BRIG.-GEN. F. L., C.B.

ORDER OF SS. MICHAEL AND GEORGE.
KNIGHT COMMANDER.

HOWARD, MAJOR-GEN. SIR FRANCIS, K.C.B., D.S.O.

COMPANIONS.

KEATINGE, RT. REV. BISHOP W. L., C.B.E., C.F.

RAWLINSON, REV. DOM B. S., O.B.E., C.F.

RIDDELL, BRIG.-GEN. E. P. A., D.S.O., Rifle Brigade.

WYNTER, LT.-COL. F. A., D.S.O., Royal Garrison Artillery.

ORDER OF THE BRITISH EMPIRE.
MILITARY DIVISION.
COMMANDERS.

LEE, COL. (HON. BRIG.-GEN.) F.

KEATINGE, RT. REV. BISHOP W. L., C.M.G., C.F.

OFFICERS.

BUTLER, REV. DOM R. U., C.F.

CAMPDEN, MAJOR A. E. J. N., VISCOUNT, Gloucestershire Regiment.

CORBETT, MAJOR D. M., R.A.M.C.

DE TRAFFORD, CAPT. R. E., Intelligence Corps.

ELWES, CAPT. F. G., Gloucestershire Regiment.

JACKSON, MAJOR R. H. H., M.C., East Surrey Regiment.

MASKELL, MAJOR W. E., Devonshire Regiment.

MURRAY, CAPT. E. G. D., R.A.M.C.

RAWLINSON, REV. DOM B. S., C.M.G., C.F.

REYNOLDS, CAPT. W. C. N., Irish Guards.

ROSS, MAJOR C., Royal Artillery.

SHARPE, MAJOR G. M., D.S.O., Berkshire Regiment.

SWEETMAN, LIEUT.-COL. M. J., East Yorks Regiment.

YOUNG, REV. DOM S. D., D.S.O., C.F.

MEMBER.

SHERLOCK, CAPT. T. D., Royal Irish Regiment.

DISTINGUISHED SERVICE ORDER.

DALY, MAJOR L. D., Leinster Regiment.

DUNBAR, MAJOR J. C., Royal Horse Artillery.

GALBRAITH, MAJOR E. D., Indian Army.

GARTLAN, CAPT. and BT.-MAJOR G. J., M.C., Royal Irish Rifles.

HANLEY, MAJOR H. A., M.C., Middlesex Regiment.

JEFFRIES, MAJOR W. F. C., Royal Dublin Fusiliers.

MARCH, MAJOR B. O., M.C., Royal Field Artillery.

MAXWELL-SCOTT, LIEUT.-COMR. M. J. R., R.N.

MURPHY, LIEUT.-COL. A. D., M.C., Leinster Regiment.

MURROW, LIEUT.-COL. H. L., Royal Garrison Artillery.

NUGENT, CAPT. J. F. H., Punjabis.

O'GORMAN, MAJOR B., Army Service Corps.

PETRE, MAJOR R. L., M.C., South Wales Borderers.

PRIOR, LT.-COL. E. R. S., M.C., South Lancashire Regiment.

RIDDELL, BRIG.-GEN. E. P. A., Rifle Brigade, attached Cambridgeshire Regiment.

ROCHE-KELLY, LT.-COL. E. J., Royal Irish Regiment.

SHARPE, CAPT. and BT.-MAJOR A. G. M., Berkshire Regiment.

YOUNG, REV. DOM S. D., C.F. (3rd class).

BAR AND SECOND BAR TO THE DISTINGUISHED SERVICE ORDER.

RIDDELL, BRIG.-GEN. E. P. A., D.S.O., Rifle Brigade, attached Cambridgeshire Regiment.

DISTINGUISHED SERVICE CROSS.

MUIRHEAD-GOULD, LIEUT. G. C., R.N.

PURCELL-GILPIN, LIEUT. G. R., R.N.V.R.

MILITARY CROSS.

AGIUS, MAJOR A. A., London Regiment.

AGIUS, CAPT. A. J., London Regiment.

BARRY, 2nd LIEUT. P. R., Irish Guards.

BERKELEY, REV. DOM O., C.F. (3rd class).

BIRD, CAPT. C. ST. J., Royal Engineers.

BRUCE, CAPT. R. W., Shropshire Light Infantry.

BULFIN, LIEUT. E. F., Yorkshire Regiment.

BURKE, CAPT. J. B., Grenadier Guards.

CAILLARD, CAPT. F. C., Somerset Light Infantry.

CHESNEY, CAPT. A. A. I., Intelligence Corps.

CLERY, LIEUT. M. J., Dragoon Guards.

CLERY, CAPT. N. C., Royal Field Artillery.

CLERY, MAJOR V. A. C., Signal Company, Royal Engineers.

CLUTTON, 2nd LIEUT. A. H., Royal Field Artillery.

COATS, CAPT. J. S., Coldstream Guards.

COATS, CAPT. M. D., Scots Guards.

CUBITT, LIEUT., C. C., Grenadier Guards.

CUMING, LIEUT. A. E. M., Royal Irish Fusiliers.

DALY, LIEUT. A., Royal Garrison Artillery.

DE LA PASTURE, MAJOR, MARQUIS, King's African Rifles.

DE STACPOOLE, MAJOR E. H., Leinster Regiment.

DILLON, LIEUT. J. J., Connaught Rangers.

DOLAN, LIEUT. H. E., Royal Air Force.

ELWES, CAPT. R. P., Coldstream Guards.

FORSTER, LIEUT. T., Royal Engineers, T.F.

GARTLAN, CAPT. and BT.-MAJOR G. J., Royal Irish Rifles.

GRATTAN-BELLEW, MAJOR W. A., Royal Flying Corps.

GUISE-BROWN, LIEUT. H., Irish Guards.

HALLINAN, LIEUT. E. V., Royal Field Artillery.

HANLEY, MAJOR H. A. O., Middlesex Regiment.

HEYDON, MAJOR G., A.M.C., Australian Expeditionary Force.

HONYWOOD, LIEUT. W. W., Lancers.

JACKSON, MAJOR H. H., East Surrey Regiment.

JAMES, CAPT. F. R., Royal Field Artillery, attached Royal Engineers.

KENYON, MAJOR J. R., Royal Field Artillery.

KILLEEN, LIEUT., Lord, Lancers.

LANGRAN, CAPT. W. H., West Yorkshire Regiment.

LEAHY, LIEUT. J. H., Royal Field Artillery.

LEVELIS-MARKE, LIEUT. P. L., Royal West Kent Regiment.

LITTLEWOOD, 2nd LIEUT. C. W., Royal Engineers.

MACARDLE, CAPT. J. R., Royal Field Artillery.

MARCH, MAJOR B. O., Royal Field Artillery.

MARTIN, CAPT. T. F., Royal Field Artillery.

MAXWELL, CAPT. G. J. C., Royal Air Force.

MOSTYN, CAPT. J. C. M., Royal Field Artillery.

MURPHY, LIEUT.-COL. A. D., Leinster Regiment.

PAULING, LIEUT. G. F., Grenadier Guards.

PETRE, MAJOR R. L., South Wales Borderers.

POWER, LIEUT. F. T., Royal Dublin Fusiliers.

PRIOR, LIEUT.-COL. E. R. S., South Lancashire Regiment.

PURCELL-GILPIN, CAPT. P. R., Scots Guards.

ROCHE-KELLY, LIEUT.-COL. J., South Irish Horse.

RYAN, CAPT. J. H. A., King's Liverpool Regiment.

SAUNDERS, LIEUT. H. ST. G., Welsh Guards.

SMITH-GRANT, CAPT. W. H., Gordon Highlanders.

STOKES, MAJOR R. R., Royal Field Artillery.

STOURTON, 2nd LIEUT. HON. W. M., Grenadier Guards.

TIDMARSH, CAPT. D. M., Royal Irish Regiment, attached R.A.F.

TREVOR-JONES, CAPT. J. E., Rifle Brigade.

TURNBULL, LIEUT. G. I., Welch Regiment.

VAN CUTSEM, MAJOR E. C. L., Shropshire Light Infantry.

WATERS, CAPT. C. L., Berkshire Regiment, attached Nigeria Regiment.

WATTS, MAJOR R. C., Royal Warwickshire Regiment.

WILKINSON, CAPT. V., Border Regiment.

WILLIAMS, CAPT. G. V., Irish Guards.

BAR TO THE MILITARY CROSS.

CAILLARD, CAPT. F. C. V. D., M.C., Somerset Light Infantry.

CLUTTON, 2nd LIEUT. A. H., M.C., Royal Field Artillery.

CUMING, LIEUT. A. E. M., M.C., Royal Irish Fusiliers.

DE LA PASTURE, MAJOR, MARQUIS, M.C., King's African Rifles.

PRIOR, LIEUT.-COL. E. R. S., M.C., South Lancashire Regiment.

PURCELL-GILPIN, CAPT. P. R., M.C., Scots Guards.

STOKES, MAJOR R. R., M.C., Royal Field Artillery.

WATERS, CAPT. C. L., M.C., Royal Berkshire Regiment, attached Nigeria Regiment.

DISTINGUISHED FLYING CROSS.

MAXWELL, CAPT. G. J. C., M.C., Royal Air Force.

AIR FORCE CROSS.

MAXWELL, CAPT. G. J. C., M.C., D.F.C., Royal Air Force.

ROYAL VICTORIA MEDAL.

QUINN, CORPORAL H. O., Motor Cyclist Despatch Rider, Reserve Special Corps, R.E.

Foreign Honours

FRENCH.

LEGION OF HONOUR.

(CROIX D'OFFICIER.)

KEATINGE, RT. REV. BISHOP W. L., C.M.G., C.B.E., C.F.

RAWLINSON, REV. DOM B. S., C.M.G., D.S.O., C.F.

(CROIX DE CHEVALIER.)

D'OILLIAMSON, LIEUT. T. E., 46th Artillery Regiment (French Army).

GALBRAITH, MAJOR E. D., D.S.O., Indian Army.

MUIRHEAD-GOULD, LIEUT.-CDR. G. C., D.S.C., R.N.

ROCHE-KELLY, LIEUT.-COL. E. J., D.S.O., Royal Irish Regiment.

CROIX DE GUERRE.

DEASE, CAPT. A. J., Red Cross, Section Sanitaire Anglaise.

DE STACPOOLE, CAPT. E. H., M.C., Leinster Regiment.

D'OILLIAMSON, LIEUT. T. E., 46th Artillery Regiment (French Army).

FFRENCH-MULLEN, MAJOR D. R., Royal Engineers.

SHARPE, MAJOR A. G., D.S.O., O.B.E., Berkshire Regiment.

STOKES, MAJOR R. R., M.C., Royal Field Artillery.

WYNTER, LT.-COL. F. A., C.M.G., D.S.O., Royal Garrison Artillery.

BELGIAN.

ORDER OF LEOPOLD.

GREIG, MAJOR H. I., Royal Garrison Artillery.

VAN CUTSEM, MAJOR E. C. L., M.C., Shropshire Light Infantry.

ORDER OF THE CROWN OF BELGIUM.

(CHEVALIER.)

SHARPE, MAJOR A. G., D.S.O., O.B.E., Berkshire Regiment.

WILLIAMS, CAPT. G. V., M.C., Irish Guards.

CROIX DE GUERRE (BELGE).

CHESNEY, CAPT. A. A. I., Intelligence Corps.

KIRKPATRICK, LIEUT. I. A., Royal Inniskilling Fusiliers.

SHARPE, MAJOR A. G., D.S.O., O.B.E., Berkshire Regiment.

VAN CUTSEM, MAJOR E. C. L., M.C., Shropshire Light Infantry.

ITALIAN.
ORDER OF THE CROWN OF ITALY.
(OFFICER.)

DUNBAR, MAJOR J. C., D.S.O., Royal Horse Artillery.

BRONZE MEDAL FOR MILITARY VALOUR.

BRUCE, CAPT. R. W., M.C., Shropshire Light Infantry.

PORTUGUESE.
ORDER OF CHRIST.

RAWLINSON, REV. DOM B. S., C.M.G., D.S.O., C.F.

ORDER OF AVIS.

STAPLETON, COMMANDER G., R.N.

RUSSIAN.
ORDER OF ST. STANISLAS.
WITH SWORDS.

SWEETMAN, LIEUT.-COL. M. J., O.B.E., East Yorks Regiment.

ORDER OF ST. ANNE.
WITH SWORDS.
(COMPANION.)

JACKSON, MAJOR R. R. H., O.B.E., M.C., East Surrey Regiment.

GREEK.
ORDER OF THE REDEEMER.
(Chevalier.)
Muirhead-Gould, Lieut.-Cdr. G. C., D.S.C., R.N.

ROUMANIAN.
ORDER OF THE CROWN OF ROUMANIA.
With Swords.
(Chevalier.)
de Trafford, Capt. R. E., O.B.E., Intelligence Corps.

ORDER OF THE STAR OF ROUMANIA.
With Swords.
(Officer.)
Murrow, Lieut.-Col. H. L., D.S.O., Royal Garrison Artillery.

SERBIAN.
ORDER OF THE WHITE EAGLE.
Martin, Lieut. C. A., Royal Dublin Fusiliers.

ORDER OF ST. SAVA.
(Officer.)
Corbett, Major D. M., O.B.E., R.A.M.C.

CHINESE.
ORDER OF WEN-HU.
O'Gorman, Major B. O., D.S.O., R.A.S.C.

MENTIONED IN DESPATCHES.
Agius, Major A. A., M.C., London Regiment.
Agius, Capt. A. J., M.C., London Regiment (twice).
Agius, Rev. Dom T. A., C.F. (4th class).

BANON, BRIG.-GEN. F. L., C.B., Assistant Adjutant-General (twice).

BERKELEY, REV. DOM O., M.C., C.F. (3rd class).

BIRD, CAPT. C. ST. J., M.C., Royal Engineers.

BOYD, CAPT. F. H., Royal Engineers.

BRITTEN, LIEUT.-COL. T. X., Mahratta Light Infantry.

BROWNE, LIEUT. HON. M. D., Coldstream Guards.

BUTLER, REV. DOM R. U., O.B.E., C.F. (2nd class).

CAILLARD, CAPT. F. C. V. D., M.C., Somerset Light Infantry.

CLERY, CAPT. N. C., M.C., Royal Field Artillery.

CLERY, MAJOR V. A. C., M.C., Royal Engineers (twice).

COATS, CAPT. and ADJUTANT J. S., M.C., Coldstream Guards.

CORBETT, MAJOR D. M., O.B.E., R.A.M.C. (twice).

COVENTRY, CAPT. J. J., R.A.S.C.

CRYAN, CAPT. R. W. W., North Staffordshire Regiment.

DALY, LIEUT. A., M.C., Royal Garrison Artillery.

DALY, MAJOR L. D., D.S.O., Leinster Regiment (four times).

DE ARTIMÉ, CAPT. P., R.A.S.C.

DE LA PASTURE, CAPT. C. E. M., Scots Guards.

DE STACPOOLE, MAJOR E. H., Leinster Regiment (twice).

DE STACPOOLE, 2nd LIEUT. R.A., Royal Field Artillery.

DE TRAFFORD, CAPT. R. E., Intelligence Corps (twice).

DILLON, Lieut. J. J., M.C., Connaught Rangers.

DUNBAR, MAJOR J. C., D.S.O., Royal Horse Artillery (three times).

FFRENCH-MULLEN, MAJOR D. R. ST. J., Royal Engineers (twice).

GALBRAITH, MAJOR E. D., D.S.O., Indian Army (twice).

GARTLAN, CAPT. and BT.-MAJOR G. J., D.S.O., M.C., Royal Irish Rifles (three times).

GOULDSBURY, CAPT. H. C., Royal Berkshire Regt., attached King's African Rifles.

GRATTAN-BELLEW, MAJOR W. A., M.C., Royal Flying Corps.

GUISE-BROWN, LIEUT. H., M.C., Irish Guards.

HANLEY, MAJOR H. A. O., D.S.O., M.C., Middlesex Regiment (three times).

HAWKINS, MAJOR A. E., Royal Field Artillery.

HAY, CAPT. L. F., Black Watch.

HAYDON, LIEUT. J. C., Irish Guards.

HONYWOOD, LIEUT. W. W., M.C., Lancers (three times).

HOUNSELL, CAPT. R. S., Royal Engineers.

HOWARD, MAJOR-GEN. SIR FRANCIS, K.C.B., K.C.M.G., D.S.O.

JACKSON, MAJOR R. H. H., East Surrey Regiment (twice).

JEFFRIES, MAJOR W. F. C., D.S.O., Royal Dublin Fusiliers (twice).

KEATINGE, RIGHT REV. BISHOP W. L., C.M.G., C.B.E., C.F. (five times).

KENYON, MAJOR J. R., M.C., Royal Field Artillery.

KIRKPATRICK, LIEUT. I. A., Royal Inniskilling Fusiliers (twice).

LAMBERT, LIEUT. C., London Regiment.

MACDERMOT, MAJOR E. T., Assistant Inspector Q.M.G. Services S.C.

MACDERMOT, MAJOR F. C., Royal Army Service Corps (four times).

MARCH, MAJOR B. O., D.S.O., M.C., Royal Field Artillery.

MARTIN, LIEUT. C. A., Royal Dublin Fusiliers.

MARTIN, MAJOR R. R., Royal Irish Rifles (twice).

MOSTYN, CAPT. J. C. M., M.C., Royal Field Artillery.

MOSTYN, LIEUT. J. P., Royal Sussex Regiment, attached Royal Air Force.

MOYSEY, CAPT. F., Suffolk Regiment.

MUIRHEAD-GOULD, LIEUT. G., R.N., Armoured Trains Service.

MURPHY, LIEUT.-COL. A. D., D.S.O., M.C., Leinster Regiment (four times).

MURROW, LIEUT.-COL. H. L., D.S.O., Royal Garrison Artillery.

NUGENT, CAPT. J. F. H., D.S.O., Punjabis (twice).

O'GORMAN, MAJOR B., D.S.O., Royal Army Service Corps.

O'GORMAN, LIEUT.-COL. M., C.B., Royal Field Artillery.

PETRE, MAJOR R. L., D.S.O., M.C., South Wales Borderers (seven times).

PRIOR, LIEUT.-COL. E. R. S., D.S.O., M.C., South Lancashire Regiment.

RAWLINSON, REV. DOM B. S., C.M.G., O.B.E., C.F. (five times).

RIDDELL, BRIG.-GEN. E. P. A., C.M.G., D.S.O., Rifle Brigade (four times).

ROCHE-KELLY, MAJOR E. J., D.S.O., Royal Irish Regiment (twice).

ROCHE-KELLY, LIEUT.-COL. J., South Irish Horse.

ROSKELL, LIEUT.-COL. W. J., North Staffordshire Regiment.

RYAN, LIEUT. J. H. A., M.C., King's Liverpool Regiment.

SAUNDERS, CAPT. P. C., Ludianah Sikhs.

SHARPE, MAJOR A. G. M., D.S.O., O.B.E., Royal Berkshire Regiment (three times).

SUMNER, LIEUT. G. J., Remount Department.

SWEETMAN, LIEUT.-COL. M. J., O.B.E., East Yorks Regiment (twice).

SWEETMAN, MAJOR M. J. J. (Hamish), Worcestershire Regiment.

TIDMARSH, CAPT. D. M., M.C., Royal Irish Regiment.

TURNBULL, LIEUT. BERTRAND, Royal Garrison Artillery.

VIAN, LIEUT. C. A., Coldstream Guards.

WATERS, CAPT. C. L., M.C., Royal Berkshire Regiment.

WATTS, MAJOR R. C., M.C., Royal Warwickshire Regiment.

WESTLAKE, PRIVATE A. M., Artists' Rifles.

WILKINSON, LIEUT. S. J., Royal Army Service Corps.

WILKINSON, CAPT. V., M.C., Border Regiment.

WILLIAMS, CAPT. G. V., M.C., Irish Guards.

WILSON, CAPT. C. J., East Kent Regiment.

WYNTER, LIEUT.-COL. F. A., C.M.G., D.S.O., Royal Garrison Artillery (four times).

YOUNG, REV. DOM S. D., D.S.O., C.F. (3rd Class) (three times).

YOURELL, CAPT. J. R., Royal Army Medical Corps.

Roll of Honour

SUMMARY

SERVING IN THE FORCES	506
KILLED IN ACTION, OR DIED ON SERVICE	109
WOUNDED	111
PRISONERS OF WAR	11
TOTAL HONOURS	154
C.B.	1
K.C.M.G.	1
C.M.G.	4
C.B.E.	2
O.B.E. (MILITARY DIVISION)	14
M.B.E.	1
D.S.O.	18
BARS TO D.S.O.	2
D.S.C.	2
M.C.	65
BARS TO M.C.	8
D.F.C.	1
A.F.C.	1
ROYAL VICTORIA MEDAL	1
FOREIGN HONOURS	33
MENTIONS IN DESPATCHES	141

Official Record of Awards

The following is a list of the official statements concerning awards of the D.S.O., D.S.C., M.C. and D.F.C. to Old Gregorians during the War.

The rank given in each case is that which was held at the time of the award, and the date is that of publication in the *London Gazette*.

Distinguished Service Order

DALY, CAPT. L. D., 2nd Batt., Leinster Regiment.

" For exceptional coolness and courage throughout the campaign. By his personal cheerfulness and example under heavy fire has been a most successful commander. Specially recommended for exceptional courage and coolness during the most severe shelling whilst the Battalion was in the Hooge trenches in August, 1915." (January 14th, 1916.)

DUNBAR, MAJOR J. C., Royal Artillery.

" Commanded his battery at Chocolate Hill with courage and skill above the average, holding his own against the enemy artillery and refusing to be silenced. Invaluable work as Brigade-Major R.A., Right Flank, 9th Corps. Untiring in all his staff work, and did much good work as Observing Officer for the Navy." (June 3rd, 1916.)

GALBRAITH, MAJOR E. D., 55th (Coke's) Rifles, Frontier Force, Indian Army.

" For conspicuously good work as D.A.A.G. of the Corps during the operations leading up to and including the battle of Arras, and subsequent fighting between April and June, 1917. His energy and devotion to duty were invaluable in a time of great pressure. His services throughout the period under review were invaluable." (January 1st, 1918.)

GARTLAN, CAPT. and BT.-MAJOR G. J., Royal Irish Rifles.

" This officer was indefatigable as Brigade Major in the actions near Henin in March, 1918, and near Bethune in April and June, 1918. The success of the Brigade was in great measure due to his untiring zeal and energy." (January 1st, 1919.)

HANLEY, CAPT. (A./MAJOR) H. A. O., *M.C.*, 1st Batt., Middlesex
   Regiment.

   " Has served continuously in France since November, 1914.   Present
at all the operations around Ypres from May, 1915, to November, 1915,
including the second battle of Ypres.   Commanded the 1st Batt. Middlesex
Regiment with distinction from March, 1917, to September, 1917, including the actions around Arras in April and May.   Is a most efficient,
reliable and very brave officer."   (January 1st, 1918.)

JEFFRIES, CAPT. (A./MAJOR) W. F., Royal Dublin Fusiliers, Special
   Reserve.

   " Although suffering from the effects of gas poisoning at a time when
a portion of the line was penetrated, he mustered all scattered troops, and
with skilful leadership led them forward and restored the line. His example
of courage and contempt of danger had the most inspiring influence on the
men."   (July 26th, 1918.)

MARCH, CAPT. (A./MAJOR) B. O., *M.C.*, Royal Field Artillery (Special
   Reserve), attached 158th A Brigade.

   " This officer took over one of the Batteries of this Brigade after
severe fighting at Arras in March, 1918, when all its officers save one, and
a large percentage of the personnel were out of action.   The battery was
in consequence more or less disorganised ; he quickly pulled it together
and did excellent work, both at Robecq and Givenchy.   On 23rd June,
1918, at Givenchy, while doing an important and dangerous reconnaissance, he was severely wounded.   His courage and coolness in danger
were an excellent example to his men."   (January 1st, 1919.)

MAXWELL-SCOTT, LIEUT.-COMMANDER, M. J. R., R.N.

   " For valuable services in minelaying operations in proximity to the
enemy's coast defences in the Eastern Mediterranean."   (February
16th, 1917.)

MURPHY, MAJOR (Temp. LIEUT.-COL.), A. D., 2nd Batt. Leinster
   Regiment.

   " With great presence of mind he moved up troops to fill a gap,
which he had discovered by means of a personal reconnaissance, between
his unit and the next division, afterwards handling his Battalion with
exceptional skill and personally selecting the best positions under heavy
fire.   His reports were invaluable and accurate, clearing up an obscure
situation, and he has on all other occasions set a splendid example of
fearlessness and ability."   (August 25th, 1917.)

MURROW, MAJOR H. L., 35th Siege Battery, Royal Garrison Artillery.

" For continuous good work in command of the 35th Siege Battery since its arrival at this front in September, 1915. This battery has done much valuable work in many parts of the line." (January 1st, 1917.)

NUGENT, LIEUT. (Temp. CAPT.) J. F. H., 28th Punjabis, Indian Army.

" This officer brought the Regiment out of action at Umm-el-Hannah on the 21st January, 1916, after the Commandant had been wounded, and showed much ability. On the 6th April, 1916, in the attack on Sannaiyat position, he was very forward in the attack, and again brought the Regiment out of action and commanded the Regiment with great ability and coolness after three officers senior to himself had become casualties, and has proved himself a fine soldier under two trying emergencies. I strongly recommend that this officer's excellent work should be rewarded, as he has been a great example to the men, and has been a great factor in keeping up their morale." (December 22nd, 1916.)

O'GORMAN, Temp. MAJOR B., General List.

" Conspicuous good work and tact in handling coloured labour under heavy bombing by enemy air craft. He has carried out all his duties in a commendable manner." (January 1st, 1918.)

PETRE, MAJOR R. L., *M.C.*, South Wales Borderers.

" For distinguished service in the field in Mesopotamia." (August 25th, 1917.)

PRIOR, Temp. MAJOR (A./LIEUT.-COL.) E. R. S., *M.C.*, 8th Batt., South Lancashire Regiment.

" For conspicuous gallantry, able leadership and devotion to duty, whilst commanding his Battalion during the fighting at Messines and Ypres from June to September, 1917. In the battle of Messines his Battalion captured and consolidated all its objectives and took numerous prisoners and machine guns. At Ypres, after the attack on July 31st, Colonel Prior held the Westhoek Ridge for six days, under very heavy shell fire and the most adverse weather conditions, and during the period August 7th to August 18th his Battalion was continually in the forward area, and did excellent work in consolidating captured positions and carrying up stores. The energy and cheerfulness of this officer have set a very fine example to the officers and men of his Battalion." (January 1st, 1918.)

RIDDELL, MAJOR (Temp. LIEUT.-COL.) E. P. A., Rifle Brigade, attached 1/1st Batt., Cambridgeshire Regiment, T.F.

" For conspicuous gallantry in action. He showed the greatest skill and foresight in assembling his Battalion and subsequently launching them to the attack without a casualty, in broad daylight, on ground observed by the enemy. His personal bravery, energy and example exercised great influence over all ranks. (Schwaben Redoubt, 14th October, 1916.)" (December 11th, 1916.)

ROCHE-KELLY, MAJOR (Temp. LIEUT.-COL.) E. J., Royal Irish Regiment.

" For conspicuous gallantry and devotion to duty in commanding his Battalion through an attack, in which he displayed great fearlessness and exceptional skill. He moved up through very heavy enemy barrage, personally reconnoitred two advanced positions, and supervised all details of consolidation, all the while exposed to very heavy shell fire. His splendid personal example and disregard of danger imbued all ranks with a spirit that swept away all opposition." (September 17th, 1917.)

SHARPE, CAPT. and BT.-MAJOR A. G. M., Royal Berkshire Regiment.

" For conspicuous gallantry and devotion to duty during a week's operations. When the enemy had launched a heavy attack and driven back the Brigade on the right, laying open the right flank, this officer went forward under heavy fire to clear up the situation, selected positions, and led up reserve companies to form a defensive flank. He also rallied leaderless men of other units and led them forward into the line. He gave a clear and accurate report of the situation on his return to Brigade Headquarters. (Wytschaete, 10-16th April, 1918.)" (September 16th, 1918.)

YOUNG, REV. S. D., Temp. C. F., 3rd Class, Army Chaplains' Department.

" He has acted as 2nd Assistant to the Principal Chaplain since September, 1915, and has rendered invaluable services. I consider he well merits distinction." (June 4th, 1917.)

Bar to the Distinguished Service Order

RIDDELL, MAJOR (Temp. LIEUT.-COL.), E. P. A., *D.S.O.*, Rifle
  Brigade.

"For conspicuous gallantry and devotion to duty when in command
of a battalion in reserve during an attack. He threw in a counter-attack at
a counter-stroke by the enemy, and held on to an eminence of the highest
tactical importance throughout the afternoon. His dispositions not only
allowed the Brigade to fall back in order before superior numbers, but
materially reduced the enemy's strength, as he held off three counter-
attacks and inflicted crushing casualties on the enemy. He eventually
assumed command and reorganised two other units of the Brigade and
passed four times through a heavy hostile barrage to his Brigade Headquarters to report on the situation. He handled a most difficult situation
with consummate skill, and his utter disregard of danger not only encour-
aged the men to further effort but was a magnificent example of courage
and determination." (December 26th, 1917.)

Second Bar to the Distinguished Service Order

RIDDELL, MAJOR and BT. LIEUT.-COL. (Temp. BRIG.-GEN.)
  E. P. A., *D.S.O.*, Rifle Brigade.

"During the several days of severe fighting in rearguard actions he
repeatedly organized counter-attacks, and personally led two of them.
After the whole of his staff had become casualties, and two of his commanding officers had been hit, his magnificent example and total disregard
of danger had the greatest effect in steadying his command." (July 26th,
1918.)

Distinguished Service Cross

MUIRHEAD-GOULD, LIEUT. G. C., R.N.

"For services on the Mediterranean Station, between January 1st
and June 30th, 1918." (December 11th, 1918.)

PURCELL-GILPIN, LIEUT. G. R., R.N.V.R.

"For valuable services in the British Aegean Squadron Auxiliary
Patrol Service during 1917." (May 17th, 1918.)

Military Cross

AGIUS, CAPT. A. V., 3rd Batt., London Regiment, T.F.

"For extreme gallantry in leading his company in the attack of
the 16th May, 1915, and subsequently on the night of the 16th/17th
May, searching as far as the enemy's wire and bringing in wounded."
(January 14th, 1916.)

AGIUS, LIEUT. (Temp. CAPT.) A. J., 1/3rd Batt., London Regiment.

" Has always shown great energy and commanded the Battalion in action for three weeks. Has been previously recommended for good work." (January 1st, 1917.)

BARRY, 2nd LIEUT. P. R., Irish Guards.

" For conspicuous gallantry and devotion to duty on September 27th, 1918, near St. Leger. Throughout the fighting he was calm and collected, acting as Adjutant, making all arrangements, and assisting in the reorganization. The next day, when there was some confusion owing to the hostile barrage at the crossing of the Hindenburg line, he did fine work in reorganizing the men and giving them the right direction." (February 1st, 1919.)

BERKELEY, REV. O. J., Temp. C.F., 4th Class, Army Chaplains' Department.

" For excellent work with the 17th Division for the past two and a half years. During that period he has shared the hardships of front line life, although over 50 years of age. His unalterable cheerfulness under all circumstances has been an example to officers and men." (March 8th, 1918.)

BIRD, Temp. LIEUT. (A./CAPT.) C. ST. J., Royal Engineers.

" For consistent good work and devotion to duty whilst Adjutant. He has done excellent work in the front line, showing gallantry and resource." (June 3rd, 1918.)

BRUCE, CAPT. R. W., Shropshire Light Infantry, Special Reserve, attached 2nd Batt.

" Performed consistent good work in command of his company in the field during period August, 1917, to November, 1918. He is a fearless leader of men, and sets a fine example to all ranks by his coolness and demeanour under fire. Various raids and patrols on the Struma and Varoar fronts were carried out by Capt. Bruce and his company, and the success attending these was due to the initiative and leadership displayed by him. The most efficient Company Commander in the Battalion, whose services strongly deserve recognition." (December 12th, 1919.)

BULFIN, LIEUT. E. F., Yorkshire Regiment, attached 2nd Batt., Leicestershire Regiment.

" For consistent good work during the operations of 1917–1918–1919. He has displayed great keenness and energy in the performance of his duties both in camp and in action, and has always shown disregard of personal safety under fire." (June 3rd, 1919.)

BURKE, 2nd LIEUT. J. B., Grenadier Guards.

" For conspicuous gallantry and devotion to duty when in charge of Battalion communications. At a moment when his men had been caught by hostile barrage and most of them hit, he reorganized them with great gallantry and coolness under heavy shell fire, and was able to maintain a constant flow of valuable information as to the progress of the attack. On reaching the final objective he rapidly opened communication with the troops on either flank and maintained them throughout the day in spite of continuous and heavy shelling. (Yser Canal, 31st July, 1917.)" (January 8th, 1918.)

CAILLARD, LIEUT. (Temp. CAPT.) F. C., 1st Batt., attached 6th Batt., Somerset Light Infantry.

" For conspicuous good work in March, 1917, when acting Brigade Major during preparations prior to the battle of Arras. During this period two raids were carried out by the Brigade, and, by his foresight, energy and hard work in assisting to arrange details, he greatly contributed to the successful issue of the operations. He was with his Battalion—6th Somerset Light Infantry—during the retirement of the enemy near Beaurains in March, 1917, and most skilfully led forward his men and occupied positions which caused enemy's rear parties to withdraw. He showed great initiative in ascertaining the situation whilst under fire, and thus enabled our troops quickly to follow up the enemy. He was wounded on 8th April, while reconnoitring ground over which the advance was to be made on 9th April near Arras. On rejoining the Brigade in August he again carried out a reconnaissance under very difficult circumstances, and thus greatly assisted the operations about Inverness Copse on 22nd/24th August." (January 1st, 1918.)

CHESNEY, Temp. CAPT. A. I., General List, attached Intelligence Corps.

" Capt. A. I. Chesney has been Intelligence Officer of the 35th Division for over two years, and at all times has performed his duties conscientiously and well, at no time sparing himself or having regard for his personal safety. He did particularly good work during the operations between September 28th and November 11th, 1918." (June 3rd, 1919.)

CLERY, LIEUT. M. J., Dragoon Guards.

" In command of a dismounted troop he displayed the greatest courage and determination in holding on to an advanced post for over two hours, although nearly surrounded by greatly superior numbers, thereby enabling infantry to withdraw and take up a position further back." (July 26th, 1918.)

CLERY, LIEUT. N. C., Royal Field Artillery.

" For excellent reconnaissance and observation work in the infantry front trenches, especially at Wolverghem on 19th and 23rd January, 1915, and near Spanbrock Molen on 7th March, 1915, and also for conspicuous gallantry on several occasions during the last 11 months, especially on night of 11th/12th March, 1915, when he laid his telephone wire to the front trenches under considerable difficulties, whilst subjected to a heavy fire all the time. During the attack on Spanbrock Molen the next day he was F.O.O. in the front trenches, and was the means of sending back valuable information and observations during the day. Again for conspicuous gallantry on the night of 11th/12th April, 1915, whilst he was out mending wires in an exposed position east of Ypres his telephonist was severely wounded. Lieut. Clery got him conveyed away to a place of safety and then continuing to mend the wire, had communication established by daylight." (January 14th, 1916.)

CLERY, LIEUT. V. A. C., 4th Signalling Co., Royal Engineers.

" For great gallantry in personally superintending the laying of the telephone lines every night over a large area of country which was continually shelled. It was due to his personal exertions and example during the period of April 27th to May 3rd, 1915, that the communications with the Brigade were kept up so well." (July 3rd, 1915.)

CLUTTON, 2nd LIEUT. A. H., Royal Field Artillery, Special Reserve.

" For conspicuous gallantry and devotion to duty when commanding a section of trench mortars, and afterwards taking his section to the front line, where for some hours he fought with the section as infantrymen. Throughout the day he showed complete disregard for his personal safety under very heavy shell fire, and showed a fine example of courage and coolness to his men." (September 16th, 1918.)

COATS, CAPT. J. S., 2nd Batt., Coldstream Guards.

" This officer became Adjutant to the Battalion in October, 1916. During the time he has been Adjutant he has shown the greatest zeal in carrying out his duties, however arduous. He took part in the operations on 31st July during the advance from Boesinghe, being responsible for maintaining communication. He has always displayed a fine example of energy and cheerfulness in all circumstances. In the trenches he always shows the utmost contempt for the enemy's shell fire, and sets a fine example to all ranks. He came out in the early part of the war, and was wounded, returning to France in January, 1916. He has completed twenty-six months of war service." (January 1st, 1918.)

COATS, LIEUT. (A./CAPT.) M. D., Scots Guards.

" Though in bad health, this officer refused to go sick, and stuck to his work with the Battalion throughout three weeks' fighting. On several occasions he carried messages of great importance, crossing open ground swept by fire, and thereby enabled the Battalion to carry out successful movements." (July 26th, 1918.)

CUBITT, LIEUT. C. C., Grenadier Guards (Special Reserve), attached 2nd Batt.

" For conspicuous gallantry and good leadership on 4th November, 1918, in command of one of the leading companies in the attack on Wargnies-le-Petit. In the face of intense machine gun fire he led his company forward, and, when seriously wounded in the leg, and lying out in the open, refused to be carried back, and continued to control his company and sent back information to Battalion Headquarters." (December 10th, 1919.)

CUMING, LIEUT. A. E. M., Royal Irish Fusiliers.

" When on patrol with four other ranks he engaged an enemy patrol, killing four and dispersing the remainder in a hand-to-hand struggle. On this and other occasions this officer was the means of rendering valuable information to the Brigade." (September 16th, 1918.)

DALY, 2nd LIEUT. A. J., Royal Field Artillery, Special Reserve.

" For conspicuous gallantry and devotion to duty. While he was helping to drag two guns out of the gun position, a shell burst, killing and wounding fourteen men. Though himself wounded, he managed to carry all the wounded off the track into shell holes. He later collected two teams and got his guns into the new positions. (N. of Zillebeke Lake, 6th/7th September, 1917.)" (March 18th, 1918.)

DE LA PASTURE, Temp. LIEUT. (Temp. CAPT.) G. H., 1/3rd Batt.,
King's African Rifles.

" This officer showed great resource and initiative in holding off
the enemy's counter-attack, and it was mainly due to his gallantry and
handling of his company that the other company, which took part in
the fight, was able to extricate itself from a very perilous position." (June
4th, 1917.)

DE STACPOOLE, CAPT. E. H., Leinster Regiment.

" For gallantry and consistent devotion to duty at all times and
in all places. This officer has shown outstanding capacity and energy
as Brigade Major from September, 1917. He has displayed conspicuous
gallantry in carrying out his duties under heavy shell and machine gun
fire on several occasions during the period February to September, 1918."
(January 1st, 1919.)

DILLON, LIEUT. J. J., Connaught Rangers (Special Reserve), attached
47th Trench Mortar Battery.

" This officer has served in the 47th Light Trench Mortar Battery
since June, 1916; in various operations and bombardments in which
the Battery has co-operated. Lieut. Dillon has always distinguished himself by his courage and resource under hostile retaliatory fire, provoked on
many of these occasions. He has, by his personal courage and devotion to
duty, set a fine example to all ranks in the Battery." (June 4th, 1917.)

DOLAN, Temp. LIEUT. H. E., H.Q., 104th Brigade, Royal Field
Artillery.

" For continual good service during past year in personally superintending the Brigade communications, often under heavy shell fire. A
very gallant officer—on one occasion he continued at his work under
shell fire after he had been wounded." (January 1st, 1917.)

ELWES, LIEUT. (A./CAPT.) R. P., 3rd Batt., Coldstream Guards.

" During the recent operations near Cambrai in November, 1917,
this officer has shown conspicuous initiative and powers of leadership
whilst commanding his company. His complete disregard of danger
and coolness in difficult moments has been of the greatest example to his
men. I cannot speak too highly of his conduct whilst in command of
his company throughout the hard fighting of the autumn of 1917."
(June 3rd, 1918.)

FORSTER, LIEUT. T., Royal Engineers.

" For conspicuous gallantry and devotion to duty when in charge of a large party laying a duck-board track towards the front line. On three occasions he had to withdraw his party owing to heavy bombardment of gas and other shells, but eventually, though wounded, completed his work." (January 18th, 1918.)

GARTLAN, LIEUT. G. I., Royal Irish Rifles.

" For gallant conduct at Neuve Chapelle with his machine guns during the advance on the 10th March, 1915, keeping up with the attacking line in spite of many obstacles, and frequently bringing his gun into action under great difficulties." (June 23rd, 1915.)

GRATTAN-BELLEW, CAPT. W. A., Royal Flying Corps.

" For conspicuous gallantry and skill on several occasions, notably the following : (1) With three other machines he attacked and drove off eight enemy machines, forcing one to the ground. (2) He attacked four Fokkers, forcing one down to 2,500 feet. Another was seen to crash to the ground during the fight. (3) When on a bombing raid two of the machines got behind owing to clouds, and were attacked by Fokkers, Captain Grattan-Bellew returned and attacked three Fokkers, one of which his observer shot down, and the others made off." (July 27th, 1916.)

GUISE-BROWN, Temp. CAPT. P. H., 7th South African Infantry.

" For general efficiency and devotion to duty. As a Company Commander he has always displayed zeal and manifested marked ability as a leader in action. He has on several occasions acted as Adjutant, and performed his duties with exceptional ability. His services during the fight at Narungombe on July 19th, 1917, in organizing resistance against counter-attacks merit award." (January 1st, 1918.)

HALLINAN, 2nd LIEUT. E. V., Royal Field Artillery.

" He gallantly led forward a party of infantry, whose officer had become a casualty, took the trench in front of him, and repelled a bombing attack. Later he repaired telephone wires under heavy fire." (April 17th, 1917.)

HANLEY, CAPT. (A./LIEUT.-COL.) H. A. O., Middlesex Regiment.

" For conspicuous gallantry and devotion to duty. He was in command of his Battalion which had just taken over the front line, when the enemy delivered a heavy counter-attack. He organized a defence which held up the enemy, and then counter-attacked. By his coolness at a critical moment he checked the enemy's advance, which, had it succeeded, would have jeopardized the success of operations which were to be undertaken on the following day. (E. of Ypres, 25th September, 1917.)" (April 6th, 1918.)

HEYDON, CAPT. G. A. M., Australian Army Medical Corps, attached 8th Batt., Australian Infantry.

" For conspicuous gallantry and devotion to duty during protracted operations. For four days he attended the wounded under incessant fire, carrying them to his dressing station when the stretcher-bearers had become casualties. (Pozieres, 24th/27th July, 1916)." (September 22nd, 1916.)

HONYWOOD, 2nd LIEUT. (Temp. LIEUT.) W. W., Lancers.

" When patrolling with an armoured car, he opened fire on a large enemy force, and wounded six of them. At great personal risk, under heavy fire, he placed one of the wounded men in the car, and returned, having obtained valuable information." (April 26th, 1917.)

JACKSON, CAPT. (Temp. MAJOR) R. H. H., *O.B.E.*, East Surrey Regiment, Special Reserve, and Machine Gun Corps.

" For gallantry and devotion to duty under fire, on the 12th March, 1920, at Ushun. Major Jackson, observing that the situation on the right was critical owing to enemy reinforcements, and that our line was beginning to waver, at once proceeded there, and, by his personal example under heavy machine-gun fire, inspired the attack." (September 27th, 1920.)

JAMES, Temp. LIEUT. F. R., Royal Field Artillery, attached 4th Field Survey Company, Royal Engineers.

" He has shown great energy and initiative in command of a group of Survey Posts throughout the operations. He has kept his posts continually in action in circumstances of great difficulty. It is largely due to his energy and skill that, in spite of numerous moves, posts being damaged, and telephone communications interrupted by shell fire, etc., his group has kept continually in action and results obtained little, if anything, inferior to those obtained before the battle, during ordinary trench warfare." (January 1st, 1917.)

KENYON, CAPT. J. R., Royal Field Artillery, Territorial Force.

"For conspicuous gallantry and devotion to duty during the action at Gaza on 26th and 27th March, 1917. To this officer was entrusted the task of making a very hurried reconnaissance of route for withdrawal of his Brigade on the night of 27th March, 1917, which he did with marked ability, and the whole Divisional Artillery was withdrawn without incident or delay along the route reconnoitred and marked by him and his orderlies. During the action of 18th and 19th April, 1917, this officer showed conspicuous devotion to duty in pushing forward with, and often in front of, the infantry, for observation." (January 1st, 1918.)

KILLEEN, LIEUT. (Lord), Lancers.

"During an engagement with 14 men and a Hotchkiss rifle, he held up the enemy, and inflicted heavy casualties. He held his ground with great courage and determination under close-range machine-gun fire, and so gained time for the infantry to take up a new defensive position. When outflanked on both sides and forced to withdraw he extricated his men with great skill." (June 22, 1918.)

LANGRAN, CAPT. W. H., West Yorkshire Regiment.

"In recognition of gallant conduct and determination displayed in attempting to escape from captivity." (January 30th, 1920.)

LEAHY, 2nd LIEUT. J. H., Royal Field Artillery, Special Reserve, attached 48th Brigade.

"For conspicuous gallantry and devotion to duty. In spite of very heavy hostile fire and the most difficult conditions, he succeeded in establishing and maintaining communication throughout the operations. (Wancourt, 9th/14th April, 1917.)" (June 18th, 1917.)

LEVELIS-MARKE, 2nd LIEUT. P. L., Royal West Kent Regiment.

"For conspicuous gallantry and devotion to duty while Intelligence Officer. When all the officers of a company had become casualties he took command and reorganized the company, and refused to be relieved until operations were concluded. He displayed the greatest zeal and energy." (December 2nd, 1918.)

LITTLEWOOD, 2nd LIEUT. C. W., Royal Engineers.

"For conspicuous gallantry and devotion to duty. He carried out the strengthening of a brick bridge under hostile barrage. His coolness and example enabled the work to be completed without cessation, despite casualties." (July 18th, 1917.)

MACARDLE, Temp. LIEUT. J. R., Royal Field Artillery.

" For conspicuous gallantry and devotion to duty. His Battery came under heavy fire, and the camouflage at one of the gunpits was set on fire. He at once ran in and extinguished it, and thus prevented the fire from spreading to the ammunition. It was largely due to his gallant act that the Battery was able to keep all its guns in action. (N. of Hollebeke, 19th September, 1917.)" (March 22nd, 1918.)

MARCH, CAPT. B. O., Royal Field Artillery, Special Reserve.

" During the operations round Guillmont from 21st July to 2nd August, 1916, inclusive, Capt. March did most valuable work as F.O.O., particularly on 30th July, at Arrow Head Copse, when as F.O.O. he sent several reports on the situation which were the first ones to get through, and were consequently of great value." (February 15th, 1917.)

MARTIN, LIEUT. (A./CAPT.) T.F., H.Q., 84th Brigade, Royal Field Artillery.

" For excellent work as Adjutant of the Brigade during the period under review. Capt. Martin did his business in a most satisfactory way, often under extremely trying circumstances. He gave excellent decisions on occasions, ran the tactical portion very well as required, and took an enormous amount of trouble to get efficiency. He was up night after night on the 'phone, always kept cheerful, and gave an excellent example to the men. His services have been brought up before for good work performed." (June 3rd, 1919.)

MAXWELL, CAPT. G. J. C., Royal Flying Corps.

" He has taken part in 43 offensive patrols, in 14 of which he acted as leader. He has destroyed at least three enemy aircraft, and driven down nine others completely out of control. He has consistently shown great skill in aerial combats, and his fearlessness and fine offensive spirit have been a splendid example to others." (March 7th, 1918.)

MOSTYN, CAPT. J. C. M., A/72nd Brigade, Royal Field Artillery.

" For conspicuous ability and devotion to duty during the period 1st May to 20th September, 1916. A fearless, energetic Battery Commander, who, on numerous occasions, has rendered conspicuous service, and has always had his Battery in a high state of efficiency." (January 1st, 1917.)

MURPHY, LIEUT. (Temp. CAPT.) A. D., 2nd Batt., Leinster Regiment.

" For continuous good work throughout the campaign. He is particularly cool under fire, and his work as Adjutant has been very good." (January 14th, 1916.)

PAULING, LIEUT. G. F., 1st Batt., Grenadier Guards.

" For conspicuous gallantry in action. He led his company and formed a strong point on the left flank, displaying great courage and initiative. Later, he maintained himself for 24 hours, causing considerable loss to the enemy until relieved. (Les Boeufs, September 25th, 1916.)" (November 14th, 1916.)

PETRE, CAPT. R. L., South Wales Borderers.

" For continuous excellent staff work and especially devotion to duty during November inclement weather, when his example and energy were invaluable." (February 2nd, 1916.)

POWER, LIEUT. F. T. A., Royal Dublin Fusiliers.

" As Brigade Forward Signalling Officer, he pushed forward through enemy barrage and maintained communication with the firing line for 48 hours in a very exposed position under continuous enemy shell fire. Through his initiative and resource communication was successfully kept up with our troops whilst advancing for a mile over very difficult country. He set a splendid example of pluck and ability." (September 17th, 1917.)

PRIOR, Temp. CAPT. E. R. S., South Lancashire Regiment.

" For seven days his company held a point in the trenches under continuous shell fire. The trench was repeatedly blown in, but he rebuilt it each time, and also captured hostile patrols consisting of an officer and six other ranks. He set a splendid example to his company under trying circumstances." (October 20th, 1916.)

PURCELL-GILPIN, LIEUT. (A./CAPT.) P. R., Scots Guards, Special Reserve.

" When the situation was very obscure after an enemy attack he carried out a daring and valuable reconnaissance over difficult and unknown ground, and in pitch darkness. He located the enemy and enabled the Battalion to take up a defensive position. He did splendid work during the following day and night, helping to clear the situation and reorganizing scattered parties of men." (July 5th, 1918.)

ROCHE-KELLY, CAPT. J., South Irish Horse.

" For continuous good service since the commencement of the war. This officer took part in the retreat from Mons in 1914, and has served continuously in France since then." (January 1st, 1917.)

RYAN, LIEUT. J. H. A., 1st Batt., Liverpool Regiment.

" For gallantry and great ability whilst in command of a company from the 31st October to 8th November, 1914." (February 18th, 1915.)

SAUNDERS, LIEUT. H. A. ST. G., Welsh Guards (Special Reserve), attached 1st Batt.

" For conspicuous gallantry and devotion to duty near Bavay on 6th November, 1918. In the attack, after a long fire fight, he led his platoon in a charge against an enemy post, being the first to reach it, and killing two and capturing the remainder of the garrison. The rest of the day he was always well in advance with his platoon, and finally succeeded in consolidating a position further forward than any other part of the Battalion line." (December 10th, 1919.)

SMITH-GRANT, LIEUT. (A./CAPT.) W. H., Gordon Highlanders.

" When in command of a raiding party, although wounded, he continued to direct operations, bombed a hostile machine gun, and killed two of the enemy. He set a splendid example throughout, and was largely responsible for the success of the raid." (April 17th, 1917.)

STOKES, 2nd LIEUT. R. R., Royal Field Artillery.

" After the F.O.O. of his Battery had been killed, he took his place and restored communication with the Battery under intense fire. Accompanied by a gunner, he went out several times on a most exposed ridge and mended the telephone lines, which were being repeatedly cut. Each time they returned they carried a wounded man to cover." (March 7th, 1918.)

STOURTON, LIEUT. (Hon.) W. M., Hussars.

" When on patrol he came under heavy rifle and machine-gun fire, but remained in touch with the enemy all day, displaying great coolness and initiative, and sending back most valuable information. It was due to his gallantry that a trooper, whose horse had been shot, was able to rejoin the patrol." (July 26th, 1918.)

TIDMARSH, 2nd LIEUT. D. M., 4th Batt., Royal Irish Regiment (Special Reserve), and Royal Flying Corps.

" For conspicuous gallantry and skill when attacking hostile aircraft on several occasions, notably on one occasion when he dived at an enemy machine and drove it down wrecked to the ground. (Near Peronne, 2nd and 30th April, 1916.) " (May 31st, 1916.)

TREVOR-JONES, 2nd LIEUT. J. E., Rifle Brigade, Special Reserve.

" Accompanied by two men, he cut a lane through our wire under very heavy fire. Later, he organized a bombing party and drove off an enemy attack. On another occasion he established a block under heavy fire, thereby saving a critical situation." (April 17th, 1917.)

TURNBULL, Temp. LIEUT. G. I., Welch Regiment.

" When acting as Battalion Scout Officer, he carried out a series of daring reconnaissances into the enemy lines for six days and nights without rest, bringing back information of the greatest value." (September 16th, 1918.)

VAN CUTSEM, CAPT. E. C. L., Shropshire Light Infantry, Spec. Res.

" Has performed the duties of Town Major, Poperinghe, with energy, discretion and tact, throughout a period of unusual stress. (Period July, 1916, to September, 1917)." (January 1st, 1918.)

WATERS, CAPT. C. L., Royal Berkshire Regiment, attached Nigeria Regiment.

" Though suffering severely from fever, he handled his company with great coolness and ability throughout an engagement, and set a most inspiring example to all." (April 25th, 1918.)

WATTS, Temp. CAPT. R. C., 14th Batt., Royal Warwickshire Regiment.

" For distinguished conduct and consistent good work. Has served continuously with the Battalion in France for 22½ months, firstly as Signalling Officer and secondly as Adjutant, which appointment he took over on the 9th August, 1916, and still holds. Has throughout shown great devotion to duty, cheerfulness, energy and a disregard for danger. During the period under review he has shown marked ability. At Vimy on the 9th April, 1917, he volunteered to command carrying parties taking S.A.A.

forward to leading Battalions in response to urgent calls. At La Culotte on 24th April, 1917, displayed considerable pluck and energy in clearing up the situation and assisting companies to organize the line. At Oppy, on 2nd May, 1917, rendered great help in organizing the front line after taking over from a composite Battalion of the 2nd Division, whose attack had failed. Again on the 7th May, 1917, rendered the greatest assistance in clearing up the situation after the enemy's counter-attack on Fresnoy." (January 1st, 1918.)

WILKINSON, Temp. CAPT. V., 9th Batt., Border Regiment.

" For conspicuous devotion to duty, and the conscientious manner in which he carries out all the work entrusted to him. He is an excellent organizer, full of energy and keenness. He sets, at all times, a fine example to all under his command." (June 3rd, 1918.)

WILLIAMS, 2nd LIEUT. G. V., Irish Guards (Special Reserve), attached 1st Batt.

" For conspicuous gallantry in action. He took over command of a company early in the action, and showed great determination during the consolidation of the first objective and the advance to the second. Later he pushed right forward several hundred yards under heavy fire, in order to clear up the situation. (Near Ginchy, 15th/16th September, 1916)." (November 14th, 1916.)

Bar to the Military Cross

CAILLARD, LIEUT. (Temp. CAPT.) F. C., *M.C.*, Somerset Light Infantry.

" He made frequent reconnaissances under much sniping and machine-gun fire, and brought back accurate information as to the dispositions of troops." (September 16th, 1918.)

CLUTTON, 2nd LIEUT. A. H., *M.C.*, Royal Field Artillery, Special Reserve.

" Owing to heavy bombardment by the enemy all communications were cut. Through intense fire of gas and high explosive this officer volunteered to go forward on three different occasions during the day to discover what he could, and brought back useful information. Later, after the withdrawal of the Battery, he returned to the vacated positions to fetch ammunition. He set a splendid example of fearlessness." (September 16th, 1918.)

CUMING, LIEUT. A. E. M., *M.C.*, Royal Irish Fusiliers.

" When in charge of a party of scouts raiding an enemy post to obtain an identification, he led his men through a gap in the wire, and charged the post. Two of the enemy stood their ground, but he wounded one and dragged him struggling 200 yards back to our lines. In this enterprise he displayed fine courage and determination." (September 16th, 1918.)

DE LA PASTURE, Temp. CAPT. (Temp. MAJOR) G. H., *M.C.*, 1/3rd Batt., King's African Rifles.

" For the very gallant and able manner in which he handled officers and men throughout the action when in charge of the firing line." (January 1st, 1918.)

PRIOR, Temp. CAPT. E. R. S., *M.C.*, South Lancashire Regiment.

" For conspicuous gallantry in action. He led the assault with great courage and initiative, gaining his objective and consolidating the position. (Regina Trench, 21st October, 1916.)" (November 25th, 1916.)

PURCELL-GILPIN, LIEUT. (A./CAPT.) P. R., *M.C.*, Scots Guards (Special Reserve), attached 2nd Batt.

" During an attack this officer set a wonderful example of utter disregard of personal danger, well-directed energy, and coolness to all engaged in the operation, and his reports to the Battalion Commander and to the gunners were invaluable." (January 11th, 1919.)

STOKES, LIEUT. (A./CAPT.) R. R., *M.C.*, Royal Field Artillery.

" This officer, who was acting in command, was engaged in withdrawing the Battery in accordance with orders he had received, when they were suddenly caught by a very heavy barrage from the enemy, who launched an attack. Notwithstanding many difficulties and very bad ground he managed to get a section away, and in spite of heavy casualties withdrew the detachments of the other guns after rendering them unserviceable to the enemy. He afterwards brought his guns into action again, handling them with great courage and skill under difficult circumstances, and by the observations he made personally in exposed places he was able to give valuable support to the infantry." (September 16th, 1918.)

WATERS, CAPT. C. L., *M.C.*, Royal Berkshire Regiment, attached Nigeria Regiment.

" He has commanded frequent patrols and has shown initiative and skill in leading. At the capture of Mkindu on 18th January, 1917, this officer was in command of the supporting company. By his skilful leading of his company and his support fire with rifles and maxims, he greatly aided the capture of the position." (January 1st, 1918.)

Distinguished Flying Cross

MAXWELL, CAPT. G. J. C., *M.C.*, Royal Air Force.

" This officer has at all times shown exceptional skill and gallantry, and on numerous occasions has fought against greatly superior numbers. During the last six weeks he has brought down five enemy aeroplanes. Recently he approached to within ten yards of three Fokker triplanes, one of which he shot down. He was chased for about nine miles by the remaining two until he met a formation of six Camels; these he led to attack some enemy aircraft, although he had only twenty-five minutes' petrol left." (August, 1918.)

Designed by Leonard Stokes, F.R.I.B.A.

MEMORIAL CROSS
Facing main School

Memoirs

LIEUT. CHARLES ARTHUR CAMPBELL, 1st Cheshire Regiment, elder son of Mr. Arthur Campbell, who lived for some years at Lynch House, Old Down, was born in 1891. With his younger brother, Cyril, who served in the Royal Field Artillery and was wounded during the war, he entered the School on September 16th, 1901, as one of the youngest boys, and after more than eight years, passed out of it to Sandhurst in December, 1909. In 1911 he received his commission in the Cheshire Regiment, and was quartered in Ireland.

At the outbreak of war his battalion was sent to the front and took part in the fighting at Charleroi and Mons in the latter part of August, 1914. On the 24th of that month he was shot at the head of his men in the battle which took place near Mons, and was killed instantly. In the evening of the same day his body was brought into the village of Audregnies by some pious Belgian peasants and buried by the curé of the place, close to the wall of the church there. He had been gazetted as Lieutenant a few months before the outbreak of hostilities, and was the first Old Gregorian to give his life for his country in the Great War.

LIEUT. C. A. CAMPBELL

1st Cheshire Regiment

Killed in Action   *August 24th, 1914*

2nd LIEUT. J. D. SHINE
1st Royal Irish Regiment

Killed in Action   *August 27th, 1914*

2nd LIEUT. JOHN DENIS SHINE, Royal Irish Regiment, second son of Colonel J. Shine, R.A.M.C., was born on September 10th, 1894, and came to Downside in September, 1905. Throughout his school career, " Gozo " Shine, as he was almost invariably called, distinguished himself in all the games and sports, and in 1911 he was awarded his First Eleven colours for Cricket, Association Football and Hockey. For three years he was a member of the Football Eleven, playing on the left wing with much success ; he was an excellent centre-forward at Hockey, and in 1911 scored sixteen of the twenty-seven goals registered by the team ; at Cricket he played for the Eleven for two seasons, and was Captain in 1912. He took part in the sports contest with Bruton in 1911, and twice won the School Tennis Championship. He was also a sergeant in the O.T.C., and attended two camps.

During his last year at Downside, he was a member of the School Committee, and of the Committees of various games ; in other spheres of activity, he was on the staff of *The Raven*, and on the Committee of the Petre Library, and he was a useful member of the Choir for several years, first as a treble, and afterwards as a bass.

In the summer of 1912, he passed into Sandhurst, where he played in the Football Eleven, in his old position on the left wing. He received his commission in the Royal Irish Regiment in 1913. On the outbreak of war in 1914, he went to the front on mobilization, and was wounded in the groin at Mons on August 27th. He was carried off the field to a neighbouring church, which was being used as a hospital. Almost immediately after his arrival the building was destroyed by shell fire, and everyone in it perished. At the time of his death, John Denis Shine was within a few days of his twentieth birthday.

2nd LIEUT. EDWARD JAMES VIBART COLLING-WOOD-THOMPSON, 2nd Royal Welch Fusiliers, only son of the late Mr. E. J. Collingwood-Thompson, of Limerick, and nephew of the Right Rev. Dom Gregory Thompson, O.S.B., Bishop of Gibraltar, was born in 1894, and came to Downside in September, 1904. He remained with us for only one term, going on to the Oratory School, Edgbaston, whence he passed into Sandhurst. In 1913 he received his commission in the Royal Welch Fusiliers, and went to the front at the outbreak of hostilities in August, 1914. He took part in the fighting at Mons, St. Quentin and the River Marne, and on September 9th was seriously wounded at La Ferté, being shot in the stomach while clearing the village of German troops. He was carried to the field hospital, where he received the last Sacraments, and died on the following day.

2nd LIEUT. E. J. V. COLLINGWOOD-THOMPSON

2nd Royal Welch Fusiliers

Died of Wounds   *September 10th, 1914*

LIEUT. A. G. R. SMITH-SLIGO

Cameron Highlanders

Killed in Action   *September 14th, 1914*

LIEUT. ARCHIBALD GEORGE R. J. SMITH-SLIGO,
3rd Cameron Highlanders, eldest son of Mr. A. D. Smith-Sligo, of Inzievar, Oakley, Fifeshire, was born in 1887, and came to Downside in September, 1903, with his younger brother, Ronald. He left the School in July, 1907, for Exeter College, Oxford, and after taking his degree received a commission in the Cameron Highlanders, Special Reserve Battalion. On the outbreak of war he went to the front with his regiment, and saw much fighting ; on September 14th, his twenty-seventh birthday, he was twice wounded at the battle of the Aisne, and was at first reported as " wounded and missing." For some time it was hoped that he might have been picked up by a German ambulance, but nothing further was heard of him, and information received from his brother officers soon left no reasonable doubt as to his death. The following details are taken, with permission, from a letter written by his father ; the captain referred to in the extract being Captain D. N. C. Capel Miers (O.G.) :—

" George's name, as you know, appeared in the casualty list of the Cameron Highlanders as 'wounded and missing,' at the battle of the Aisne on September 14th. In this fight our men advanced a long way and won much ground from the Germans, but at the close had to retire about 400 or 500 yards and entrench. From letters, written by George's captain, we learned that he had been twice hit, in the arm and leg, that he had not retired at the end, and that he had done 'awfully well.' Captain Miers also said that a burial party of the South Wales Borderers had been over the ground and had not found him, and that he hoped a German ambulance might have picked him up. To-day (November 18th) I have a letter from an officer who was badly wounded the same day, and who lay on the ground for three days before being picked up. He says that he was told that George got up and advanced to take prisoner some Germans who had raised the white flag. The latter waited until he was quite near and then shot him. He also says it was commonly believed in the regiment that he was killed."

LIEUT. ROBERT DE STACPOOLE, Connaught Rangers, fourth son of the Duke de Stacpoole, was born in 1892, at Mount Hazel, county Galway, and in September, 1902, came to Downside, where his three elder brothers were already at school. He left in the autumn of 1909, entered Sandhurst the year following, and was gazetted to the Connaught Rangers in 1911. He went to the front with his regiment in the British Expeditionary Force, taking part in the engagement at Mons on August 23rd, and in all the subsequent fighting until the German stand at the river Aisne. On September 20th he was shot in the head and killed instantly, at Verneuil (Aisne), some 15 miles from Soissons. Sir Gerald Burke (O.G.), who saw him on the evening of the 19th, spoke of him as " in excellent spirits ; extremely popular amongst the men owing to his cheerful disposition, unselfishness and bravery." He was promoted to be Lieutenant a few days only before his death.

LIEUT. R. DE STACPOOLE

Connaught Rangers

Killed in Action   *September 20th, 1914*

CAPT. D. N. C. C. MIERS

Cameron Highlanders

Killed in Action   *September 20th, 1914*

CAPTAIN DOUGLAS NATHANIEL CARLETON CAPEL MIERS, 1st Cameron Highlanders, of Crinant, Glamorganshire, eldest son of Lieut.-Colonel C. H. Miers, late 79th the Queen's Own Cameron Highlanders, was born in 1875 and came to Downside in May, 1890. He was only in the School for two terms, leaving us in December of the same year for the Oratory School, Edgbaston. In 1896 he was gazetted to the Cameron Highlanders from the Militia, and obtained his company in 1901. In 1898 he was with the Nile Expedition at the battle of the Atbara, and during the South African War was present in the actions at Vet River, Zand River, Wittebergen and Ladybrand. His services were mentioned in despatches, and he received the Queen's medal (four clasps) ; he also received the Royal Humane Society's bronze medal for saving life (1900). He went to the front at the outset of the war and was slightly wounded in the leg about September 20th, during the fighting on the north bank of the river Aisne. At that time the Camerons were using a large cave in the river bank for their mess, which, as it faced southwards, was not exposed to the German fire. To this Captain Miers was carried and a doctor was brought to attend to him. While his wound was being dressed a high explosive shell fell and burst just above the roof of the cave. The shock of the explosion shattered the water-worn rocks and the whole mass collapsed, burying all who were in the cave at the time, Captain Miers among the number. The debris was cleared away and the bodies recovered as quickly as possible, but every one was dead. It is believed that all were killed instantly by the mass of rock as it fell. Among those who perished in this disaster was Captain Alan Cameron, of Lochiel, who had been sent for by Captain Miers to take over command of the battalion in his absence. In 1901 Captain Miers married Margaret, youngest daughter of the late Mr. J. E. Christie of Forthbank, Stirling, and is succeeded by a son born in 1902.

2nd LIEUT. GEOFFREY PHILIP JOSEPH SNEAD-COX, Royal Welch Fusiliers, second son of Mr. J. G. Snead-Cox, Lord of the Manor of Broxwood, Herefordshire, was born in 1895, came to Downside in September, 1909, and left in July, 1912. During his last year at school he played regularly for the Association Football Eleven, and several times for the Cricket Eleven. He took great interest in the work of the O.T.C., in which he held the rank of sergeant ; he attended three camps, and was a conspicuous member of the Roberts team which won the inter-house competition in 1912. His favourite subject was History, and he showed a special aptitude for anything connected with this subject. He was on the committee of the Abingdon Society, and was a member of *The Raven* staff. In the summer of 1911 he played the part of the Duchess in " The Gondoliers " with much success. He passed into Sandhurst from the School in July, 1912, and received his commission in the Royal Welch Fusiliers a year later. When the war began his battalion was stationed at Malta, and he himself was in hospital recovering from the effects of a polo accident. At his own earnest entreaty he was allowed to travel home with the rest ; the voyage did him good, and after a few days in Netley Hospital he was able to go home on sick leave. Before his leave was over he heard that his regiment was under orders for the front and he at once rejoined, leaving for Belgium on October 4th. He was killed in action near Ypres on October 21st, 1914. The following account of his death is reproduced with permission from a letter by Mr. J. G. Snead-Cox:—

" Soon after landing, the regiment was ordered to the front, and after several days of forced marching, in which they covered 105 miles, took part in an attack upon the town of Menin. The place was held by a greatly superior force of Germans, and the attack was beaten back with heavy loss. Geoffrey's company was in reserve. One of his brother officers, who was being carried back wounded, saw him at the end of the day standing at the head of his men, guarding the line of retreat, and heard him call out, ' Are you the last ? '

" That night what was left of the regiment occupied some trenches near the village of Zonnebeke. As the enemy had again

2nd LIEUT. G. P. J. SNEAD-COX
Royal Welch Fusiliers

Killed in Action   *October 21st, 1914*

been reinforced, orders were sent to the Welch Fusiliers to fall back. Unfortunately the order never reached them, and they held the trenches all day against an overwhelming force. A soldier, who is now in the London Hospital, states that on the afternoon of the 20th, in the trench where Geoffrey was, he and sixteen men were the only ones left alive. There was a lull in the fighting and Geoffrey went along the trench, encouraging his men, sharing his ration with them, giving them some chocolate and dividing the contents of his brandy flask.

" When the bullets began to hum again, Geoffrey, whose duty it was to direct the fire of his men and give the range, stood up and looked through his field glasses. A sergeant, who was next to him, begged him not to expose himself. Geoffrey, still looking through his glasses, exclaimed, ' All right, I see them now.' At the same moment a bullet struck him in the middle of the forehead.

" After his death, the men consulted among themselves and decided not to put up the white flag, but to bolt back ' every man for himself,' and to trust to the gathering darkness for safety. A little later the Germans advanced and took the trench. During the night British reinforcements came up, and in the morning drove the Germans out. Geoffrey and four other officers were buried in a part of the trench which had been widened by a shell. The German losses on the 20th were enormous. They came on in dense masses, and men fell in rows before the rifles in the trenches, but the enemy never got within fifty yards of the trenches held by the Welch Fusiliers, until they were abandoned at the end of the day. My boy was only nineteen at the time of his death."

2nd LIEUT. RICHARD SNEAD-COX, 2nd Royal Scots, eldest son of Mr. J. G. Snead-Cox, of Broxwood, Herefordshire, was born in 1893, and was at Downside from September, 1906 until July, 1911. He was an able boy, and won an entrance scholarship into the School ; subsequently, he passed the Higher Certificate on three consecutive occasions, with distinctions in French, and in 1909 he won the Ferrers Essay Prize. He was a member of the staff of *The Raven*, and was on the committees of the Petre Library and the Abingdon Society. He was a good athlete, and took part in the Bruton Sports Competition in 1911. During his last year at school, he played in the Hockey, Football and Cricket Elevens, and won the quarter-mile in the School Sports.   In 1912 he went up to New College, Oxford, and was still an undergraduate when war began. At once obtaining a commission in the Royal Scots, he was sent to the front early in October, and was killed in action near Neuve Chapelle on October 28th, 1914, at the age of twenty-one. The following details are taken, with permission, from a letter written by his father, Mr. J. G. Snead-Cox :—

" He was reading for Honours, and hoped some day to enter the Civil Service. He had no idea of joining the army. At the end of July he was in Scotland, staying with friends. Just before war was declared he sent a postcard to his mother with these words, ' The day England goes in, I volunteer.' Three or four days later he obtained a commission in the Royal Scots. He was one of a draft of eight officers who went to France early in October to join the 2nd Battalion, which was at the front. By the morning of October 28th all of them, except Richard, had been either killed or wounded, and Richard was shot dead on the afternoon of the same day.

" He was in action for the first time on October 12th, and again on the 13th and on the 14th. On the latter day his captain was wounded and afterwards wrote to tell me that Richard had ' behaved very well indeed, under very trying circumstances.' For the next ten days he was almost continuously in the trenches. In one of his letters he said, ' Being under fire for the first time is rather

2nd LIEUT. R. SNEAD-COX
2nd Royal Scots

Killed in Action   *October 28th, 1914*

terrifying, but it is wonderful how quickly you get accustomed to it.' In a later letter he said he could now sit in the trenches and watch the shells overhead, and find time to note how beautiful they were as they burst in the blue sky. One morning, when his company was in the reserve trench, the men in the advance line suddenly signalled that they were running short of ammunition. Richard at once went with two of his men and, crossing the 300 yards which separated the two lines of trenches, brought a fresh supply.

" On October 28th the Royal Scots were supporting the Northumberland Fusiliers in an attack upon a position held by the enemy near Neuve Chapelle. Things did not go well, and there was a good deal of confusion and some uncertainty as to what the Royal Scots were expected to do. To make matters worse the Royal Scots found they were being fired upon from behind. In these circumstances Richard's company was told to go forward and join the Northumberland Fusiliers in their trenches. He was leading his platoon (fifty men) and had just reached the trench, when he fell back, shot through the heart.

" His last letters, two of them received after his death, were full of high spirits and of pride in his regiment. An officer, under whom he served, writes that Richard ' had a great deal of hard work to do, which he always did very well and very cheerfully.' Another who knew him very well writes : ' Richard was brave to the point of rashness and he had the makings of a splendid soldier.' In spite of all privations and dangers he had come to love life in the army, and in his last letter wrote : ' I am becoming more and more military every day.' He was buried that night in the field where he fell."

CAPTAIN LOUIS EDMUND HARRINGTON MOLY-NEUX-SEEL, 2nd Border Regiment, son of the late Henry Harrington Molyneux-Seel, Richmond Herald, was born in 1872, came to Downside in January, 1885, and left in July, 1891. Passing through Sandhurst, he received his commission in the Border Regiment in 1894, and obtained his company in 1902. He took part in the South African War and was mentioned in despatches. From 1910 to 1913 he was British Vice-Consul at Van, Turkey-in-Asia, where for some time he was also Acting French Consul. Rejoining his regiment, he went to the front, and was killed in action near Ypres on October 29th, 1914. In the *Gazette* of November 16th, for no apparent reason, the official statement of his death was corrected, and he was reported as wounded and missing. No evidence to justify this correction ever appears to have been forthcoming, and, later on, the original announcement was reaffirmed.

Captain Molyneux-Seel's medals, set into a handsome memorial tablet, have been placed in the School near to the portraits of the Old Gregorians who fell in the war, with a suitable inscription concluding with the words : " These medals are placed here by his mother, for the love he bore to his old School."

CAPT. L. E. H. MOLYNEUX-SEEL
2nd Border Regiment

Killed in Action   *October 29th, 1914*

CAPT. C. E. M. DE LA PASTURE

1st Scots Guards

Killed in Action   *October 29th, 1914*

CAPTAIN CHARLES EDWARD DE LA PASTURE, 1st Battalion, Scots Guards, eldest son of the late Marquis de la Pasture, was born in September, 1879, and was at Downside from September, 1892, until December, 1895. After a short time at the Jesuit College, Wimbledon, he joined the army, and in May, 1898, received a commission in the Oxfordshire Light Infantry. He served with Colonel Plumer's Rhodesian column in the South African War, after which he was gazetted to the Scots Guards. He obtained his company in 1907, and was A.D.C. to General Sir F. Forestier Walker, Governor of Gibraltar, from 1907 to 1910. In 1911, he married Agatha, daughter of Mr. Alexander Mosley, C.M.G., of Gibraltar.

He went to the front at the outbreak of hostilities, and took part in all the important engagements up to October 29th, when the whole right flank company, which he commanded, together with a company of the Coldstreams, was surrounded by the Germans, and lost heavily. This took place between Becelaire and the Menin Road, at the first battle of Ypres. Captain de la Pasture's name was among the list of those officially reported missing on November 1st, and he was mentioned in Sir John French's despatch of February 18th, 1915. It afterwards became clear that he had fallen in the engagement of October 29th, 1914. On that day he was seen lying dead in the trench, next to a brother officer, by one of his sergeants who was taken prisoner and was helping to carry out a wounded German.

His younger brother, Hubert, the present Marquis de la Pasture, who was in the School from 1899 to 1903, was in British East Africa when the war broke out, and at once joined the East African Mounted Rifles. He took part in many engagements, and was awarded the M.C. and Bar.

LIEUT. GEORGE NOEL McGRATH, 2nd Dragoon Guards, son of Mr. George McGrath, Charlemont, Jamaica, B.W.I., was born on December 12th, 1885, came to Downside in September, 1898, and left in July, 1899. He received a commission in the Dragoon Guards, was sent to the front, and died of wounds received in action on November 5th, 1914.

In Memoriam

LIEUT. G. N. McGRATH

2nd Dragoon Guards

Died of Wounds   *November 5th 1914*

PRIVATE E. A. WILLETT

1st Sportsman's Batt. Royal Fusiliers

Died on Service   *February 9th, 1915*

PRIVATE EDWARD ARCHIBALD WILLETT, 1st Sportsman's Battalion, Royal Fusiliers, was the eldest son of the late Mr. A. E. Willett, a well-known solicitor at Bromley, Kent, for many years Clerk to the Magistrates and Registrar. He was born on January 11th, 1880, and came to Downside in September, 1891. His School record was uniformly successful. He won the Gregorian Medal in 1894, and was unquestionably the best classical scholar of his generation at Downside. He was a member of the Football Eleven in 1896, and in the following summer secured the best bowling average in the Cricket Eleven. He left in July, 1897, entered the law, and became a partner in the firm of Willett & Latter on his father's death in 1906. He was a fine all-round sportsman, a good cricketer and tennis player, excellent at golf and billiards, and at one time no mean Rugby footballer. On the formation of the Sportsman's Battalion he at once enlisted, and was in training at Hornchurch Camp, Essex, at the time of his death. Early in February he caught influenza ; other maladies followed, and he died at Hornchurch on Tuesday, February 9th, 1915. He was buried at Bromley Old Cemetery, with full military honours, on Thursday, February 11th.

His brother, John Wickham Willett (O.G., 1901-1908), held a commission during the war in the London Regiment, and was wounded.

2nd LIEUT. FRANCIS CHICHESTER TYRRELL, 4th Coldstream Guards, younger son of Sir William Tyrrell, G.C.M.G., K.C.V.O., C.B., Permanent Under-Secretary of the Foreign Office, and nephew of Mr. F. F. Urquhart, Dean of Balliol, was born on November 21st, 1892, and came to Downside in May, 1904. His life at school was a successful and happy one. He was an able and attractive boy, of fine character, straightforward and plucky, and always bright and cheerful, on the best of terms with his masters and companions. He passed the Higher Certificate Examination on three occasions, and in 1911 secured distinction in French. During his last year at Downside he played hockey, football and cricket in the First Elevens, and was a member of the Games Committee. In other spheres of activity he also did excellent work, and was on the staff of *The Raven*, on the Petre Library Committee, and Secretary of the Abingdon Society. He held the rank of sergeant in the O.T.C., and attended two camps. In July, 1911, he left the School, and in the following autumn went up to Balliol College, Oxford. On the outbreak of hostilities in 1914, he applied for a commission, was gazetted to the Coldstream Guards, and after some months' training, went to the front in North-Eastern France. He died of wounds on February 16th, 1915, at the age of twenty-two, after he had received the last Sacraments. The following account of his death is taken from a letter written by Colonel G. Fielding, *D.S.O.* :—

" Yesterday morning he was in charge of a working party, who were improving one of the communication trenches, when he was shot by a stray shot through the abdomen just below the heart. He was at once bound up and carried down to the dressing station, and they were luckily able to send him in a motor ambulance at once to the officers' hospital at Béthune. From the first, I fear, they considered his case a very critical one. He had lost a lot of blood, I suppose one of the main arteries had been cut, and he died at 3 a.m. this morning. He saw a Roman Catholic priest before he died. The doctor tells me that he was conscious when he was brought in and almost up to the end, and that he was most remarkably brave and calm. The doctor gave him morphia to stop any pain, but he had lost too much blood to be able to hold out.

2nd LIEUT. F. C. V. TYRRELL
4th Coldstream Guards

Died of Wounds   *February 16th, 1915*

" I cannot tell you how very grieved we all are, for we all liked him so very much, and personally I am very grieved, as he was an excellent young officer, always so anxious to do anything that he could and helping to look after his men. He was buried this afternoon in the cemetery at Béthune, the Catholic priest officiating. Most of the officers managed to get away to the funeral."

A requiem Mass was sung for him at Oxford, in the presence of the Master of Balliol and many other friends, who deeply mourned his death. " His development at Oxford," wrote one who knew him very well, " was a thing to watch, and only those who followed him there from Downside could fully value it. He was rapidly widening his circle of friends, which he could always do, without forgetting the old ones ; and the charm and power of his character, always latent in him, were becoming very well known . . . . We have lost the perfect Downside boy . . . . there are few who had more of the spirit of ' pietas ' in all its meanings than had Frank."

The following fine poem was written to his memory by his schoolfellow and much-loved friend, Stephen Hewett :—

To F. C. T.

2ND LIEUT., COLDSTREAM GUARDS.

To you, old friend, whose letter came,
  Your final letter, when the day
  Was done, and you had passed away
From the laborious manly game,

The bitter sweetness of the fight,
  From love and laughter, shame and strife,
  The colours and the shades of life,
To peace and dawn of endless light,

Who knew that all which others prize,
  The fruit of learning, nature, art,
  Ambition, and gay pride of heart,
Are but a pageant for the eyes ;

That all the golden hopes of youth
  Are by a single deed outdone,
  And in a single moment won
The Life that gave the shadows truth,

Who knew that naught is foul or fair
  But man and what he wills to make,
  Himself his own perfection,—Take
This poor late answer, and a prayer

For strength of heart and courtesy,
  A will to lead, a smile for Fear,
  As your own downs of Sussex clear,
As your own Sussex breezes free :

That not in vain may Downside send,
  That Balliol be not in vain,
  That memory of old days remain
To make me worthy of my friend.

British Expeditionary Force,
  Easter, 1916.

S. H. H.

2nd LIEUT. CYRIL FRANCIS BURNAND, 1st Grenadier Guards, only son of Mr. and Mrs. Charles Burnand, and grandson of Sir F. C. Burnand, for many years the Editor of *Punch*, was born July 31st, 1891, and came to Downside in April, 1904.

He took a prominent part in School affairs, displaying much character and energy. He played in the Second Eleven at Football and Hockey (1908-9), and won the School Challenge Cup for Swimming four years in succession (1905-8). In 1909 he passed the Higher Certificate. He sang in the Choir and took a keen interest in all musical activities. His inherited gifts as an actor won him great success on the Downside stage, notably in the parts of the retired Butterman in " Our Boys " and Benjamin Goldfinch in " A Pair of Spectacles."

In July, 1909, he left Downside and went up to Trinity College, Cambridge. In 1911, he received his " blue " for rowing in the Cambridge Eight, the well-known critic, Guy Nicholls, writing of him in the *Morning Post*, " Burnand rowed in better style than anyone in either crew." After taking his degree he decided to go in for railway engineering, and obtained a position with the Midland Railway Co. The following letter from Sir W. Guy Granet speaks for itself :—

" General Manager's Office,
Midland Railway,
16, Great George St., S.W.,
March 16th, 1915.

" Dear Mr. Burnand,—I feel that I must write at once to tell you how much I feel for you and Mrs. Burnand in the terrible sorrow that has come to you.

" I think perhaps, in some ways, I can feel for you more deeply than many of your more intimate friends, for I had watched and tried your boy very carefully, and had come to the conclusion that he was quite the best young man that had ever come to me on the Midland.

" I had the utmost belief in him and, as I wrote to him only the other day, I missed him very often and very much. I was looking forward to his becoming one of my most useful assistants,

2nd LIEUT. C. F. BURNAND
1st Grenadier Guards

Killed in Action   *March 11th, 1915*

and I know that he was assured of a most successful career. He had most unusual gifts for a young man, great force of character, adaptability, capacity for dealing with men both above and below him, and I cannot tell you how greatly I shall feel his loss.

"I know that those with whom he worked had the same opinion of him, and the Midland will be very much the poorer for his loss. I never met a young man in whom I had greater confidence."

At the outbreak of hostilities he obtained a commission in the Grenadier Guards, and after a few months of training went to the front in December, 1914. In the following February he came home on short leave, returning to Flanders on March 4th, to lose his life there in action near Neuve Chapelle on March 11th, 1915, at the age of twenty-three. We are indebted to Mr. Charles Burnand for the following particulars of his son's death :—

"So far as we can learn the plan was that the Brigade in support, comprising the Guards, should go into the trenches on the 10th at night, behind those which had been successfully taken during the day, and that the next morning the fresh troops should go through those men who had fought on the 10th and carry on further, thus keeping the enemy on the run. On the 11th, they had to advance over ground which the Germans were shelling hard, they having brought up reinforcements and machine guns during the night. I am told the Guards carried out their orders and that Cyril had done remarkably well, but in leading his men on to the parapet of the trenches he was shot in the stomach and died almost immediately. He fell into the arms of another officer, but unfortunately he, poor fellow, was killed the next day, so that we have never heard anything more definitely."

Father R. Watt, Catholic Chaplain with the 23rd Field Ambulance, 7th Division, B.E.F., wrote of him :—

"He was the only Catholic officer in the 1st Grenadiers, and was always of the greatest help to me in my ministrations ; to the Catholics of his regiment and still more to me, his loss is a great disaster."

2nd LIEUT. RODERICK ALGERNON DE STACPOOLE, Royal Field Artillery, fifth and youngest son of the Duke de Stacpoole, was born on August 11th, 1895, came to Downside in January, 1905, and left in December, 1911. He was a bright and cheerful boy, very popular with all who knew him throughout his short life. After passing through Woolwich, he was gazetted to the R.F.A. on August 12th, 1914, and went to the front soon afterwards in the 1st Battery, R.F.A., 8th Division. On March 11th, 1915, he was killed in action, being only nineteen years of age at the time. We are permitted by the Duke de Stacpoole to print the following extracts from two letters received from Major A. E. M. Head, R.F.A., giving further details :—

" March 11th, 1915.—It is with the greatest regret that I have to write to you that Roderick was killed to-day. He was acting as forward observation officer, and was shot while laying out a telephone line from the Battery to the infantry lines. The man who was with him tells me that he was shot in the right side, became unconscious almost at once, and died very shortly afterwards, so I am glad to be able to believe that he cannot have suffered very much. We all feel his loss terribly, as we were all so very fond of him. It is such a pity, as I feel sure he would have had such a good career in front of him.

" March 16th, 1915.—I can now give you some further details about poor Roderick. He was sent out as forward observing officer on the morning of the 11th to set telephonic communication to the front. He got quite close to the place from which he was to observe quite safely, and there was an open bit he had to cross. He waited for a lull in the fire, but unfortunately a volley was fired while he was crossing. I told you in my last letter, which I hope will have reached you, that he was shot low down in the right side and died almost at once.

" We succeeded in recovering his body, and I had him brought back to the Battery and buried him behind the guns ; I was fortunately able to get a Roman Catholic Chaplain. His grave is on the south side of the Rue du Bacquerot, 300 yards N.E. of the

2nd LIEUT. R. A. DE STACPOOLE
Royal Field Artillery

Killed in Action   *March 11th, 1915*

Rouge Croix cross roads, on the main Estaires—La Bassée roads. We all feel his loss terribly as we were all devoted to him."

His name was among those of the R.F.A. mentioned in Sir John French's despatch of May 31st.

His brother Robert was killed at the Aisne on September 20th, 1914, and his three remaining brothers, George, Hubert and Francis all served in the war, the two latter being wounded.

2nd LIEUT. BRENDAN JOSEPH FOTTRELL, 3rd Royal Irish Regiment, only son of Mr. and Mrs. J. G. Fottrell, of Richlieu, Sydney Parade, Dublin, was born on October 12th, 1885, and came to Downside in January, 1899. At school he was conspicuous for his energy and public spirit, and took a prominent part in the various games. He played right half-back in the Association Football Eleven in 1901-2, and was a member of the Sports Committee in 1902. In the Abingdon Society he was a vigorous and capable debater. He left Downside in April, 1902, and later on passed into Trinity College, Dublin. Subsequently he entered the Law, and was practising as a solicitor in Dublin at the outbreak of the war. He immediately volunteered for service, was gazetted to the Royal Irish Regiment on August 15th, 1914, and went to the front in the following February. We are indebted to Mr. J. G. Fottrell for the following account of his son's death in action on March 15th, 1915, in his thirtieth year :—

" He was called up at 2.30 in the morning of March 15th to take part in an attack on the ' Mound ' near St. Eloi. While leading his men, coming out of the village, he was shot dead by a machine gun which the Germans had installed. His body could not be recovered for several days, but finally it was brought in and buried at a spot nearly opposite where he fell."

2nd LIEUT. B. J. FOTTRELL
3rd Royal Irish Regiment

Killed in Action   *March 15th, 1915*

PRIVATE A. FOX
National Guard

Killed in Accident   *March 29th, 1915*

PRIVATE ANTHONY FOX, National Guard, second son of the late Mr. Anthony Fox, of Runnemede, Dundrum, Co. Dublin, was born in 1851, came to Downside with his brothers Richard and Edward on September 26th, 1864, and left in July, 1868. In the School he was a contemporary of Abbot Ford. On the outbreak of war in 1914, although well over sixty years of age, he offered himself for military service and became a Private in the National Guard. Whilst on patrol duty with the Home Reserve, he was accidentally killed as he was crossing the railway line at Hayward's Heath, on the morning of March 29th, 1915. At the time of his death he was in his sixty-fourth year. The following further information was obtained through the kindness of a relative :—

" He was run down at Hayward's Heath by the express train to Brighton, and was quite lifeless when the body was found. He had been on patrol all night, and crossed the line with another man to get something needed for the men's breakfast. When his companions noticed he was missing, prompt search was made and the dead body found. With regard to his career since he left Downside, his sister reports it to have been happy and uneventful, marked only by great devotedness and affection for his mother and father ; a quiet family life, even in its tenour, chiefly prosperous. He was never married.

" When the war broke out, he showed remarkable energy and capacity for rising to an emergency, joining the Volunteers when quite beyond the fighting age, and being enthusiastic in his devotion to our country. They speak highly in his regiment, both of his military zeal and ability, and of his genial disposition. He was well liked by all."

The only photograph of Anthony Fox which we were able to obtain was taken shortly after he left Downside.

LIEUT.-COL. THOMAS XAVIER BRITTEN, 110th Mahratta Light Infantry, son of the late Major-General T. E. Britten, of the Indian Army, was born November 21st, 1867, at Bhusawal, India, and came to Downside in September, 1879. He left in July, 1882, and, after a short time at Oscott, entered the Army, receiving a commission in the Gloucestershire Regiment, from which he transferred into the old Indian Staff Corps, doing duty in the Bombay command. He was promoted Major in 1905, became Double Company Commander in the 110th Mahratta Light Infantry in 1908, and second in command in 1910. At the outbreak of hostilities the regiment was stationed at Belgaum, India, and for three months it waited impatiently in the hope of being ordered to Europe, until on November 4th it left for the Persian Gulf.

By kind permission of Mrs. Britten, a large part of the letters she received from her son describing his experiences in Mesopotamia appeared in the War Supplement of the *Downside Review* for July, 1915. On April 14th, 1915, Colonel Britten was wounded very seriously during the engagement at Shaiba, and died early on the following morning, at the age of forty-seven. The following extracts from a letter of Col. Frazer to Mrs. Britten give some account of the circumstances of his death :—

" Long before this letter reaches you, you will have received the terribly sad news of your son's death. I cannot express to you how very sorry I am for you in your loss. It has been a great shock to all of us. All the Indian ranks of the regiment rightly looked on him as the Father of the regiment. He had been in it longer than anyone else, and has always shown such fine soldierly qualities. During every action in this war your son has exhibited the most dashing bravery and judgment. He was the only British officer who gained actual entrance to Kurna, before that place surrendered on December 9th. On many occasions, in India and since the regiment came to Mesopotamia, I have reported that I could not wish for a better second in command. He would have been a splendid Battalion Commander. His double company was the best trained in the regiment.

LIEUT.-COL. T. X. BRITTEN
110th Mahratta Light Infantry

Died of Wounds   *April 15th, 1915*

" He was so cheerful when he was wounded. When I first saw him after this, he was lying on a stretcher and, though I fear he was in pain, he smiled at me most cheerfully as I went up to speak to him.   Just as I was bending over him I was struck in the back of the shoulder myself, and very much regret I had not an opportunity of talking to him again.   My wound was very slight and is already healed.   Your son was wounded towards the end of a long hard day's fighting, but he looked cheerful, smart and just as always, when he was lying wounded on the stretcher.   The Turks came down in great force to Shaiba on April 12th, and during the 13th and 14th we had several attacks and made counter-attacks against them, which were very successful.   On April 14th, most of our force started off at 9 a.m. to look for the enemy's main forces.   We found them in position about four miles from Shaiba and attacked them.   Your son was wounded about 4 p.m., and the enemy were defeated and retreating by 5.30.   He died in the Field Ambulance at Shaiba at 5.30 a.m. on April 15th.   All the officers were buried together in one cemetery at 12 noon on April 15th.

" The whole regiment will always miss your son very greatly.   It is so sad ; he would have succeeded me in command of the regiment next October, or on the conclusion of the war.   Like so many excellent soldiers, he was one of the kindest of men and always so considerate to others.   The whole regiment joins with me in expressing our most heartfelt sympathy in your loss.   There is no one in the whole regiment whose loss we would deplore so much as we do your son."

CAPTAIN EDWIN MIDLETON HALE MURPHY, 2nd Leinster Regiment, son of Mr. and Mrs. Jerome Murphy, of 37, Cadogan Street, S.W., was born on December 31st, 1881, and came to Downside in September, 1895. He was a capable and attractive boy, who played his part well in every branch of school life. During his last summer term he was a member of the Cricket Eleven. He left Downside in July, 1899, and subsequently entered the Army. He served in the South African War, being awarded the Queen's medal with five clasps, received his company in February, 1911, and was placed on retired pay in May, 1913. On the outbreak of hostilities in the following year, he rejoined his regiment and went to the front early in 1915. He died of wounds received in action near Armentières on May 6th, aged thirty-three years. Major Bullen-Smith, who was in command of the 2nd Leinsters at the time, wrote of the circumstances as follows :—

" On May 5th, near Armentières, he was going to the assistance of a wounded man of his own company, and just as he reached him was shot in the back, probably by the same German sniper, the bullet passing right through the abdomen. The doctor decided that he should not be moved, so he was made as comfortable as possible in the breastwork. Yesterday afternoon the doctor thought him a little better, but the end came very suddenly about 11.15 p.m. last night (May 6th). He was a very gallant and capable officer, and a great favourite with us all."

The following extracts from letters written by two of his brother officers are printed by kind permission of Mr. and Mrs. Murphy :—

" I knew your son slightly at Passage West, but only well since I came out here three months ago. I shall always be happy to think that we were great pals during this time, and his company, ' A ' Company, were devoted to him, as were indeed the whole regiment. I am sure I may say without exaggerating that he was by far the most efficient and most popular officer in the whole regiment. I know that Murphy's advice was sought, not only by the C.O., but by the General, who had a very high opinion of him. He

CAPT. E. M. H. MURPHY
2nd Leinster Regiment

Died of Wounds   *May 6th, 1915*

died like a soldier, peacefully, and I was with him till within about twenty minutes of his death, which occurred at 11.20 p.m. on the 6th inst. . . ."

" I would like you to know how we all appreciated him, how we regret his loss and share with you your great sorrow. Indeed, we all mourn for him as a brother, for he always showed himself as such to us. An admirable soldier, one whose loss cannot be made good, while getting his men well in hand he yet won their love and respect, so that I assure you there was not a dry eye among all the men of his company who were allowed to come to the funeral. Among the officers of his company, too, he was unfailingly popular, and it couldn't be otherwise, for he always insisted in sharing alike with them any work that had to be done, no matter how unpleasant, and he continually took the young officers' duties for them, so that they might go and amuse themselves. I could tell you a hundred instances of his courage and carelessness of personal danger. He hated shells and yet, when part of his company was shelled, you always found him there, helping and encouraging his men.

" Of course the greatest instance of this was the one in which he lost his life. The instant he heard that one of his men was hit, he at once walked fearlessly across the open to the place, and it was just as he reached the wounded man that he was hit himself. You have heard that we did all that could possibly be done for him, and it will comfort you to know that he did not suffer, as he was under morphia the whole time. I visited him as often as my duties permitted, and he always had a smile for me. I saw him about fifteen minutes before he died, and he was very peaceful and tranquil, even saying ' Good night ' to me when I left at 11.0 p.m. on the 6th. So he just passed away quietly, helped by the last rites of the Church.

" For myself, I feel his loss and miss him terribly. Ever since my childhood I have had a great admiration for Edwin. At school (Downside) he was my *beau ideal* of everything, and he went out of his way to be nice to me. Out here, when we were both men doing men's work, my admiration grew to real affection, and now I mourn for him and always shall as a well-beloved brother."

CAPTAIN ILTYD EDWIN MAITLAND WATKINS, 2nd Monmouthshire Regiment, only son of Mr. John Maitland Watkins, himself an Old Gregorian (September 1865—July, 1870), was born on March 25th, 1890, and came to Downside in September, 1904. He was a clever boy of sterling character. He left Downside in July, 1908, and in the following autumn went up to King's College, Cambridge, where he took his degree (Law Tripos) in 1911. He passed the Solicitors' Final Examination in June, 1914. In March, 1909, he joined the 2nd Battalion Monmouthshire Regiment, T.F., as 2nd Lieutenant, and threw himself enthusiastically into the work, qualifying in musketry at Hythe in 1911, in signalling at Bulford in 1913, and receiving the appointment of Brigade Signalling Officer in August of that year. He was gazetted Captain in July, 1914, and volunteered for service abroad immediately on the outbreak of war. For a few months he was stationed at Northampton, commanding Section 4, Welsh Divisional Signal Company, Royal Engineers, T.F., whence he went to the front with the 2nd Monmouths. He was killed in action near Ypres on May 7th, 1915, aged twenty-five, and was buried on the battlefield near the village of La Brique St. Jean, about one mile northeast of Ypres.

Shortly afterwards, Colonel Cuthbertson, *M.V.O.*, *C.M.G.*, commanding officer of the regiment, wrote of him as follows:—

" Dear Mrs. Watkins,—I have not had time to write before to tell you how deeply my sympathies lie with you and Mr. Watkins on the loss of your gallant son.

" He was killed on the morning of the 7th, just at the end of the German attack, and his death was instantaneous and painless.

" Of his qualities as a soldier and a gentleman I cannot speak too highly. Cheerful, gallant and unselfish, he died as he would have chosen to die, with his face to the enemy and in the middle of his men whom he loved and commanded so well.

" We buried him on the battlefield, and any of his effects will be sent in the official way. His loss is deeply deplored by all ranks."

CAPT. I. E. M. WATKINS
2nd Monmouthshire Regiment

Killed in Action   *May 7th, 1915*

" He knew no fear," wrote a subaltern who was beside him when he fell, " his every thought was for his men. On the march he was up and down the ranks speaking cheering words to them, and even carrying the rifles of the weaker ones." And his parents received the following fine tribute to his memory from one of the Catholic soldiers of the regiment : " He was worshipped by his men ; in our view he was a priest and a saint and the pride of the regiment."

2nd LIEUT. EVERARD JOSEPH DRUITT, 2nd Battalion, Royal Berkshire Regiment, only son of the late Lieut.-Col. Edward Druitt and Mrs. Druitt, of 91, Iverna Court, W., was born on July 7th, 1895, and came to Downside in January, 1906. He was a boy of very upright and high-principled character, deeply influenced by religion ; sensitive and affectionate, his courage was of a high order, and he held his course due-on, little influenced by the fluctuations of public opinion, whilst his own influence, which steadily increased year by year, was excellent. A fine all-round athlete, he distinguished himself at all the games and sports from his earliest days at school. After a most promising apprenticeship in various Junior teams, he played for three years in the Cricket, Hockey and Association Football Elevens with equal success. On the introduction of Rugby Football at Downside in September, 1912, Druitt, who played right wing three-quarter, was chosen to captain the First Fifteen, and had the satisfaction of leading his team to victory in their first match. He was also captain of the Hockey Eleven, in which he played centre-half. In 1912 he was awarded his " Colours " for Cricket, Football and Hockey. When the new school buildings were opened at the beginning of the Summer Term, 1912, he became a Barlow House Prefect, and in the following September he was appointed a School Prefect and Head of his House, in which position he proved a most successful leader, captaining the Barlow Hockey, Cricket, Gymnastic and Sports Teams and commanding the Barlow section in the O.T.C. He also represented his House at golf. In the inter-house Sports of 1913 he brought off a fine triple success by winning the hundred yards, the long jump and putting the weight. He attended camp in 1911, 1912 and 1913, as private, lance-corporal and sergeant respectively.

For several years he sang in the choir, first as a treble and later on as a bass. In 1912 he took the part of Dick Deadeye in " H.M.S. Pinafore."

On leaving the School in July, 1913, he went in for railway work on the London and North Western, and on the outbreak of hostilities enlisted as a private in the H.A.C., and went to the front soon afterwards. In March, 1915, he received his commission in the Berkshires, and was killed in action at the head of his platoon, near Fromelles, on the following May 9th, being

2nd LIEUT. E. J. DRUITT
2nd Royal Berkshire Regiment

Killed in Action   *May 9th, 1915*

nineteen years of age at the time. The evening before he had received Holy Communion, the Papal blessing, and a plenary indulgence for the hour of death. The following letter, which we have been permitted to make use of in this memoir, is a wonderful testimony to his character and influence:

" A Company, 2nd Royal Berkshire Regiment,
25th Brigade, 8th Division, British Expeditionary Force,
May 13th, 1915.

" Sir,—It is with the deepest regret and sorrow that I am writing these few lines to you regarding the sad death of your son who, as you have no doubt been informed officially by this time, was killed in action on the 9th inst. I hope, sir, you won't mind my presuming in writing to you, but I was sure you would like to know how he died. Mr. Druitt had only been with us a short time, but I can honestly say every man in the platoon loved him and would have followed him anywhere, as during our few tours of duty in the trenches he had proved himself to be absolutely without fear and had gained the assured confidence and respect of his men.

" On the morning of the assault he was full of confidence, and when the order came for us to assault the position he was first over the parapet at the head of his platoon and was smiling and cool as if on parade. He shouted ' Come on, boys,' and started to lead us across the open, but had only advanced a few yards when he fell dead, shot straight through the heart. He was killed instantaneously and I am sure suffered no pain, for I looked at him as I went on and I saw that the smile was still on his face, and he was quite dead.

" Sir, I have seen many officers and men die since I came out here, some of them comrades I had known for years, but none affected me so much as the death of my platoon commander, your son, and a lump comes into my throat as I try to find words to express my sympathy and sorrow, for I loved him, sir, and can perhaps understand a little of what your feelings must be at the loss of so brave and noble a son.

" I hope you will not mind my writing to you, sir, and I hope it will cheer you a little to know that your son died as he had lived, a very gallant British gentleman. I am platoon sergeant of the platoon which Mr. Druitt commanded, and all the N.C.O.'s and men of the platoon wished me to write and tell you how he died, and all send their deepest sympathy in your sad bereavement.

" Please accept these few lines as a slight acknowledgment of the esteem and regard in which we held your son, and our deep regret at the loss of such a brave and gallant officer."

No less striking is the following from one who had been for years a schoolfellow of his at Downside:

" I got to know Everard very intimately out here, and conceived not only a very great affection for him, but also a great admiration for the strength of his character. I have never met anyone who cared less what others might think of his actions, or anyone with a greater devotion to the practice of his religion.

" He hardly ever missed a chance of hearing Mass and receiving Holy Communion, and I have known, again and again, occasions on which he has dragged himself up early in the morning, on the very first day of a ' rest ' in order to hear Mass, when we had only arrived at billets late the night before, feeling absolutely tired out after a long and trying period of trench life.

" His example in this way was altogether wonderful, and I have no hesitation in saying that I know it bore good fruit. God has not seen fit to leave longer on this earth one whose influence must have been so much for good, but Everard must now be most happily in Heaven, for I have never met a purer mind or more upright character."

2nd LIEUT. HUGH PATRICK SHINE, 1st Royal Irish Fusiliers, third and youngest son of Col. J. Shine, R.A.M.C., was born on August 20th, 1896, and came to Downside in September, 1905. Full of life and energy, he was a fine athlete and distinguished himself in every branch of sport. During his two last years at school he played regularly in the Hockey and Cricket Elevens, and in the Rugby Football Fifteen; he was also a good boxer, and was runner-up in the singles in the School Tennis Tournament in 1913. At Cricket he was a very useful player with both bat and ball, giving invaluable aid to his side at critical moments. Needless to say, he rendered excellent service to his House, representing Caverel at Cricket, Hockey, Golf and Gymnastics. He was a lance-corporal in the Corps.

He left Downside for Sandhurst in December, 1913, received his commission in the Royal Irish Fusiliers on October 1st, 1914, and went to the front early in the following year. About the second week of May he was wounded slightly in the hand, but did not leave the firing line. The last report about him was: " Fearless—succoured a wounded man under fire," and his name was sent up for mention. On May 21st he wrote to the Headmaster at Downside, and after mentioning several " Old Gregorians," contemporaries of his own, whom he had met in France, some of whom had since been killed, the letter concluded with the words : " It does not seem as if there will be many left when the war is over." Three days later he was killed himself. He fell in action at the Battle of Ypres on May 24th, 1915, being only eighteen years of age at the time of his death.

We have received permission to print the following extract from a letter of Capt. E. H. Fforde to Col. Shine, which gives a short account of his son's death.

" June 14th, 1915. I was commanding ' A ' Company, in which your son was, at the time of his death, and am about the only officer left who was present. On the morning of the 24th, at 2.30 a.m., the Germans started a heavy gas attack, followed by artillery. My company was about 200 yards behind the front line, in support, and we were all ' standing to,' awaiting orders and

2nd LIEUT. H. P. SHINE

1st Royal Irish Fusiliers

Killed in Action   *May 24th, 1915*

being shelled at the same time. About five minutes after the attack commenced a shrapnel shell killed your son. He was hit in the head and rendered unconscious at once, and died in about five minutes.

"I may add that your son was very popular with his men who, I could see, were genuinely sorry at losing him. As for the officers, we all liked him; he was so young and it seemed so fine of him coming out. Major Kentish, who commanded the company before me, always spoke highly of him, especially after the attack on St. Julien on April 25th."

His brother, John Denis, Col. Shine's second son, was killed at Mons on August 27th, 1914.

2nd LIEUT. HUGH MAURICE MACDERMOT, 6th Royal Irish Fusiliers, only son of The MacDermot, of Coolavin, Monasteraden, co. Sligo, was born September 29th, 1896, came to Downside in April, 1906, and left in December, 1908. He received his commission in 1915, and sailed for the Dardanelles in July, landing at Suvla Bay in the first days of August. On August 9th he was killed in action while leading his men in a charge against the Turkish position on " Chocolate Hill." He had not yet reached his nineteenth birthday at the time of his death. The division in which he was fighting was practically annihilated, an officer writing to The MacDermot as follows :—

" The 10th Division did what they were set to do, and when it was done there was no 10th Division. There was no braver or more gallant young soldier in all the King's Services than your son, or one who carried his boyish spirit more gloriously to the very end."

Full of youthful enthusiasm, ennobled by religious faith, Hugh MacDermot was well prepared in every respect for his great sacrifice, and a few days before sent a high-spirited and affecting letter to his mother. The Catholic chaplain wrote of him : " On August 7th your son's was the last confession I heard before the regiment went into action, and he was shot dead leading his men in a charge on August 9th, carrying to the feet of God a pure soul and the unblemished courage of a soldier." He was wearing a Benedictine medal around his neck when he was killed at Suvla Bay. A little later, The MacDermot wrote to say that a friend of his had met an officer who had returned wounded from the Dardanelles who was recounting the bravery of the subalterns in the fight. " It was really a wonderful thing," he said, " to see a young officer of the Irish Fusiliers named MacDermot—a mere child—leading his men." He was referring to the subject of this memoir.

2nd LIEUT. H. M. MacDERMOT

6th Royal Irish Fusiliers

Killed in Action   *August 9th, 1915*

LIEUT. A. E. CHISHOLM

11th Royal Scots

Killed in Action   *September 25th, 1915*

LIEUT. ALASTAIR E. CHISHOLM, 11th Royal Scots, attached 1st Royal Scots Fusiliers, was born October 14th, 1893, came to Downside in September, 1904, and left in July, 1908, when he went to Ushaw College. He received his commission in the 11th Royal Scots in November, 1914, and went to the front in the following year. On September 25th, 1915, he was killed in action during the British attack on Hooge. The following extracts from the letter of a brother officer, which we are kindly allowed to print, give all the known details of his end :—

"The battalion did not know till a short time before that they were to be in the attack. Alastair, being Bombing Officer, had to help the artillery in clearing the trenches. At the first moment possible, Alastair and a few men under him went out of the trenches and attacked the Germans by themselves, driving them out of three lines of trenches. Three times the Germans rushed forward to bayonet him, and three times Alastair drove them back. Standing on the third German parapet he kept the enemy back for more than two and a half hours by throwing bombs at them. 'He seemed to have a charmed life,' the men told me. Shells were bursting all round him, numberless Germans were shooting at him, and yet he stood there, right up on the enemy's parapet, calling and encouraging his men and throwing bombs with deadly aim at the enemy in front of him. At last the Germans tried to make a sally out to stop him by throwing bombs back at him, but, as the men told me, to every one bomb thrown by them Alastair threw three, and his men merely kept up the supply, handing bomb after bomb up to him, and he threw them as quickly as they were given to him.

"In this way he held back any number of men for two and a half hours, throwing in all about five hundred bombs. How many Germans he accounted for may never be known.

"The Major said to me : 'The regiment to which most credit is due is the Royal Scots Fusiliers, but still more credit is due to a most gallant and brilliant officer, to a man I am most proud to have known, and whose wonderful exhibition of self-sacrifice has impressed many men who will never forget him.' So said one of his officers and such is the opinion everyone holds of him, such was his bravery and his wonderful spirit, which has made so great and deep an impression on all round about him.

" His last words were to a man who had been with him all the time, called King. He called out to him, ' Look here, King, you carry on, I'm struck badly.' With that he fell back and died immediately, a bomb having exploded in front of him, wounding him in the stomach."

The Colonel of the 1st Royal Scots Fusiliers wrote concerning him :—

" All the men who managed to come out of the attack on September 25th are loud in his praises, and I am of opinion that his services are deserving of the highest reward."

This is fully borne out by the words of one of his men :—

" Mr. Chisholm is dead ; he died game, and like the perfect gentleman he was. He was killed on the third line, leading the way, as fine a leader as one could have. He was the nicest, happiest officer we had, always cheery and always had a good word to say."

Knowing that there was great danger before him, he had been to confession and Communion a few days before.

CAPT. J. H. A. RYAN, M.C.

1st King's Liverpool Regiment

Killed in Action   *September 25th, 1915*

CAPTAIN JAMES HENRY ALOYSIUS RYAN, 1st King's Liverpool Regiment, younger son of W. H. Ryan, Esq., of Tilecote, Roade, Northampton, was born on September 15th, 1892, and came to Downside in September, 1905. A fine all-round athlete, he distinguished himself in the School sports and in all the games, becoming successively captain of the Football, Hockey and Cricket teams. An actor of ability, he took part in performances of " Our Boys " and " A Pair of Spectacles," and in his last term he introduced and organised a semi-dramatic concert which took place with much success on the last night. He passed the School Certificate in 1909, and in December, 1910, passed twenty-fourth on the list into Sandhurst, where he subsequently received his Colours for Football, Hockey and Cricket. He played Cricket for Northamptonshire in 1912 and 1913 ; won the Officers' half mile at the Army Athletic Meeting, 1913 ; played Association Football for Army v. Navy, and v. Dutch Officers, 1914 ; and played Hockey for Army v. Navy, 1914. He went to the front at the outbreak of hostilities, and passed through fourteen months' continuous fighting without being wounded in any way, though he was constantly exposed to danger, and every other officer in the Battalion was either killed or wounded.

He was mentioned in despatches by Sir John French, received the Military Cross in January, 1915," for gallantry and great ability," and a little later was promoted Captain. On the occasion of the big attack in the neighbourhood of Loos and Hill 70, Ryan was put in charge of one of the companies leading the attack, and was killed in the engagement which followed, on September 25th, 1915. He was twenty-three years of age. Being warned that the post was one of extreme danger, he took the opportunity to go to confession and Communion the day before. The following letters, which we are permitted to print, give the true account of his death and show how greatly he was loved by his fellow officers and men:

" October 5th, 1915.—Although I feel the utter inadequacy of words in such a bereavement as yours, as officer commanding the battalion, may I express to yourself and family the heartfelt sympathy and regret of all ranks in the loss of your gallant son ?

"On 25th September the battalion was ordered to attack a very strong position which the enemy have held for many months. 'B' and 'C' Companies led the attack, the former commanded by your boy. The attack, though unsuccessful, was most gallantly carried out. Nothing could have exceeded the coolness and bravery of your son who directed his company under the heaviest fire with coolness and determination until instantly killed by a wound in the head. Our only consolation is that he can have felt no pain whatever.

"Once again, please accept the deepest sympathy of us all who, knowing your son's worth as a fine sportsman, a valued friend and gallant soldier, can realise something of his family's tremendous loss."

"October 13th.—. . . He was killed instantaneously, and could not have felt any pain, shot through the head. His men said that he was absolutely wonderful; under a murderous fire he led his men three times across to the German trench, perfectly cool and calm. By losing him the regiment has suffered a loss far greater than any other casualty. His company and everybody who knew him are heartbroken, no officer was loved more by his men. I don't believe anyone else could have led men across that terrible piece of ground, but they would follow Jim anywhere."

"September 29th.—Although a good many more have been killed since I joined, he was the only one that really mattered to me, nor do I think that I will ever have the same feeling in the Regiment since he is gone. When it is my turn to go, I only hope that I may face it as well as he did. We were to attack with gas at 5 a.m., but up to the last the wind, such as it was, was unfavourable. However, as it happened, the wind was all right for most of the line, so we had to carry on. 'B' Company was one of the attacking companies, and a lot of men were promptly gassed, and there was a lot of confusion, but Ryan worked wonders, and was everywhere at once, and got all his men well out. He was shot through the head and must have died instantly. He was an officer who always was ready to make sacrifices for the Regiment, and I am sure that he himself does not regret or grudge his death. I was talking to him late at night the night before we went up to the trenches, and he was saying how his religion stood to him in a time like this (I myself do not belong to the Old Religion) and how he felt quite ready for death if necessary."

LIEUT. THE HON. M. D. BROWNE

1st Coldstream Guards

Killed in Action   *September 29th, 1915*

LIEUT. THE HON. MAURICE DERMOT BROWNE,
1st Coldstream Guards, second son of the Earl of Kenmare, was
born on July 25th, 1894.   In May, 1905, he came to Downside,
and, before leaving it, he had become Head of the School, holder
of the School Challenge Cups for Golf and Boxing, a member of
the Cricket Eleven, in which he played well with both bat and ball,
and the recognized leader among his schoolfellows in every matter
of public interest.   In 1912 he was appointed the first Head of
the newly-established Roberts House.   He sang in the choir as
an alto, and took part with distinction in several plays and farces.
He was captain of the Boxing Club and secretary of the Golf
Club, and in the Officers' Training Corps he held the rank of
sergeant, attending camp in the summer of 1912.   In the same year
he also took part in the successful Roberts team in the O.T.C.
inter-house competition.

In July, 1912, he passed into Sandhurst, was gazetted to
the Coldstream Guards in the following year, and went to the
front with his regiment on the outbreak of hostilities in August,
1914.   He took part in the fighting at Mons, during the strategical
retreat to the south of Coulommiers and the subsequent advance,
in all of which the Coldstreams played a very distinguished part,
and on September 14th, 1914, was wounded in the right forearm
during the battle of the Aisne, and invalided home.   In the
following November he rejoined his regiment, remaining with it
in France, except for some short intervals of leave, and acting
as Adjutant for some weeks before his death, which took place
in action near Loos, on September 29th, 1915.   It is well known
that the Brigade of Guards took a very prominent part in the
British advance in September, 1915, and in the capture of Hill
70, the Coldstreams coming in for a full share of the fighting.
On September 29th, while their trenches were being heavily
shelled, an urgent call was sent to the Commanding Officer, who
at once came out of his shelter, taking Dermot Browne, his adjutant,
with him.   At that moment a German shell fell directly upon the
two officers, killing both of them instantly.   A brother officer
wrote as follows :—

" We buried them on the battlefield last night, side by side ; Father Knapp, Irish Guards, R.C. Chaplain, read the service for Dermot. The guns and maxims were firing all the night, and rockets were going up by which we could see."

Thus ended, only two months after his twenty-first birthday, the life of one who seemed destined for the highest command. As a boy every form of sport appealed to Dermot Browne ; he was a splendid rider, with all the Irishman's love of horses, and at School he set the tone and led his fellows inevitably, without being in the least aware of the high example he was giving or the influence he had upon others. When, in the war, he came to face danger and death, the same force of character, high spirits, and compelling fulness of life carried him on, and with him those he led.

" I knew him very well," wrote a private of his company, " and he died a perfect gentleman, the coolest man on the battlefield ; for he went after the Germans with a whip in one hand and a revolver in the other."

" I went up and saw him in his cellar the night before he was killed," wrote an officer of the Coldstreams ; " The battalion had had a terrible day, but Dermot was just himself—brave and cheerful as ever—the life and soul of all those around him. I simply cannot believe that I have said good-bye to him for ever ; he was the very finest type of officer and gentleman that I have ever known. None of those who knew Dermot in time of peace will ever forget the wonderful influence he had over all with whom he came in contact. None of those who have served with him out here will ever forget the example he has set us all. He and his colonel lie side by side, not very far from the place where they fell, and close to the village of Loos. Their troubles, their dangers, are past, and we are left to face our own without their help. God grant that the memory of how Dermot himself would have faced such trouble and sorrow may give us strength to face the future without him."

CAPT. L. G. LORD PETRE
4th Coldstream Guards

Died of Wounds   *September 30th, 1915*

CAPTAIN LIONEL GEORGE LORD PETRE, 4th Coldstream Guards, only son of the fifteenth Baron, was born on November 3rd, 1890, came to Downside in September, 1902, and left in July, 1905, when he went to the Oratory School, Edgbaston. He had been at the front for a considerable time without receiving any injury, and had passed unscathed through the great battle which began on Saturday, September 25th, 1915. Some days later, in the neighbourhood of Loos, he was in charge of a company of his regiment who were entrenching themselves in ground taken from the Germans. In the course of the work one of the men drove his pick into an unexploded shell which had buried itself in the ground. The blow, of course, exploded the shell, and a piece of it struck Lord Petre in the head. He was taken to the Duchess of Westminster's hospital at Le Touquet, and died there on September 30th, 1915, without regaining consciousness. He was twenty-four years of age. His body was brought home and buried at Thorndon on Saturday, October 9th.

In 1913 Lord Petre married Catharine, daughter of the Hon. J. R. de Clare Boscawen and grand-daughter of the sixth Viscount Falmouth ; and was succeeded by his son, born in 1914.

2nd LIEUT. ROBERT EMMET, 1st Life Guards, eldest son of Major Robert Emmet, Warwickshire Yeomanry, of Moreton Paddox, Warwickshire, was born on September 25th, 1897, and came to Downside in September, 1911. He played in the First Fifteen at Rugby Football, and in the Second Eleven at Cricket in 1913 and 1914, and in the same years also played for his House (Barlow). He was a lance-corporal in the Officers' Training Corps, and in 1913 was awarded a silver medal as one of the successful competitors in the Shooting Competition.

He left Downside in October, 1914, on receiving a commission in the Warwickshire Yeomanry. Early in 1915 he transferred into the 1st Life Guards, and in the following October was taken ill with typhoid fever, contracted while serving with his regiment. He received every care at a nursing home in London, but died, after three weeks' illness, on October 29th, 1915, fortified by the rites of the Church. He was eighteen years of age at the time of his death. On November 2nd he was buried with full military honours at Kensal Green, after a solemn Requiem at Farm Street Church.

2nd LIEUT. R. EMMET

1st Life Guards

Died on Service *October 29th, 1915*

MAJOR M. J. SWEETMAN
2nd Worcestershire Regiment

Died of Wounds   *November 22nd, 1915*

MAJOR MICHAEL JAMES J. (HAMISH) SWEETMAN, 2nd Worcestershire Regiment, attached 2nd Dorsetshire Regiment, eldest son of the late Michael James Sweetman, J.P., of Lamberton Park, Queen's County, was born in 1864, came to Downside in September, 1877, and left in December, 1884. He took his B.A. degree at London University, and subsequently entered the Army, being gazetted to the Worcestershire Regiment. He received his captaincy in 1896, and acted as Superintendent of Gymnasia for the Western District from 1895 to 1899, filling the same post later on at Gibraltar and Cork. He saw service in the South African War, and, soon after its close, retired with the rank of Major, and was placed on the reserve of officers. On the declaration of war he at once rejoined and, after working for some weeks in the recruiting and remount departments, he was sent to his old regiment and battalion, the 2nd Worcestershires, which he joined at the Aisne on September 30th, 1914. About a fortnight later they were moved to Belgium to oppose the advance of the German forces which had taken Antwerp, and Major Sweetman was wounded in the fighting near Ypres in October. On recovering from the effects of his wound he was attached to the 2nd Dorsetshire Regiment, and went to Mesopotamia. On November 21st, during the battle of Ctesiphon, he was mortally wounded in the groin, the same bullet injuring his spine. In spite of this grievous wound he remained with his men until the end of the battle, which was then thought to have been won. On the next day he was taken to a hospital ship on the Tigris. He was then unconscious, and never rallied, dying before the ship reached Kut-el-Amara. His sister, who kindly supplied these details, received many letters from his brother officers in which they spoke enthusiastically of his gallantry in the field, his kindness and his great personal modesty. The men under his command spoke of his kindliness and pluck— how he would help them to put up his tent in the blazing sun of the desert and then assist them in making their own dug-outs. His name was sent in three times for the D.S.O., and after the capture of Kut-el-Amara, by the 2nd Dorsets, of which he took command when the C.O. was wounded, he received the congratulations of the General and the Commander-in-Chief. He is buried at Kut-el-Amara.

LIEUT. CHARLES ANDREW MARTIN, 6th Royal Dublin Fusiliers, second son of the late Mr. T. Martin, of Greenbank, Monkstown, Co. Dublin, was born in 1895, came to Downside in January, 1906, and left in April, 1912. He played in the Hockey Eleven, 1911-12, and won the Golf Challenge Cup in 1912. After leaving Downside, he passed into Trinity College, Dublin. At the beginning of the war he joined the Dublin Fusiliers, and went out to Gallipoli in July, 1915. He was wounded in the arm at Suvla Bay in the following August, but not seriously enough to necessitate a return home. Later in the year he went with his regiment to Salonika, where he took part in the fighting against the Bulgarians. After a very heavy engagement on December 8th, 1915, he was reported " wounded and missing " ; it has since been ascertained that he was taken prisoner by the Bulgarians, and died of wounds about two days later, probably on December 10th. He was twenty years of age at the time. From information supplied by his Commanding Officer it appears that Lieut. Martin was in command of one of two companies sent forward to hold an advanced position on what is called the Rivet Ridge, in order to delay the Bulgar advance. With great gallantry his men succeeded in holding up the enemy from 8 o'clock in the morning till about 3.30 in the afternoon, being all the time practically unsupported by artillery fire, as the British guns were moving to new positions. " This check to the enemy was of the greatest importance to the remainder of our troops, and also the French."

The following further details were related to the American Consul General in charge of the American Legation at Sofia by some of the British prisoners who were under Lieut. Martin's command during the engagement :—

" He displayed the greatest coolness and bravery. On the morning of the 8th he received a severe bullet wound in the leg, but notwithstanding remained at his post, directing and encouraging his men until the Bulgarian bayonet charge in force made it impossible to hold out longer with the few available men under his command. Then he ordered all who were able to retreat in good order. He helped some of the men out of the trench, and called ' Good-bye, boys,' to the wounded men lying there."

LIEUT. C. A. MARTIN
6th Royal Dublin Fusiliers

Died of Wounds   *December 10th, 1915*

He was last seen going up a slight hill with the retreating men, and as his company was then under a very heavy rifle, machine gun and artillery fire, it is probable that he was again wounded about this time.

The following extract is from a letter written in August, 1917, by an English officer, then a prisoner of war in Bulgaria :—

" I have learned the following facts. He was hit in the arm and leg, but carried on ; subsequently he was hit again, as far as I can gather, in the stomach, the bullet lodging somewhere in the spine. He was picked up on the morning of December 9th, 1915, by the Bulgarians and taken to a dressing station, when it was found that he was paralysed from the hips downwards. Everything was done for him, but he died probably on December 10th. The above facts were given to me by a Bulgarian medical student, a candidate officer, who attended to Lieut. Martin, doing all that was possible under the circumstances. . . . Not long ago I met this gentleman in Philippopolis ; he recalled our meeting and told me all about Lieut. Martin. He did not know Martin's name, but from the description he gave of the officer he answered my recollection of Lieut. C. A. Martin, Royal Dublin Fusiliers."

Charles Martin was a most successful officer ; he was mentioned in despatches " for gallant conduct," and received the Order of the White Eagle from the Crown Prince of Serbia. His commanding officer wrote of him as follows :—

" To me and the regiment he is a great loss. He was a most promising officer, and led and handled his men most skilfully that morning in a very difficult situation."

One of his fellow officers described him as " a great favourite with both the officers and men, who speak highly of him," and the Catholic chaplain referred to him as " one of my dearest friends."

MAJOR FRANCIS WILLIAM JOSEPH MACDONNELL,
12th (attached 9th) West Yorkshire Regiment, eldest son of F. E. J. MacDonnell, J.P., of Dunfierth, co. Kildare, by his second wife, Georgina, daughter of James Gernon, Esq., of Athcarne Castle, co. Meath, was born in November, 1870. He came to Downside in September, 1881, left in July, 1887, and subsequently entered the Army. He saw service in South Africa during the years 1901 and 1902, taking part in operations in the Transvaal and Orange River Colony, as Captain in the 3rd Royal Dublin Fusiliers, and receiving the Queen's Medal with four clasps. He had retired from the Army some years since, but rejoined at once on the outbreak of hostilities, being posted to the 12th West Yorks, with the rank of Major, in November, 1914. In the following July he was transferred to the 14th battalion, and later still was attached to the 9th for service with the Mediterranean Expedition. In Gallipoli he contracted dysentery and was removed to hospital at Malta, where he died on December 13th, 1915, aged forty-five.

In 1898 Major MacDonnell married Teresa, daughter of the late Sir John Lawson, and leaves issue two sons and one daughter.

MAJOR F. W. J. MacDONNELL
12th West Yorkshire Regiment

Died on Service   *December 13th, 1915*

2nd LIEUT. C. M. FENDALL
Royal Field Artillery

Killed in Action   *December 14th, 1915*

2nd LIEUT. CHARLES MAGRATH FENDALL, Royal Field Artillery, elder son of Col. C. P. Fendall, *D.S.O.*, R.A., of Wokingham, Berks, was born on August 29th, 1892, came to Downside in September, 1905, and left in July, 1908. After studying for a year or so in London he went out to Alberta, Canada, where he was working on a ranch at the outbreak of war. He at once came home, obtained a commission in the R.F.A., and went to France some months later. On December 14th, 1915, his battery was heavily shelled for some time, and Fendall was killed instantly by a shell which struck the office where he was working. He was twenty-three years of age at the time. The following letters, which Mrs. Fendall kindly permits us to publish, give details of his death :—

" It happened by the merest chance—if there be such a thing as mere chance—that it occurred to me to go round the Cameron Highlanders' trenches on the morning of December 14th. There was really no reason why I should have done so, as I had been with the Camerons almost daily. In passing your son's battery I saw the medical officer, whom I knew pretty intimately, and stopped to chat with him. Your son joined us, and subsequently I asked him about the Catholics of the battery. He knew them all well, so I ventured to ask if he were not a Catholic himself. We talked for some time, and he made his confession while we walked to the little wood where his battery was. It was a great shock to me when I heard early in the afternoon that he had fallen. It must have been within an hour of my leaving him.

From the captain in charge of his battery :—

" It is extremely difficult for me to write to you in your great grief in losing your dear son, who was such a good soldier and so beloved by his men. I will try and explain how he met his death, which took place on December 14th. He was the subaltern on duty in the battery, and usually sat in the office. At about 2.15 p.m., just as I had returned from the trenches, four or five German shells came straight into the battery, one going through the office roof. On rushing there I found your son had been killed, and the brigade doctor, who was also sitting there, very badly wounded ; he has since died. I can't tell you what a gloom it has cast over us all, as we were all so fond of him. He was buried at 10 a.m. the following day, a Roman Catholic chaplain officiating, the Brigade Commander and all the officers attending."

Another officer of the battery wrote to Col. Fendall :—

" The boy was killed by a shell, instantaneously, on the 14th. All our batteries have been getting rather heavily shelled lately. We know no particular reason except that we are in a salient and, as the leaf comes off the trees, we possibly become visible—flashes at all events—to some enemy points, or observation balloons, or aeroplanes. I saw him myself about two days before. There is not much consolation in my telling you how much we all liked the boy. He was the most modest, likeable, quiet, shy, amenable boy. The cruel part is that we were just going out to ' rest,' so called, and next week would have seen us out of this and in a back line temporarily. The division has lost a gallant soldier and a good gunner. I can't bring myself in these times to pity a youngster who dies a gallant death for his country, but I do pity his father and mother."

SURGEON J. BARRETT, R.N.V.R.

H.M.S. " Imperieuse "

Drowned in North Sea   *December 18th, 1915*

SURGEON JAMES BARRETT, M.B., R.N.V.R., was born in 1885, came to Downside in January, 1898, and left in July, 1899. He was a good athlete, played in the Cricket Eleven in 1899, and distinguished himself in the Aquatic Sports. At the time of his death he was Medical Officer on H.M.S. *Imperieuse*. He was washed overboard and drowned at sea, whilst on active service, on December 18th, 1915. His brother, Tim Barrett (O.G.), wrote as follows :—

" As far as we can learn, the ship he was attached to was a victualling ship (H.M.S. *Imperieuse*) somewhere in the North Sea, and on the night of December 18th, 1915, he was washed overboard and never seen again. . . . The captains of the different ships on which he served seem to have held, from the letters we received, a very high opinion of him."

2nd LIEUT. RICHARD SHIRBURNE WELD-BLUNDELL, 7th King's Liverpool Regiment, elder son of Mr. Charles J. Weld-Blundell, of Ince Blundell Hall, Lancashire, was born in 1887, came to Downside in September, 1902, left in April, 1905, and at a later date went up to Pembroke College, Oxford. He was a fine sportsman and good at games ; at Downside he played in the Cricket and Association Football Elevens, and at Oxford he played football for his college. He was very interested in English Literature, especially in the Elizabethan dramatists.

Soon after the war began he received a temporary commission in the Coldstream Guards, from which he subsequently transferred to the King's Liverpools. On January 1st, 1916, fortified by the rites of the Church, he died in camp at Ramsgate from the effects of an accident.

At the inquest it was stated that he was last seen at his billeting quarters at ten o'clock on the night of Friday, December 31st, and soon after eleven was found lying unconscious in the road outside his quarters, with a severe wound in the back of the head. It was a wild, stormy night, and owing to the war regulations the sea front was in complete darkness, and it is thought that he must have slipped on the steps and in his fall have struck his head on an iron rainpipe at the edge of the kerb. He never recovered consciousness, and died the following morning, at the age of twenty-eight. The funeral, with full military honours, took place at Ince Blundell on January 8th, the Archbishop of Liverpool officiating.

In February, 1915, he married Mary Angela, eldest daughter of Capt. Jasper Mayne, of Tumbricane, Ipswich, by whom he left an infant daughter, born less than a month before her father's death.

2nd LIEUT. R. S. WELD-BLUNDELL

7th King's Liverpool Regiment

Died on Service '   *January 1st, 1916*

CAPT. B. P. NEVILE

7th Lincolnshire Regiment

Killed in Action   *February 11th, 1916*

CAPTAIN BERNARD PHILIP NEVILE, 7th Lincolnshire Regiment, youngest son of the late Mr. R. Nevile, of Wellingore Hall, Lincoln, was born in 1888, came to Downside in April, 1902, and left in July, 1905. He distinguished himself in all branches of athletics, and was an excellent all-round cricketer. At Downside he was a prominent member of the Football, Hockey and Cricket Elevens. After leaving school he studied engineering at Birmingham, and, a few years later, went up to Trinity College, Cambridge, where he took his degree in 1913. Besides playing regularly for his college at hockey and cricket, he played cricket for the University on several occasions, and won his " blue " for both hockey and golf. He also played cricket for Worcestershire, and in 1913 headed the bowling averages for the county. In September, 1914, he received his commission in the 7th Lincolnshires, becoming Lieutenant a month or two later, and Captain in January, 1915. After many months' service in France he was shot through the head on February 11th, 1916, at a point about three miles south of Ypres. He was twenty-seven years of age.

One of the men in his company described the circumstances as follows :—

" There was no attack, merely the usual sniping and desultory shelling characteristic of a normal day in the trenches. Captain Nevile was in the firing line, looking over the parapet, superintending the placing of some barbed wire, when a German bullet struck him through the head. He died shortly after without suffering."

His commanding officer wrote of him :—

" We have lost a really good officer, whose first consideration was always for those under his command, and a good friend, whose interests were very much centred in the battalion. . . . Bernard will be missed by all ranks. I have just returned from our dressing station, where I saw and spoke to several of his company, and it was most gratifying to hear them say how much they will miss him."

A priest who was his chaplain until a fortnight before he was killed gave a striking testimony to his character :—

" He was shot right through the head about 8.30 one night. He was at once unconscious, and died about an hour later. He had served Mass the preceding Sunday, and had been to Holy Communion. . . . You can have no idea of the value to a Catholic chaplain of a man like Nevile. Personally he was a saint, absolutely simple and child-like and a regular communicant. He thought little of getting up at six in the morning after his regiment had returned from the trenches—arriving perhaps at midnight, muddy, wet, and tired, to come and serve Mass and have Communion. . . . I simply can't give you any adequate idea of the man. He was just a Christian gentleman and soldier. There is one thing that strikes me more and more every day about him. It was a gentlemanly humility that kept him from ever mentioning anything about himself. I have been with him constantly, I have talked to him for hours, and yet not till I saw in a recent paper some references to his sporting powers had I the remotest idea of his qualifications in that respect."

MIDSHIPMAN G. A. H. DE BLESS

H.M.S. " Revenge "

Died on Service   *March 23rd, 1916*

MIDSHIPMAN GERVASE ANTHONY H. DE BLESS,
H.M.S. *Revenge*, son of the late Mr. A. H. de Bless, was born on
October 20th, 1897, came to Downside in May, 1908, and left
in January, 1915. An exceptionally clever boy of very active
mind and many interests, during his time in the School he dis-
tinguished himself in all branches of study, winning the Gregorian
Medal in 1912. He passed the Higher Certificate three times,
twice gaining distinction in French and twice in Roman History.
For three years he played in the Junior Cricket Eleven, which he
captained in 1912. From 1908 to 1912 he sang in the choir as
a treble, and he took a leading part with much success in " The
Gondoliers," and in " H.M.S. Pinafore." In 1914 he was
Editor of *The Raven*, and was on the committee of the Petre
Library. In this year also he was awarded the Higher Certificate
Latin Prose Prize given by St. Gregory's Society. On leaving
Downside he spent two terms at Cambridge under the tuition
of Mgr. Barnes. Sensitive and somewhat retiring, and with
health far from robust, he faced the situation created by the war
with splendid courage, and obtained a cadetship in the Royal
Navy. A skilful angler, fishing had ever been his favourite recrea-
tion, and on this pleasant pastime he wrote some charming verses
which were afterwards collected in a little booklet. The last of
these refers to his Great Adventure, so soon to be accomplished.

" R.N.

" Happy by the silvery Coln,
　The hours I spent at Fairford dear ;
　Now those April days are flown,
　I learn to serve and know no fear.

King of rivers, Test immortal !
　Yet I thrill at thoughts of thee.
　Traversed now in Fate's dark portal—
　Fate that leads me to the sea.

Test and Coln, each stream and valley
　That my boyhood happy made,
　Farewell ! No more may I dally,
　God of battles grant thy aid ! "

Early in February, 1916, he was gazetted midshipman, and joined H.M.S. *Revenge* on March 21st. Shortly before this he had been suffering from influenza, a relapse ensued coupled with complications, and he died on board ship on March 23rd, aged eighteen, fortified by the rites of the Church, which were administered to him by Dom Jerome Tunnicliffe, of St. Mary's, Liverpool, a monk of Downside.

2nd LIEUT. B. H. WORSLEY-WORSWICK

2nd King Edward's Horse

Killed in Action   *April 29th, 1916*

2nd LIEUT. BASIL HENRY WORSLEY-WORSWICK, 2nd King Edward's Horse, son of the late Major Worsley-Worswick, of Normanton Hall, Hinckley, and younger brother of Dom Peter Worsley-Worswick, of Downside Abbey, was born on April 20th, 1881, and came to Downside in May, 1894. He played in the Cricket Eleven in 1899. On leaving the School in July, 1899, he went up to Christ Church College, Oxford, and later on was articled to Messrs. Witham & Co., but being unable to bear the indoor life of an office, he went out to a farm in Rhodesia, and subsequently migrated to Canada. He returned from Canada just before the war, and enlisted in the 2nd King Edward's Horse in August, 1914. He served for one year as a trooper, during which time he was doing infantry work in the trenches for five months. He took part in the fighting at Festubert, was given a commission in his own regiment, and sent to the Cavalry Reserve at the Curragh.

On Easter Monday the Sinn Fein rising took place in Dublin, and King Edward's Horse, among other regiments, was called in to quell the disturbance. Basil Worsley-Worswick's death was the result of the general confusion prevailing during that tragic time. It appears that a detachment of the Dublin Fusiliers was stationed at the malt-house of Guinness' Brewery, and Lieut. Lucas, who had been on duty for four days and nights, was sent to relieve the officer in charge. According to the evidence given by Sergeant Flood and his men of the Dublin Fusiliers, when Lieut. Lucas arrived they took him to be a Sinn Feiner, and shot him in cold blood. Basil Worsley-Worswick was in the next picket, and, suspecting that something was going wrong in the malt-house, asked his superior officer for permission to investigate. He was told to wait until morning, and so did not arrive at the malt-house until dawn. It is probable that he found out that Lieut. Lucas had been shot and, his suspicions thoroughly aroused, on being challenged by Sergeant Flood, he knocked him down. In the confusion and misapprehension that followed, he was fired upon by the guard and killed. Thus, through a succession of misunderstandings, this gallant officer lost his life on April 29th, 1916, being thirty-five years of age at the time.

CAPTAIN GILBERT MEADE GERARD, 2nd (attached 1st) Highland Light Infantry, only son of the late General Sir Montagu Gilbert Gerard, K.C.B., K.C.S.I., of Rochsoles, Airdrie, Lanarkshire, was born in 1889, came to Downside in April, 1904, and left in July, 1906. After passing through Sandhurst he was gazetted to the 2nd Battalion of the Highland Light Infantry in 1908. He was promoted lieutenant in September, 1911, and captain in April, 1915. He went out to France with the British Expeditionary Force in August, 1914, and in November of that year he was sent home with a very severe wound, from which, however, he recovered sufficiently to rejoin his regiment at the front, but in May of the following year he was again sent home wounded. In February, 1916, he was again sent to the front attached to the 1st Battalion of his regiment, where, however, he contracted the serious illness which ended in his death on May 2nd, 1916. He was the last survivor of the original officers of this battalion who went out during the war.

One of the officers of his regiment wrote as follows :—

" You will have heard before this of the death of Captain Gerard ; his illness was diagnosed as ' acute enteritis,' and he died after being moved down to the Field Ambulance Hospital from one of the more advanced ones. He was commanding us for the few days before his illness. We miss him very much indeed. I especially feel his loss very much, as the only officer here who knew him in peace time. He was always very good to me from the day I joined, and it seems cruel luck just when we thought he had pulled through. He had been seedy for three days before, but would not go sick, but eventually had to go on April 27th. He died at 6 a.m. on May 2nd.

" In the name of the regiment I wish to express our great sorrow at his loss, and sincere sympathy with all his friends."

Lady Gerard received a special telegram of condolence from the King and Queen.

CAPT. G. M. GERARD

2nd Highland Light Infantry

Died on Service   *May 2nd, 1916*

MIDSHIPMAN J. H. G. ESMONDE

H.M.S. "Invincible"

Killed in Action   *May 31st, 1916*

MIDSHIPMAN JOHN HENRY GRATTAN ESMONDE, H.M.S. *Invincible*, younger son of Sir Thomas H. Grattan Esmonde, Bart., M.P., was born on May 2nd, 1899, came to Downside in January, 1910, and left in December, 1911, when he passed into Osborne. His period of training at Osborne and Dartmouth was barely completed at the outbreak of war in August, 1914, but he was at once gazetted midshipman and attached to H.M.S. *Invincible*. He took part in several naval engagements, including the battle off Heligoland and the fight at the Falkland Islands, in which the *Invincible* sank the armoured cruiser *Scharnhorst*. Of this fight he wrote the brilliant description which appeared in The *Downside Review* for March, 1915. He died on May 31st, 1916, when the *Invincible* was sunk during the battle of Jutland. Sir Thomas Grattan Esmonde received the following letter from one of the surviving officers :—

" This Kodak belonged to your son ; he gave it to the signalman who was stationed aloft, to try and take some photographs of the action. The signalman was one of the survivors, and happened to have the Kodak secured to his person. He gave it to me to return to you.

" Your son was at his old station in ' A ' turret, and died as I am sure he would have wished to die, full of fight and enthusiasm. The guns of ' A ' turret were doing excellent work at the time, and we were giving the *Derfflinger* much more than she bargained for. There was a tremendous explosion on board at 6.34 ; the ship broke in half and sank in ten or fifteen seconds. Death must have been almost instantaneous and painless to your son, and his end was one you may well be proud to think of."

The chaplain of the Battle-Cruiser Squadron sent the following letter :—

" I wish to express to you and Lady Esmonde and family my sincerest sympathy with you in your dreadful loss. Since February of 1915 I have been Catholic chaplain to the 2nd and 3rd Battle Cruiser Squadrons, and during that short time came to know and appreciate your boy. He was always on the spot for Confession and Mass, and went to no end of trouble to make arrangements, and to induce his men to come to the Sacraments. The Sunday before the action I had arranged to join the *Invincible*, but owing to lack of accommodation we put it off till the following Sunday.

" We were following the ship when she blew up. His death was swift and painless—the death of a true Catholic gentleman and officer fighting in a just cause. May God rest him and comfort you and your family."

Sir Thomas Grattan Esmonde received a telegram of condolence from the King and Queen.

The *Daily News* published the following tribute to the literary abilities of the dead midshipman, the letter referred to being that which appeared in the *Downside Review* :—

" One of the personal losses in Wednesday's action that calls for more than ordinary sorrow, in that it involves the sudden ending of a life of much more than ordinary promise, is that of Midshipman John H. G. Esmonde, of the *Invincible*. The dead midshipman was the son of Sir Thomas Esmonde, M.P., and his brilliant account of the battle of the Falkland Islands can be forgotten by no one who read it in the *Daily News* or the *Manchester Guardian*, the two papers to whom Sir Thomas Esmonde courteously supplied copies of his son's letter. The description of the battle—in particular the duel between the *Invincible* and the *Scharnhorst*— as seen from the top of a turret, was characterised by many competent judges as the most effective narrative of a naval engagement that the war had up to then produced. Put at the lowest it was a remarkable piece of writing for a boy under sixteen, arguing powers of observation and presentation that the future must have brought to a notable maturity. ' I hope I shall never have to go through it again,' young Esmonde wrote of the scenes he witnessed on the sinking *Gneisenau*. The words come back with an even more tragic ring to-day. But we cannot doubt that if the story of the *Invincible's* end could be known, the boy who flinched honourably at the death of others would be found to have gone unflinchingly to meet his own."

LIEUT. PRINCE ALFRED MARIA SAPIEHA

Killed in Action   *June 5th, 1916.*

PRINCE ALFRED MARIA SAPIEHA, eldest son of Prince Paul Sapieha, of Siedliska, Rawaruska, Poland, was born at Jaslo, in Galicia, Austria, on February 19th, 1896, came to Downside in January, 1908, and left in July, 1913. Descended from an ancient Polish family, he was a clever and capable boy, strong-willed, high-spirited, and courageous. His school life at Downside, where he made many friends, was a very successful one. He passed the Higher Certificate twice, gaining distinction in German on both occasions. On the opening of the new school buildings at the beginning of the Summer Term of 1912, he was placed in Roberts House, and was a member of the Roberts O.T.C. team which won the inter-house competition in 1913. He sang in the choir from 1908 to 1911. His ancestral home was in the Austrian dominions, and on the outbreak of the Great War in August, 1914, he joined the Mounted Artillery of the Austrian Army, and left for the war front against the Russians, with the 7th Division of the Imperial Horse Artillery, early in November. He was a patriotic Pole, inevitably opposed to the inveterate enemies and oppressors of his race, but although circumstances placed him against the Russians, who were our allies in the first stages of the conflict, he had the highest regard for England, and was devoted to his old school, and it is in accordance with the unanimous desire of those who knew him at Downside that he has been included in this record of " Old Gregorians," who fought nobly and died gallantly for their country in the war, that he may be honoured along with his schoolfellows and share in the prayers and Masses offered up for them in perpetuity. As a soldier he displayed great ability and courage, was decorated with the silver Medal of Valour in 1914, and again in 1915, and was promoted Lieutenant in his division of the Mounted Artillery in May, 1916. In spite of the difficulties in the way, he managed to get a letter through to one of the monks who had been a contemporary of his in the School. It is dated April 6th, 1916, and shows how strong was his affection for Downside. We have been permitted to print the following extract :—

" You don't know what immense pleasure your letter gave me. At last a piece of news from Downside after almost two years. A little news I had through Tarnowski, but that was only a rumour ;

unfortunately I see it was true as regards the many who have fallen. I am so sorry for them all and hope that K. has quite recovered. I am serving ever since the first day, and am at the front from November, 1914. I have had many close shaves, but immense luck throughout. I know very little of what has happened to most of the other Poles, as we are continually separated—that is our terrible tragedy. At home there are ruins and plundered remains ; as one would expect, it is hard. I am writing to you from a kind of shed (much worse than the *old* bikeshed by the monks' refectory at D.). I am at present having two days' rest three miles away from the lines, and it is only in honour of this letter which is going over sea that I am writing in ink. Almost my only amusements are a gramophone and a small rifle, with which I have already shot two crows . . . . The first thing I shall do when the old state of things is restored is to come to Downside. . . . It is a funny coincidence that just as I got your letter I was reading Belloc's *Path to Rome*. Are there matches and sports as usual ? I should be infinitely grateful to you if you tried to send me a copy of the latest *Raven*, but I fear it is impossible. . . . If this ever gets to you at all, please answer me. I am always so glad to hear something of Downside."

Alfred Sapieha was killed in action at the age of twenty, on June 5th, 1916, whilst defending the trenches of Sapanow, near Krzemieniec, in Wolhynia (Russia), in the first days of the offensive of General Brusilow against Austria. He fought with the greatest determination and courage, inspiring his fellow soldiers to hold on to the uttermost, and resolutely refusing to surrender. His body was never found, but near to the place where he was killed a cross was erected by Prince Roman Sanguszko, who was himself afterwards slain by Russian peasants, who also destroyed the cross. The last report of Alfred Sapieha from the officer in charge of him and his battalion at the end was as follows : " He performed his duties in action with incredible bravery."

What has been said above applies also to another " Old Gregorian," Anthony de Skrzynski, a Polish boy of outstanding ability, who was born on March 21st, 1892, and was at Downside from September 1906 to July 1907. He afterwards studied at Breslau University. He was killed in action at the battle of Lodz, fighting against the Russians, in the autumn of 1914. He was twenty-two years of age.

2nd LIEUT. E. E. TREVOR-JONES

6th Rifle Brigade

Killed in Action *July 1st, 1916*

2nd LIEUT. EVAN EDWARD TREVOR-JONES, 6th (attached 1st) Rifle Brigade, elder son of Major E. J. Trevor Cory, M.D., R.A.M.C. (T.), of Aberdare, was born on January 15th, 1896, and came to Downside in September, 1906. He was a very attractive boy, thoughtful, unselfish and brave. A hard worker of considerable ability, he secured the first place in his class in 1912 and 1913 ; and during his last year at School he was a House Prefect, Librarian of the Petre Library, and a sergeant in the O.T.C. In 1913 he was awarded a silver medal as one of the successful competitors in the Shooting Competition. He was a member of the School Eleven at Cricket in 1914, and he won the Second Division Tennis Singles in 1912. For three years he played for Caverel House at Cricket, Hockey and Rugby Football, and he also took part in the House Sports and Gymnastic Competition. After leaving Downside in July, 1914, he went to Clare College, Cambridge, for the Michaelmas Term, at the end of which he obtained a commission in the Rifle Brigade. In June, 1915, he went to the front, where for some time he acted as bombing officer. He was killed in action at Serre in the early days of the Somme Battle, on July 1st, 1916, at the age of twenty. His younger brother, Eric, whilst in the same battalion, was killed at the same place in April, 1918. One of Edward Trevor-Jones' fellow officers supplied the following account of his death :—

" . . . We have learnt some of the details of his gallant behaviour on that day, and all agree that his conduct was magnificent. He was wounded in the upper part of his left arm during the first advance, but kept on with his men and led them most gallantly to our objective ; he here did excellent work consolidating our position under heavy machine and shell fire. During the next three hours he was wounded twice more, though not seriously, in getting wounded men under cover.

" Eventually he was ordered to go back by the commanding officer of another regiment, and he and another of our officers who was wounded in the right arm started across ' no man's land ' towards our line ; they got another wounded man out of a shell hole and started him crawling back, and then finding a man with a shattered thigh, began to bring him in between them with their wounded arms. They had just reached our parapet when a shell burst and killed your son instantly (the other two were untouched).

" I have been in the same company as your son since February of this year, and I can assure you that he was an example to us all for coolness, courage and energy ; his men all loved him and respected him, and I am expressing the sentiments of every member of the battalion when I say that we have lost in him a most valuable and beloved officer and comrade."

The colonel under whom he was trained before leaving for France, referring to a description of his death, wrote as follows :—

" I am having it copied and am sending it to the *Rifle Brigade Chronicle*. I hope you will not mind my doing this. I am anxious that the particulars of your son's gallant conduct and splendid death should be recorded for the benefit of the regiment. The officer who was with him at the time has got the *D.S.O.*, so if your brave boy had been spared, he would also have had the *D.S.O.* Last June I had a letter from the officer commanding the 1st Battalion of the Rifle Brigade at the front about the officers of the Battalion who were serving with him, and he said of your boy, ' He is a very capable officer, and I recommend him for promotion.' "

It was Edward Trevor-Jones' desire to enter the Noviciate at Downside at the end of the war. The two following extracts from letters written after his death will help to show the affectionate regard in which he was held at school. A member of the community who knew him well wrote of him thus : " I have never known a better boy, modest, devout, with a high and strong sense of duty, generous, chivalrous, unselfish, without any self-assertion, but strong to hold his own when duty called."

And this tribute was from one of his schoolfellows :—

" He died, as I expected, most gallantly, and showing the spirit of self-sacrifice which was so noticeable in him when we were all together at school."

2nd LIEUT. C. A. STONOR
Royal Inniskilling Fusiliers

Killed in Action   *July 1st,* 1916

2nd LIEUT. CUTHBERT A. STONOR, Royal Inniskilling Fusiliers, youngest son of the late Mr. Charles Joseph Stonor, J.P., of Anderton Hall, Lancashire, was born on August 13th, 1887, came to Downside in May, 1901, and left in July, 1905.

He was killed in action on July 1st, 1916, when leading his men in a charge, after being less than two months at the front. He was twenty-eight years of age. On leaving school he spent several years in the East, but returned from Colombo directly he heard that war had been declared. After a year's training he obtained his commission and was sent to the front on May 10th, 1916. On July 1st he was reported missing, and some weeks later his body was found lying in the midst of his own men. A letter from his mother was the only means of identification. The feelings of all who knew him, both here and in the East, were expressed in the many letters of sympathy received by his parents. One sentence sums up all :—

" Nobody could have lived a better life or died in a finer way. I am sure he has very few things to regret having done in this life, and that everybody who knew him will always remember his friendly, cheerful disposition."

LIEUT. HUGH GILBERT CLIFFORD, 2nd Lincolnshire Regiment, only son of Sir Hugh Clifford, G.C.M.G., Governor-General of Ceylon, was born on January 20th, 1897, came to Downside in January, 1908, and left in April, 1913. He was a pleasant, cheerful, straightforward boy, well liked by all. During his last year at school he was a Caverel House Prefect, he played hockey for Caverel, and sometimes for the School Eleven, and he was awarded his House Colours for sports. He went to Sandhurst in August, 1914, received his commission in the 2nd Lincolns in the following December, when he joined his regiment at Grimsby, and went to the front in March, 1915, receiving his baptism of fire at Neuve Chapelle. He was wounded on May 9th in the Fromelles attack, being hit in the leg by a splinter of shell. On the same day, and at the same place, Everard Druitt was killed in action. Hugh Clifford was sent home at once, arriving two days later at the Royal Free Hospital, Gray's Inn Road, where the piece of shell was extracted. He recovered quickly and rejoined his regiment at Grimsby on July 1st. Exactly a year later, on July 1st, 1916, having returned to the front, he was killed in action, at the age of nineteen.

LIEUT. H. G. CLIFFORD
2nd Lincolnshire Regiment

Killed in Action   *July 1st, 1916*

2nd LIEUT. K. C. MACARDLE

17th Manchester Regiment

Killed in Action   *July 9th,* 1916

2nd LIEUT. KENNETH CALLAN MACARDLE, 17th Manchester Regiment, eldest son of Mr. T. Callan Macardle, D.L., of St. Margaret's, Dundalk, was born on April 21st, 1890, and was at Downside from September, 1901, till July, 1902. After completing his school career, he spent two years learning hop-growing, and then went to California, where he joined Clemens, Horst & Co., an important firm of hop growers. Later on he left the firm and became a member of the staff of the Canadian Bank of Commerce in San Francisco. At the outbreak of the war he came to England and obtained a commission in the Manchester Regiment. He went to France early in 1916 with the 17th Battalion, and was killed on July 9th, in one of the attacks on Trones Wood. In this attack, he and some of his men reached an advanced post where they found themselves without supports. Nevertheless, they decided to remain there until reinforcements should arrive. Before this happened they ran short of ammunition, and Lieut. Macardle offered to go and bring assistance. Whilst crossing the open on the way back he was killed. At the time of his death he was twenty-six years of age.

LIEUT. D'ARCY JOHN JOSEPH HARTLEY, Dragoon Guards (attached Machine Gun Corps), son of Mr. Hartley, of Chorlton Hall, Malpas, Cheshire, was born on July 1st, 1890, came to Downside in September, 1901, and left in December, 1902. During his short stay at Downside he did very well in the Junior Sports, and gave every promise of distinguishing himself at athletics. Subsequently he went to Eton, and afterwards to Merton College, Oxford, in 1910. He was an excellent athlete, and represented Oxford in the Long Jump in 1911 and 1912, winning in 1911. He was also a useful cricketer and a fine horse-man, representing Oxford at Olympia in horse jumping. He had always intended to join the Army, was given a commission in the Dragoon Guards in September, 1914, and went to the front in the following February. He was killed in action on July 14th, 1916, at the age of twenty-six. The *Oxford Magazine* of November 10th, 1916, from which we have gathered most of the above facts, added that " his sunny disposition and athletic prowess won him many friends, and made him an ideal cavalry officer."

LIEUT. D'ARCY J. J. HARTLEY
7th Dragoon Guards

Killed in Action   *July 14th, 1916*

2nd LIEUT. S. H. HEWETT

11th Royal Warwickshire Regiment

Killed in Action   *July 22nd, 1916*

2nd LIEUT. STEPHEN HENRY HEWETT, 11th (attached 14th) Royal Warwickshire Regiment, son of the late Mr. John S. Hewett, of 2, Raleigh Road, Exeter, was born on January 19th, 1893. Coming to Downside as a small boy in September, 1905, and passing through all the stages of school life, there was no activity in which he did not excel. With all his rare gifts and successful achievements he was entirely free from any form of self-assertion ; a loyal and sympathetic friend and a delightful companion, brilliant, witty and unselfish, always interested in the opinions of others and appreciative of their merits. Distinguished alike in study and in games, he secured the Higher Certificate no less than five times, with many distinctions to his credit in Latin, Greek, French, English and History. He was awarded the Gregorian Medal in 1907. He gained a classical Exhibition at Balliol in December, 1909, but being considered too young to take it up, entered again the following year, when he was awarded the Senior Classical Scholarship. He played Cricket for the School Eleven in 1910 and 1911, gaining his colours and holding the position of captain in the latter year. His best achievement was a score of 93, not out, against Bruton School, in 1911, when he carried his bat through the innings. He was in the Hockey Eleven from 1908 to 1911, during which seasons he also played regularly for the Association Football team, winning his colours in both, and also for the Sports Competition with Bruton in 1911, when he represented the School in the mile. He was Head of the School for nearly two years, President of the Abingdon Society, Librarian of the Petre Library, and editor of *The Raven*, and an enthusiastic member of the choir, in which he sang for two years as treble, and later on as bass. He was an actor of quite exceptional merit, performing in many farces and plays, and crowning his dramatic efforts in his last term, when he sustained with great skill the part of the Duke of Plaza-Toro in " The Gondoliers." He was lance-corporal in the O.T.C. in 1911, when he attended camp. He went into residence at Balliol in October, 1911, and a brilliant career awaited him at Oxford. He won successively the Craven, Hertford and Ireland Scholarships, and was Jenkyns Exhibitioner in 1914. In this year he was also President of the Brackenbury and Secretary of the Jowett Societies. In athletics he played for

147

Balliol at Cricket and Hockey, and gained his " Blue " at Hockey, securing victory for Oxford by shooting the only two goals in a memorable match against Cambridge. His devotion to Downside was very deep ; he frequently returned on visits, and took a keen interest in all developments. During the Easter Holidays of 1914 he wrote the fine poem, *Patriæ domus decorem*, with which we are now so familiar. Admirably set to music by Dom Alphege Shebbeare, it was sung for the first time at the great gathering of Old Gregorians at the Centenary celebrations on Whit Monday, June 1st, 1914, was acclaimed by all with enthusiastic approval, and by right of conquest became the School Song from that day onwards.

Stephen Hewett's academic successes were cut short by the advent of the Great War, and in January, 1915, he was gazetted 2nd Lieutenant in the 11th Royal Warwickshire Regiment. For the greater part of the ensuing year he was stationed either at Blandford or Wool, in Dorset, and his happy proximity to Downside enabled him to pay us many visits. He went to France in March, 1916, and was attached to the 14th Battalion of his regiment. At the front he proved a capable officer, carrying out his duties with great energy and thoroughness. " Suscipiat Dominus sacrificium nostrum," he wrote in one of his last letters ; his prayer was granted, and he fell gallantly leading his platoon in the great Somme advance. He was twenty-three years of age.

An attack was planned for the evening of July 22nd, 1916, and Stephen Hewett volunteered with his platoon to join the first lines. The attack came off at 7 p.m. in the daylight, but it was a failure owing to the intense machine-gun fire of the enemy. Hewett did not return, and was posted as missing. At first hopes were entertained that he might be alive in the hands of the enemy, but these hopes had to be abandoned in the face of several independent reports of his death. Finally his commanding officer wrote to Mrs. Hewett as follows :—

" I have made very careful enquiries as to the accuracy of the evidence you mention, and have most unwillingly arrived at the conclusion that your poor boy is dead. It appears that his body was found by the unit relieving our own, and that it was buried by them on the actual battle ground.

Believe me that it is with the utmost regret that I have to write you this sad news, and for my own part also the blow is a bad one. Your son was one of my very best officers and such a keen soldier, energetic and hard working ; his loss will be a great one to the battalion.

Apart from his professional qualifications, I liked the boy so much for his fine, manly qualities and general cheery bearing."

And his company commander, also an Oxford man, wrote of him thus :—

" I am lucky enough to have been his company commander, and am very proud to count myself as one of his friends. He was a fine officer in every way, loved and respected by his men, and an irreparable loss to the company and regiment. . . . Things are very different without him."

Stephen Hewett's love of Downside never wavered, and as time went on he became more and more convinced that his true vocation was the Benedictine life there. " Vobis parta quies," he wrote to his sister, who had become a nun, " but not the common desire of all of us, even the least spiritual, not the mere happiness of peace and England : but that beatitude (already realised in your life) which we can only pray that we may reach through the ordeal and the fire before us—' which has power to make our noisy years seem moments in the being of the eternal silence ' . . . If we are to be spared, I know one who will give heartfelt thanks for the great gift and blessing of life, which I will enjoy unchanged, in the same old way, but even more keenly than before. And if anyone asks what is the way, he need only read your letter."

A selection of Hewett's poems, entitled *Before the Mellowing Year*, was published privately at Oxford in 1916. This collection included the beautiful verses addressed to the memory of his schoolfellow, Francis Tyrrell, and reprinted in this book at the conclusion of the memoir of that beloved friend.

Hewett was a wonderful correspondent, and a collection of his letters from France was published after his death, by Messrs. Longmans, with an introduction by Mr. F. F. Urquhart, his friend at Balliol. The letters contained in this little volume, *A Scholar's Letters from the Front*, were written with no view to publication, to his relatives and intimate friends, and—to quote one of the reviews—" portray that charm of character which endeared Stephen Hewett to all who knew him. His unselfishness and brightness; his devotion to his men; his enthusiasm for literature; his enjoyment of the lighter side of things as typified by his delight on finding that his fellow-officers all knew ' Gilbert and Sullivan'; his appreciation of natural objects; his memories of England; and above all and infusing all, the Catholic atmosphere —these qualities give to the letters a charm and a living interest which place them far above ordinary war correspondence and entitle them to a place in literature." We conclude with the following faithful and sympathetic portrait of a most brilliant and lovable personality, which appeared in the *Oxford Magazine* of November 10th, 1916 :—

Even when the War has taken so many of the best, the loss of Stephen Hewett is a specially grievous blow to his friends and to the College [Balliol]. From the time when he came up from Downside at the age of sixteen and won a classical Exhibition, he always showed a rare gift for scholarship, and this was more than confirmed when, after being elected to the first scholarship next year he took a first class in Moderations and won the Hertford, Craven, and Ireland Scholarships. He had a peculiar sensitiveness for words and language, which seemed to be part of a wide joy and delight in art and nature, and a deep, though almost childlike, understanding of persons. His work for " Greats " showed equal promise, and he was elected Jenkyns Exhibitioner in 1914. On the hockey field he was also distinguished and played against Cambridge in 1914; he was a good cricketer as well, and played for the College; but more perhaps than his games he enjoyed country walks, especially in his favourite Somerset hills. He was fond of music, too, and as a member of the Bach Choir sang in the 1914 Festival : in the previous term he had played a small but effective part in *The Acharnians*. Hewett had many friends, and though he never consciously claimed leadership and was often a rather silent member of a party, their life seemed to centre round him. He wished to be a teacher, and might probably have returned to Downside ; he loved its country, and a strong and simple piety made him feel peculiarly at home there. It was a greater wrench for him than for most to join the Army. He had strong ties at home, and he was distrustful of his own courage. A long period of training and changes from one battalion to another tried him greatly, but his letters, when once he got to the Front, showed that he had found himself and had even come to take a keen delight in the romance of a soldier's great calling.

CAPT. N. C. CLERY, M.C.
Royal Field Artillery

Killed in Action   *July 24th, 1916*

CAPTAIN NOEL CAIRNS CLERY, *M.C.*, Royal Field Artillery, younger son of the late Surgeon-General James A. Clery, C.B., was born on December 30th, 1892, came to Downside in September, 1903, and left in December, 1910. He played in the Cricket Eleven, and the Hockey Eleven, in 1909 and 1910 and for three successive seasons in the Association Football Eleven. In all three games he was awarded his colours. In 1910, he was a member of all the games committees, and was also Captain of the Boxing Club. From the School he went to the R.M.A., Woolwich, and was in the Royal Field Artillery at the outbreak of war. He saw much service at the front, and, like his brother, Captain Vyvian Clery, R.E., was mentioned in despatches and awarded the Military Cross. He was killed in action on July 24th, 1916, at the age of twenty-three. We are indebted to his brother for the following extracts :—

" On the day he was killed, there was some question of putting in a trench mortar battery, and Noel's general said that he did not think Noel ought to go up as it was too dangerous, but Noel said that it was his personal job to sight the trench mortar batteries ; so he insisted on going, and while walking with another officer, he was sniped at a long range and fell dead instantaneously. His servant was most terribly cut up and said to me that Noel was more like a brother than a master to him. . . . His Brigade-Major wrote to me and said, ' He was one of the best and bravest chaps that ever stepped.' Noel's grave is in Caterpillar Wood, near Montauban, amidst the shells and the guns, and I am sure he would have asked no more fitting place to be buried in."

There is also another remark of his brother's which we can fully endorse :—

" Those of the monks who remember him will appreciate the greatness of my loss."

2nd LIEUT. PHILIP STEPHEN KOE, 2/4th York and Lancaster Regiment, son of Mr. Digby F. Koe, of Gray's Inn, barrister, and Mrs. Koe, of 35, Blessington Road, Lewisham, was born on May 3rd, 1896, came to Downside in September, 1909, and left in December, 1914. He was an able boy of wide interests, and having passed the Lower Certificate with five First Classes in 1911, he gained the Higher Certificate in the two succeeding years. He was a member of Barlow House.

He enlisted in the Inns of Court O.T.C. in March, 1915, and obtained his commission in the York and Lancaster Regiment in the following August. At the end of May, 1916, he was sent to the French Front. He was a cheerful and effective officer, and wrote a few days before his death to a friend at Downside : " I feel very fit and am having a good time." He was killed in action by a shell on August 1st, 1916, at the age of twenty. " He was very reliable and hard-working," wrote his commanding officer, " and always set a fine example of cheerfulness to his men under the most trying circumstances."

2nd LIEUT. P. S. KOE

2/4th York and Lancaster Regiment

Killed in Action   *August 1st, 1916*

2nd LIEUT. R. WALKER
2/5th Lancashire Fusiliers

Killed in Action   *August 9th, 1916*

2nd LIEUT. RICHARD WALKER, 2/5th Lancashire Fusiliers, only son of the late Mr. Charles William Walker, of Holmshurst, Burwash, Sussex, was born on April 24th, 1883, came to Downside in April, 1894, and left in July, 1902. In his last year at school, " Dick " Walker passed the Higher Certificate in seven subjects and won the History, English Literature and Essay Prize and the French Prize. He played Cricket in the Second Eleven, and will be remembered by his contemporaries as the best boxer of his generation at Downside. He was an ideal Captain of the Boxing Club, most energetic and successful, and through his efforts boxing became very popular in the School. He himself won the Challenge Cup several times, and, being unchallenged in 1902, the cup became his absolutely. From Downside he went to Christ Church College, Oxford, and continued to distinguish himself as a boxer at the University.

Early in the war, in spite of great difficulties in the way, he joined the Artists' Rifles, volunteered for foreign service, and went to France with his battalion in October, 1914. He ultimately became a company sergeant-major, and in 1916 obtained a commission in the Lancashire Fusiliers. He was reported missing on August 9th, 1916, but, later on, was officially reported by the War Office as killed in action on that day. He was thirty-three years of age.

2nd LIEUT. PATRICK GILBERT O'HARA, 1st (attached 3rd) East Surrey Regiment, son of Major Patrick Henry O'Hara, of Mornington, Crookedwood, Co. Westmeath, was born on March, 29th, 1897, came to Downside in May, 1909, and left in July, 1914. He was a member of Barlow House, playing for it at Cricket, Hockey and Football in 1912, 1913 and 1914 ; in 1914 he also played for the School Cricket Eleven. Obtaining a commission in the East Surrey Regiment, in due course he went to the front, and was killed in action on August 14th, 1916. After he had been hit, his servant carried him back into a shell-hole, where he died almost at once. He was nineteen years of age.

2nd LIEUT. P. G. W. O'HARA

1st East Surrey Regiment

Killed in Action   *August 14th, 1916*

2nd LIEUT. C. W. DALY

3rd Rifle Brigade

Killed in Action   *August 18th, 1916*

2nd LIEUT. CECIL WILLIAM DALY, 3rd Rifle Brigade, second son of the late Mr. William Daly, of Dunsandle, was born in 1897, came to Downside in September, 1910, and left in December, 1914. He took a prominent part in the public life of the School, where his charming and frank disposition made him a universal favourite. Especially conspicuous in all branches of athletics he distinguished himself equally in the Rugby Fifteen, the Hockey Eleven, and the Cricket Eleven, in the last of which, in 1914, he secured the excellent batting average of 50.36 and the ground record for matches, 161 not out. He also rendered good services in the Sports team, and was the winner of the School Tennis Tournament for three successive years. He was a member of the Sacristy from 1911 to 1914, and was attendant on His Eminence Cardinal Gasquet during the Centenary celebrations, his natural dignity and striking appearance making him one of the most impressive figures on that great occasion. During his last year at Downside he was one of the School Prefects. After the usual course at Sandhurst he received a commission in the Rifle Brigade, and went to France early in 1916. At the front he proved himself a very competent and successful officer, and was held in high esteem by all with whom he came in contact. He was mortally wounded in an attack on the German trenches to the north of Guillemont on the afternoon of August 18th, 1916, and in spite of every effort to save his life he died just after reaching the dressing station. The deep regard felt for him by all may be seen from the following extracts from a few of the many letters of sympathy received by Mrs. Daly, who kindly permits us to publish these quotations.

From the Commanding Officer of the 3rd Rifle Brigade :—

" He had reached the German trench and had behaved in a most gallant way, earning the admiration of officers, N.C.O.s and men of his company. I saw him and spoke to him before he died, and though he was in some pain he was quite cheerful. He leaves a very big gap in this battalion, where he was thought most highly of by everyone."

From the officer commanding his company :—

" He had charge of the bombing platoon which was in the second line, but as the first line was held up he brought his men up, and while giving orders he received a bullet in the neck. He was bandaged up by his sergeant and put in a shell-hole while the battalion took the trenches, and in the evening he was taken down to the dressing station. . . . I can't tell you how much I shall miss him and what a loss he is to the company, but I am sure he died as he would have wished, leading his men at close quarters with the enemy."

From the sergeant of his platoon :—

" He was by my side in the advance, when he was struck in the neck by a bullet. . . . At the time he was hit he was standing up giving orders, and the last words I heard him say were, ' Steady, men, on the left.' I cannot find words in which to express our sympathy with the relatives, and I could not tell you in words how he was idolized by the men in his platoon. His loss was a great blow to us all, for he was an officer we would willingly have followed anywhere. By the fearless and brave example he set us, he had a way of making us feel confident in our safety everywhere."

2nd LIEUT. H. J. F. FLEMING

6th Dorsetshire Regiment

Killed in Action   *August 24th, 1916*

2nd LIEUT. HUGH JOSEPH FRANCIS FLEMING, 6th Dorsetshire Regiment, was the only son of the late Sir Francis Fleming, K.C.M.G., and Lady Fleming, of Sidney Place, Onslow Square, London. He was born on February 6th, 1896, came to Downside in May, 1909, and left in July, 1913. He was an excellent athlete, and one of the best runners we have ever had at Downside. He swept aside the existing records of the Third and Second Divisions in the School Sports of 1910 and 1911, and in the latter year he won his colours against Bruton. Great things were anticipated when he reached the First Division, but unfortunately he was prevented from taking part in any of the events in 1913 through the revival of a strain received at Football twelve months previously. He played in the first Fifteen at Rugby Football, and in the Second Eleven at Hockey in 1912 ; he also played for his House (Caverel) at Hockey and Cricket. After the outbreak of war he made continuous efforts to serve his country in the Army, but his sight was very defective, and he was medically rejected. Finally he obtained a commission in the Dorsets, and passed his period of training at Bovington Camp, near Wool. He went to the front on August 2nd, 1916, and was killed by a shell on the 24th. His colonel wrote that he had an excellent reputation, and was very popular, and a Catholic chaplain of his regiment at Bovington wrote to Sir Francis Fleming as follows :—

" Your dear son was in my company. I can assure you no one misses him more than I do. He was a true soldier and a gentleman. The men loved him."

At the time of his death Hugh Fleming was twenty years of age.

CAPTAIN HENRY CULLEN GOULDSBURY, 9th Royal Berkshire Regiment (attached King's African Rifles), was the eldest son of C. E. Gouldsbury, late Indian Police, and was born on May 9th, 1881. He was in the School at Downside from January, 1894, to December, 1896. He was also for a short period at the United Services College, Westward Ho! and at St. Edmund's College, Ware. He is remembered at Downside as a versatile and spirited boy of considerable force and marked ability. He possessed great facility in composition, both in prose and verse, and his subsequent fame as a writer came as no surprise to those who remembered him at school. He took a prominent part in the debates of the Abingdon Society and, whilst on the staff of *The Raven*, published a number of essays and poems far above the average usually found in school periodicals. On the Downside stage, he played the parts of the Queen in " Hamlet " (1895), and Clarence in " Richard III " (1896). For a considerable time after he left Downside he entertained hopes of returning as a member of the Community, but this wish was not destined to be realised, and after a period of service in the Royal Irish Militia he joined the British South Africa Company in 1902, and went to Southern Rhodesia. In 1908 he was transferred to the Northern Rhodesian Administration, and in 1910 was promoted to the rank of Native Commissioner.

On the outbreak of the war he rendered valuable assistance to the Chartered Company, especially in regard to the Belgian Battalion stationed at Mporokoso, in Northern Rhodesia. After three unsuccessful applications for employment with the Rhodesian Forces he resigned his position, and, at his own expense, returned to England to offer his services for the war. In March, 1915, he was gazetted Lieutenant in the Royal Berkshire Regiment. Three months later he was seconded to the King's African Rifles, and sent to British East Africa. After ten months in the fighting line he was placed on the Staff and appointed, with the temporary rank of Captain, Liaison Officer to Colonel Molitor of the Belgian forces co-operating with the British in Uganda. Four months later he received the appointment of Military Landing Officer at Tanga, from which he was to have been transferred, after a short interval, to the political service of German East Africa. From Uganda he travelled with his wife to Nairobi, and parted from her in perfect health on August 22nd. Three days later, he arrived at Tanga, but was almost immediately attacked by malaria, and died in

CAPT. H. C. GOULDSBURY
9th Royal Berkshire Regiment

Died on Service   *August 27th, 1916*

hospital on August 27th, 1916. He was buried with those who fell in the first attack on Tanga. He has since been mentioned in despatches by General Smuts " for meritorious service in East Africa."

In spite of the varied labours of an active and energetic life, he found time to continue his literary activities, and as a novelist and poet soon acquired a wide reputation as an interpreter of South Africa, both in its attractive and repellent moods. His novels, *Circe's Garden* (1907) and *The Tree of Bitter Fruit* (1910), are full of interest and display much power and thought, and he was joint author, with the late J. West Sheane, of *The Great Plateau of Northern Rhodesia*, a brilliant descriptive book, published by Edward Arnold in 1911. It is, however, as a writer of verse, at once vehement and strong, yet marked by great tenderness and beauty, that he is best known and most admired. His finest poems, some of which first appeared at Bulawayo, under the title of *Rhodesian Rhymes* (1909), have been collected in the two volumes, *Songs out of Exile* (1912), aptly described as " Verses of African Sunshine, Shadow, and Black Man's Twilight," and *From the Outposts* (1914), published in London by T. Fisher Unwin. These works have received a most appreciative and laudatory welcome from the English Press. The following extract from *The Western Morning News* may serve as an illustration :—

Mr. Gouldsbury has already been compared to Adam Lindsay Gordon and Rudyard Kipling. To our thinking, his muse is rather that of a chastened Swinburne, alive to all the beauty of an African earth, stricken with a sense of fate and the inexorable to-day, but quickened also by the dignity of toil and racial pride. . . . In these pages is humour, breezy and caustic as befits the wandering Odysseus who has taken his toll of men and cities. And with it there is a sense of music, a tenderness of touch, and that *curiosa felicitas* that marks all genuine poetry.

Nearly all the years of Cullen Gouldsbury's manhood were spent in the land of his " exile," which he has portrayed with so much skill and force in his writings, but it is to the land of his boyhood, to the " peaceful English days," that the most tender and beautiful of his poems belong. From these *Songs out of Exile*, from the story of his long years of toil in Africa, and of his noble death in the service of England, the thoughts of those who knew him at Downside will go back to the days of his early enthusiasms, struggles and triumphs, and recall the time when he entertained his schoolfellows with sprightly satires and parodies, or wrote in loftier vein of Life and Death :—

> Surely it falls ; and then, as if by magic,
> The trials, longings of our exile cease ;
> And Life's stern glare, blending with Death's soft twilight,
>   Fades in eternal peace.

2nd LIEUT. RODERICK ALAN EDWARD O'CONNOR, Leinster Regiment, was the youngest son of the late Mr. Justice R. E. O'Connor, of the High Court of Australia. He was born on April 21st, 1894, came to Downside in June, 1906, and left in December, 1907. After leaving Downside to return to Australia he continued his education at the Grammar School, Sydney, and was completing his second year in arts at Sydney University when war was declared. Being under age for a commission in the Australian forces he came to England, and obtained a commission in the Leinster Regiment. He was killed in action on September 1st, 1916, at the age of twenty-two.

His commanding officer wrote as follows :—

" He had just got command of his company, and was killed while leading his men in a bombing attack to recover some lost trenches. Though not with us very long, we all knew his value. I have lost one of the best of my young company commanders, and an esteemed friend."

2nd LIEUT. R. A. E. O'CONNOR

3rd Leinster Regiment

Killed in Action   *September 1st, 1916*

MAJOR N. W. LAWDER

Bedfordshire Regiment

Killed in Action   *September 4th, 1916*

MAJOR NOEL WILFRID LAWDER, Bedfordshire Regiment (attached 3rd Nigeria Regiment), son of Edward Lawder, M.D., was born on October 12th, 1886, came to Downside in January, 1898, and left in April, 1901. He adopted a military career and received his commission in the Bedfordshire Regiment. After much service on the Western Front during the Great War, he was killed in action near Falfemont Farm, south of Guillemont, on September 4th, 1916, at the age of twenty-nine. The details of his death were thus recorded by one of the Catholic chaplains :—

" I knew Major Lawder very well, and, strange to say, I was wounded at exactly the same time as he was killed. I saw him a short time before the attack, and he was as cheery and as optimistic as possible. The Bedfords attacked on that day a little to the south of Guillemont, near Falfemont Farm, and your son was one of the first to be killed. I was wounded at 3.30 p.m. on that day, and as I was brought back to the dressing station I was informed that poor Major Lawder was killed. The news was a shock for me—more than the shock of my wound. I had known him so well. I gave orders for the other Catholic chaplain to have his body brought back, if possible, to the big cemetery for burial. Wedge Wood, where you say he was buried, is one of the many small woods between Guillemont, Montauban and Hardecourt. There will be no difficulty about identifying the grave afterwards, as there is a special unit for that purpose.

" Your son was an excellent soldier and a perfect Catholic. His religion gave him such consolation that active service was a perfect joy to him. He had no fear whatsoever. In fact he was too brave, if I may say so."

2nd LIEUT. HENRY LUBIENSKI BODENHAM, 11th Black Watch, was the eldest son of the late Count and Countess Bodenham Lubienski, of Rotherwas and Bullingham Manor, Herefordshire. He was born in 1896, came to Downside in September, 1908, and left in July, 1914. He was an able boy, generous and plucky, and, after a year as a Roberts House Prefect, he was appointed Head of his House and Head of the School in September, 1913. He was in the Second Rugby Football Fifteen, and also played for his House. In 1912 and 1913 he took part, with the victorious Roberts section of the O.T.C. in the Inter-House Competitions. He was Captain of the Shooting Club and a lance-corporal in the Corps. In 1913 he was editor of *The Raven*, and was on the Committee of the Petre Library. In 1913 and 1914 he passed the Higher Certificate. Having matriculated for Trinity College, Cambridge, he was studying for a mathematical exhibition when war broke out. He obtained a commission in the Border Regiment in December, 1914, but in January of the next year was transferred to the Black Watch. After passing with distinction through the School of Gunnery he was transferred in January, 1916, to the Machine Gun Corps, and went to the front on April 28th, with a machine-gun company, as second in command. He was killed in action on September 7th, 1916. His captain, who described him as " undoubtedly my best officer," stated in a letter that, seeing Lieutenant Bodenham was overworking, he had tried to send him down to the base for twenty-four hours' rest, but that he refused to leave his men in danger. Soon afterwards he set out to visit some of his posts with two other officers. On the way out a shell burst close to them, killing him instantly, and wounding his two companions. Within three minutes a doctor and a priest came up, but he was already dead.

2nd LIEUT. H. L. BODENHAM

11th Black Watch

Killed in Action   *September 7th, 1916*

CAPT. J. O. TURNBULL

3rd Welch Regiment

Killed in Action   *September 9th, 1916*

CAPTAIN JOHN OSWIN TURNBULL, 3rd (attached 2nd) Welch Regiment, third son of Mr. L. R. Turnbull, of Raisdale, Penarth, Glamorgan, was born in 1889, came to Downside in April, 1901, and left in July, 1907. During his last two years at school, he was on the committees of the various games and was a conspicuous member of the Football, Hockey and Cricket Elevens. At cricket he distinguished himself first as a bowler, and subsequently as a bat. In 1907 he was captain of the Eleven, and was especially congratulated in the next number of *The Raven* " on the excellent manner in which, both by word and example, he captained the team." He was also on the committee of the Petre Library, 1906-7, and was a member of the School Committee in 1907. After leaving Downside he went to Exeter College, Oxford, where he graduated. He played Hockey in his College Eleven, and he obtained his " half-blue " at Billiards, successfully contending against Cambridge in 1909 and 1910. On completing his course at Oxford he joined the firm of Messrs. Vaughan & Roche, solicitors, of Cardiff Docks, and was engaged upon this work until the outbreak of the war, when he obtained a commission in the Welch Regiment. He carried out his military duties in a most able and efficient manner. He was sent to France, and was wounded at Loos, on October 8th, 1915. Returning to France in August, 1916, he was killed whilst leading a bombing party against a German trench in the early morning of September 9th, 1916. He was twenty-seven years of age.

PRIVATE WILLIAM FORSTER, Public Schools Battalion, Royal Fusiliers, second son of Mr. C. Forster, of Newcastle-upon-Tyne, and Burradon, Rothbury, was born in 1892, came to Downside in September, 1904, and left in July, 1910. Willie Forster was a boy of sterling qualities, conspicuously earnest, unselfish and self-restrained. At school he was an enthusiastic member of the Shooting Club, and secured medals in 1909 and 1910. From Downside he went to Trinity College, Cambridge, where he graduated B.A. and LL.B. in 1913. He joined the Public Schools Battalion of the Royal Fusiliers in February, 1916, and a few months later went to France. He was reported missing on October 7th, 1916, and is now ascertained to have been killed in action on that day. He was shot through the heart and died almost immediately, with a smile on his face and a prayer on his lips. The sergeant of his platoon, who was by his side, was badly wounded at the same time.

PRIVATE W. FORSTER
Royal Fusiliers

Killed in Action   *October 7th, 1916*

LIEUT. F. G. DOWNING

5th Middlesex Regiment

Died on Service   *October 27th, 1916*

LIEUT. FRANCIS GEOFFREY DOWNING, 5th Middlesex Regiment, was the son of Mr. Francis H. Downing, of Ballyvelly, Tralee, Co. Kerry. He was born in 1897, came to Downside in January, 1909, and left in September, 1914. Of a naturally cheerful and friendly disposition, and excellent at games, he was universally popular. At Cricket he played successively for the Junior, Second and First Elevens, receiving his colours in 1914. In that year he headed the bowling averages, having taken forty-five wickets during the season, thus constituting a record. He also played for the Rugby Football Fifteen, for the Hockey Eleven, and for his House (Roberts) at Cricket, Football and Hockey. From 1911 till he left the School he was a member of the Sacristy.

Having obtained a commission in the Middlesex Regiment he went to the Western Front. In October, 1916, he returned to England with some ill-defined malady, and was sent to the Military Hospital at Fulham, where meningitis developed. Though for the first few days of his arrival in London he seemed to rally, the improvement was not sustained, and he died on October 27th.

2nd LIEUT. GILBERT AUSTIN TURNER, 3rd Royal West Kents (attached 7th Loyal North Lancashire Regiment), eldest son of Mr. G. L. Turner, of 13, Chester Terrace, Regent's Park, N.W., was born in 1897, came to Downside in September, 1909, and left in July, 1915. He was a boy of fine character and excellent ability, and took an active part in the life of the School. He played for the First Eleven at Hockey and Cricket in 1915, and represented his House (Barlow) on many occasions in Cricket, Hockey, Sports, Corps, Gym. and Golf, securing the Golf Championship in 1914. He was appointed a House Prefect in 1913 and a School Prefect in 1915. For some years he sang in the choir. He passed the Higher Certificate in 1913, 1914 and 1915, was a member of the Literary Society and of the Abingdon Debating Society, and was on the staff of *The Raven*. In December, 1914, he passed his matriculation for Balliol College, Oxford, but postponed his university course on account of the war. After passing through Sandhurst he received a commission in the Royal West Kent Regiment, and shortly after was sent to France. He was killed on November 17th, 1916, together with his orderly, through the explosion of a shell which penetrated through the roof of the company headquarters, where he was stationed. His company commander wrote of him as follows :—

" The company had attacked three days previously and gained its objective. Your son had done excellent work in keeping his men well together and in using initiative when consolidating. He was cheery throughout right up to the end. We buried him in as suitable a spot as possible, near Grandcourt. . . . He died after having accomplished something of great military importance in getting forward with his men. I personally have lost a good friend and comrade in arms. He was a great help to me, for he had a very keen sense of duty."

The Catholic chaplain also wrote in the highest terms of his character and his devotion to his religious duties.

2nd LIEUT. G. A. TURNER

3rd Royal West Kent Regiment

Killed in Action   *November 17th, 1916*

CAPT. J. P. H. WOOD

22nd Manchester Regiment

Killed in Action   *January 11th, 1917*

CAPTAIN JOHN PATRICK HAMILTON WOOD, 22nd Manchester Regiment, fourth son of the late Alexander Wood, M.A., and of Mrs. Wood, 18, Antrim Mansions, Hampstead, was born in 1880, came to Downside in January, 1893, and left in December, 1896. He had previously spent three years at school at Melle, in Belgium. Jack Wood was a boy of bright and happy disposition, and took part with energy and success in the various branches of school life. In the Christmas Plays he was one of the best actors of his generation at Downside, especially distinguishing himself in the parts of Lady Macbeth (1894), the First Player in " Hamlet " (1895), and Buckingham in " Richard III " (1896). After leaving School, he took part with Paget's Horse in the South African War. In January, 1915, he joined the Artists' Rifles, London Regiment, and, in the following April, received his commission in the Manchester Regiment.

In due course he was sent to the front and was wounded in the thigh at Mametz during an attack made in the early morning of July 1st, 1916. He was in command of his company at the time.

After reaching the German third line trench, the attack was continued in short rushes, and it was here that Lieutenant Wood was wounded. After lying in a large shell-hole for several hours, while shells and machine-gun bullets passed constantly overhead, his wound was ultimately dressed by one of his men, and he was able to make his way back to the British lines. He returned to the front at the earliest opportunity, and was killed by a shell in an attack at Butrancourt on January 11th, 1917, the day after he was gazetted captain. He was buried near Beaumont Hamel. A few days before his death he attended Mass and received Holy Communion from the hands of the Senior Catholic Chaplain of the Division, who wrote to say how much impressed he had been " by his truly devout and thoroughly Catholic attitude." One of his fellow officers wrote of him as follows :—

" He has been all along one of the heroes of the war, and only those who knew him well could know all the courageousness that kept his sense of duty to such a high level. His religion was always a source of comfort and strength to him—and he was prepared to face death calmly and confidently."

2nd LIEUT. GEOFFREY LYNCH-STAUNTON, 13th Hussars, elder son of Senator George S. Lynch-Staunton, K.C., Hamilton, Canada, was born in 1896, and received his preparatory education at Highfield School, Canada. He came to Downside in February, 1911, and left in June, 1914. He was a boy of strong character, clear views and high ideals. He played in the First Football Fifteen from 1912 to 1914, and for his House (Roberts) in 1914. He was also in the Roberts' O.T.C. team in 1913. During his last two years at school he was a House Prefect. On leaving Downside he went to Merton College, Oxford, and at once joined the 'Varsity O.T.C. Desirous of serving the Empire in the war he returned to Canada, joined the Canadian Remount Department, and was sent to France. For a short time he served on the Imperial Staff, but feeling that his real duty lay in the firing line he obtained a commission in the Hussars, and with that unit left for service with the Persian Gulf expedition. He fell in the heavy fighting in Mesopotamia on March 5th, 1917, at the age of twenty.

Two days before his death, in his last letter to his parents, he wrote a most vivid and interesting account of his experiences in the campaign.

Geoffrey Lynch-Staunton, who is deeply mourned by his many friends on both sides of the Atlantic, had before him a future full of bright hopes and promise which he willingly sacrificed in the great struggle for freedom. Those who knew him at Downside will readily concur with the sentiments expressed in the following extract from a letter describing the impression he made upon one who came into close contact with him during his course of military training :—

" I was profoundly impressed with his high ideals, his broad sympathy, his wide culture, his manliness and transparent single-heartedness. . . . the heart of your son always remained the same, gentle and kind, animated with a sincere courtesy, a true piety, and a wide generosity towards others . . . he left with me a lasting impression, an impression, indeed, that still remains and will continue for many a day. At a time like this words seem empty, and have little power to soothe the heart ; but I feel it is

2nd LIEUT. G. LYNCH-STAUNTON

13th Hussars

Killed in Action   *March 5th, 1917*

something for you to know that your son has done his duty ; that the sacrifice he has made has been made willingly and freely, and that his passing was in the manner he would have chosen in this tremendous crisis in the history of our race and of the world. It is something also to know that your son was not lacking in his sense of duty to his king and country, and that that very sense of duty he possessed was able to inspire me, a very much older man, with the resolution towards a higher outlook than I had. I am sure that your son did not fail to touch others in the same way ; and, though he could not count many years, it may be said with confidence that he fulfilled his task in life, for all who knew him are the better for his association."

MAJOR WILLIAM ARTHUR GRATTAN-BELLEW, *M.C.*, Royal Flying Corps, third son of Sir Henry Grattan-Bellew, Bart., and Lady Sophie Grattan-Bellew, of Mount Bellew, co. Galway, was born in 1894, came to Downside in January, 1906, and left in July, 1911. Gifted with a frank and sunny nature and an admirable combination of courage and gentleness, no boy of his generation at Downside was held in more affectionate regard by both masters and boys, and his death came as a deep personal loss to all who knew him. At school he played occasionally in the Hockey Eleven, and regularly as goalkeeper in the Football Eleven, 1910-11. His goal-keeping is described in a contemporary number of *The Raven* as " always good, sometimes brilliant." He was also successful in the Aquatic Sports, especially at diving. An enthusiastic member of the Natural History Club, his energy and cheerfulness added greatly to the success of the expeditions into the country during the summer term. In the O.T.C. he was promoted to the rank of corporal in 1911. After leaving Downside he went to Trinity College, Cambridge, and passed Engineering Special, Part I, in 1914.

He received his first commission in the Flying Corps in January, 1915, and after some months' service at the front was invalided home, being gazetted to the Connaught Rangers in March, 1916. Subsequently, he rejoined the Flying Corps, in which he held the rank of Major at the time of his death, on March 24th, 1917, from injuries received whilst flying on active service in France. He was twenty-two years of age at the time. In July, 1916, he was awarded the M.C. for conspicuous gallantry and skill on several occasions, notably the following :—

" (1) With three other machines he attacked and drove off eight enemy machines, forcing one to the ground. (2) He attacked four Fokkers, forcing one down to 2,500 feet. Another was seen to crash to the ground during the fight. (3) When on a bombing raid two of the machines got behind owing to clouds, and were attacked by Fokkers, Captain Grattan-Bellew returned and attacked three Fokkers, one of which his observer shot down, and the others made off."

He has also been mentioned in despatches.

MAJOR W. A. GRATTAN-BELLEW, M.C.
Royal Flying Corps

Killed in Action   *March 24th, 1917*

2nd LIEUT. M. HILLIER
3rd King's Own Scottish Borderers

Killed in Action   *April 9th, 1917*

2nd LIEUT. MAURICE HILLIER, 3rd King's Own Scottish Borderers, elder son of Mr. E. G. Hillier, C.M.G., of the Hong Kong and Shanghai Bank, Peking, was born in 1898, came to Downside in September, 1911, and left in June, 1915. He was a useful and popular member of his House, and played for Roberts several times at Football, Cricket and Hockey. He was also in the House Sports, O.T.C., and Gym. teams. In 1914 he played in the Second Eleven at Cricket, and he was a member of the Second Fifteen at Football, 1913-14. From Downside, he went to Sandhurst, and in due course was gazetted to the King's Own Scottish Borderers. He was killed in action in France on April 9th, 1917, aged nineteen. The following is an extract from a letter written by Fr. P. F. Oddie, C.F., *M.C.*, the chaplain of the Brigade to which Maurice Hillier was attached :—

"The death of Hillier was a very severe blow to me, as he was without exaggeration the very best Catholic officer I had. . . . I had a parade for the K.O.S.B.'s before they went into battle, and on that occasion Hillier himself brought all the Catholics of the regiment to the Sacraments, and himself went to Confession and Communion. He never missed an opportunity of going to Mass and the Sacraments, and took endless pains to get the men of his regiment to their duties. I can assure you that I am not exaggerating when I say that he was a shining example to all of us. His excellent qualities made him popular with all ranks, and although I feel deeply for his relatives in their terrible loss, I cannot feel sorry for him. He was killed at our second objective on the morning of April 9th."

LIEUT. GERARD THOMAS MANBY-COLEGRAVE,
Royal Garrison Artillery, only child of the late Mr. Thomas Manby-Colegrave, was at Downside from October till December, 1897. He was afterwards at the Oratory School (1899-1901). He was gazetted 2nd Lieutenant in the Kent Cyclist Battalion (Territorials), in November, 1914. In the following August he was appointed transport officer, and after some months of service was transferred to the Royal Garrison Artillery. He died of wounds received in action on April 21st, 1917, at the age of thirty-one.

He married, in 1907, Hilda, eldest daughter of Mr. James W. Thunder, formerly of Bellewstown House, Co. Meath, and leaves a son and a daughter.

LIEUT. G. T. MANBY-COLEGRAVE
Royal Garrison Artillery

Died of Wounds   *April 21st, 1917*

2nd LIEUT. G. B. BATE

3rd Loyal North Lancashire Regiment, attached R.F.C.

Killed in Action   *April 29th, 1917*

2nd LIEUT. GEORGE BEAUMONT BATE, 3rd Loyal North Lancashire Regiment (attached Royal Flying Corps), son of Mr. George Bate, of The Rhyddyn, Caergwrle, near Wrexham, was born in 1895, came to Downside in May, 1909, and left in December, 1911. During his last term at school he played in the Hockey Eleven as goalkeeper. In April, 1915, he joined a Public School Brigade attached to the Royal Fusiliers, and from this he obtained a commission in the Loyal North Lancashire Regiment. After spending two winters in the trenches he applied for admission to the Royal Flying Corps. His application having been accepted he returned to England and commenced his training in March, 1917. In the following month he was sent to France, and on April 23rd, acting as observer, he went for his first flight over the German lines. In the engagement that followed he displayed great skill and gallantry, and brought down one of the enemy machines. His pilot was wounded and his own tunic was torn by a bullet, though he remained unharmed. The party to which he was attached accounted for eleven enemy machines, without losing any of their own. A few days later, whilst acting again as observer, his machine was attacked by three of the enemy at once. He brought down the first in flames, and succeeded in driving the second out of control. Whilst doing this, his machine was fiercely attacked from below by the third enemy machine, and he was shot through the heart. The pilot, with some of his controls broken, just managed to reach the British lines, although chased by the enemy. Beaumont Bate was killed on April 29th, 1917, and was buried near the front line after a funeral service conducted by a Catholic priest. The officer commanding his squadron wrote of him as follows :—

" It is almost a miracle that the pilot is alive to-day, as their machine was terribly shot about. Your son was only with us for a short time, but had already had a stiff fight with hostile machines, in which his pilot was wounded. He put up an exceptionally plucky fight, and promised to be one of our very best observers. His death is a great loss to this squadron."

The following is an extract taken from a letter written by one of his fellow officers in the Loyal North Lancashire Regiment :—

" . . . We are all proud to have been associated with him. Everybody recognised his sterling worth. I, myself, spent some time with him in the trenches. Cheerful, capable, fearless, a true friend, the highest type of British officer, and a noble example to all."

CAPTAIN HARRY EUSTACE HERRICK, 1st Royal Irish Fusiliers, was the last of the direct line of Herricks, of Shippool Castle, co. Cork, and was the only surviving son of the late Major Herrick, H.A.M., and Mrs. Herrick, of 3, Cresswell Gardens, South Kensington, and grandson of the late Major-General Herrick, R.M.L.I. He was born on September 20th, 1889, came to Downside in September, 1903, and left in July, 1908. Though of a somewhat retiring disposition he played an important part in the work and life of the School, and his natural charm and the excellent qualities of his character secured for him a considerable influence over his contemporaries. He was a leading member of the Cricket, Football and Hockey Elevens, and represented Downside in the Sports Team that played against Bruton in 1907. He was Captain of the Football and Hockey in 1907, and was elected Captain of the Cricket Eleven, but refused it. In 1908 he was at the top of the batting averages, with several splendid scores to his credit, including 90 against Lansdown C.C. and 56 and 81 not out against the Past.

For three years he was on the Games and Petre Library Committees, and was on the School Committee, 1907-8. He distinguished himself on several occasions on the Downside stage, notably in the part of Charles Middlewick in " Our Boys " (1908). From the School he passed into Sandhurst in 1908, and in the following year played in the Association Football match against Woolwich. He was gazetted to the Royal Irish Fusiliers in September, 1909. At the outbreak of war he went out with his regiment as machine-gun officer. He was in the retreat from Mons, and took part in the battles of Meteren, Messines and Ypres, being badly wounded in the jaw while advancing with his guns near St. Julien on April 25th, 1915. In the following June he obtained his captaincy. In November, Captain Herrick was passed fit for light duty, and for some months did work at the War Office, after which he went through a Staff course. In July, 1916, he received the appointment of brigade major in the Southern Command, a position which he held until March, 1917, when he returned to the front attached to the Staff. At the time of his death he had returned temporarily to his regiment, and was in

CAPT. H. E. HERRICK
1st Royal Irish Fusiliers

Killed in Action   *May 11th, 1917*

command of a company when he was killed in action on May 11th, 1917, aged twenty-seven. He was shot through the head, death being instantaneous.

His commanding officer wrote on May 14th, 1917 :—

" He was commanding ' D ' Company, and had got his company on its objective when he saw some of the Household Battalion going ahead of their objective. Knowing that they would be cut off, he gallantly went forward to recall them, but unfortunately was shot through the head whilst doing so. He suffered no pain, as his death was absolutely instantaneous. . . . The Fawn was a great personal friend of mine, and I feel his loss very much indeed. He was a very gallant and most capable officer, and will be a very great loss to the battalion in particular and the service at large."

The following is from a letter of one of his fellow-officers :—

" As Staff Captain of this Brigade, I worked with your son from early in December last until he proceeded overseas, and his death came as a great shock to me. Never have I met a more charming fellow-officer or more loveable companion, and the severance of our always pleasant relationship when he went abroad was a great grief to me, while by his death I lose a friend for whom I had more than an ordinary affection and regard. . . . The regret in this Brigade is universal. Everyone loved and respected Eustace, and his loss is keenly felt. . . . It must be some consolation to you to know that Eustace died as he lived, an officer and a gentleman, a white man through and through, serving his country in a good cause."

2nd LIEUT. CHARLES WILLIAM STEPHEN LITTLE-WOOD, *M.C.*, Royal Engineers, only son of Mr. W. Littlewood, of Cairo, Egypt, was born on August 26th, 1897, came to Downside in January, 1910, and left in July, 1915. He was a fine type of English boy, straightforward, fearless and self-restrained. Though naturally of a quiet and unassuming disposition, his all-round ability and the strength and charm of his character secured for him a prominent position in the School. After taking part with success in various Junior teams he became a member of the Football Fifteen in 1914, and played for his House (Caverel) at Cricket, Football and Hockey. He was also successful at Tennis, Boxing and Aquatic Sports, and won the High Jump in the House Sports Competition in 1915. During his last year at Downside he was a sergeant in the O.T.C., a School Prefect and Head of his House. He was also on the Committees of the Petre Library and the Scientific Society. He passed the Higher Certificate in 1913 and 1914, and in July, 1915, he gained the thirty-second place in the Entrance Exam. into Woolwich. On passing out from the R.M.A. he was gazetted 2nd Lieutenant in the Royal Engineers in February, 1916, and in the following October went to the Western Front, where he saw a good deal of fighting, and was regarded as a very capable and successful officer. In April, 1917, he was awarded the M.C. " for conspicuous gallantry and devotion to duty. He carried out the strengthening of a brick bridge under hostile barrage. His coolness and example enabled the work to be completed without cessation, despite casualties." On the night of July 10th, 1917, whilst engaged in military operations, he was hit in the head and killed instantaneously by a fragment of a field-gun shell which burst just in front of him. He was nineteen years of age at the time of his death. The circumstances are thus described by an officer in the same Field Company :

" On the night of his death he was in charge of two bridges being made across some of our trenches, about half a mile apart between the front line and the reserve line. There was a good deal of desultory firing with field guns and trench mortars that night, but in spite of this he insisted on walking about in the open from one job to another quite alone. He had just left one job and was going over to the other when he must have

2nd LIEUT. C. W. S. LITTLEWOOD, M.C.

Royal Engineers

Killed in Action   *July 10th, 1917*

been hit directly by a shell in the head. . . . He had shown a fine example to the men that night by his utter disregard of danger, as they were working on top and were in a condition to need every encouragement."

He was buried by the Catholic Chaplain of the Brigade to which his company was attached, in the Military Cemetery at Neuville Vitasse, about four miles in front of Arras, and a cross has been erected to his memory. It is abundantly evident from the letters of those who knew him on active service that he retained in full measure the characteristics that made him so loveable a personality at school.

The following extract is from a letter written by one of his senior officers :—

" He was a first-rate youngster at his work, very cool, and quite regardless of risk to himself. In the April operations he did extremely well and was awarded the Military Cross for his skill and gallantry. . . . It was a great pleasure to me to see the excellent work done by him this year. Not only was he good at the technical work during operations, but he was very good with the men, and I noticed his section was one of the best in his company, which is the best of the R.E. Companies in the Division. His C.O. spoke most highly of him always."

The officer who was second in comand of his company, and who had lived with him since September, 1915, wrote as follows :—

" I felt I must write to tell you how fond we all were of Littlewood, and how deeply we felt his death. There was something about him which made us all love him, and I don't remember ever hearing him speak ill of anyone or say anything unpleasant or unkind. . . . I have never known a man who was more quiet and unassuming in public, more kind as a friend, or keener or more fearless in action."

And the Catholic Chaplain wrote of him :—

" His company is attached to this Brigade, and I knew him well. He had been to his religious duties shortly before his death. . . . He was so well liked and respected that his loss is very much felt."

CAPTAIN JAMES OWEN WILLIAMS SHINE, 1st Royal Dublin Fusiliers, eldest son of Col. J. Shine, R.A.M.C., was born on April 23rd, 1891, came to Downside in September, 1902, and left in July, 1909. He was an able boy, gifted with considerable eloquence and humour, which made him an excellent debater in the Abingdon Society, and a successful actor on the Downside stage. He passed the Lower Certificate in 1906, and the Higher Certificate in each of the three following years. At games he played for the Hockey and Football Elevens, and was runner-up in the Tennis Tournament of 1909. In this year he passed direct to Sandhurst, and, after completing his course at the R.M.C., he was gazetted to the Royal Dublin Fusiliers and joined his battalion in India. During the present war he was sent to the Western Front, and, in July, 1916, whilst leading his company into action on the Somme, he was wounded in the left leg by a machine-gun bullet. After a short leave he rejoined his regiment in France and was killed in action on August 16th, 1917. At the time of his death he was in his twenty-seventh year. His two brothers, 2nd Lieut. J. D. Shine, Royal Irish Regiment, and 2nd Lieut. H. P. Shine, Royal Irish Fusiliers, had already been killed in the war.

CAPT. J. O. W. SHINE
1st Royal Dublin Fusiliers

Killed in Action   *August 16th, 1917*

2nd LIEUT. J. S. MORRISS
Royal Warwickshire Regiment

Killed in Action   *October 5th, 1917*

2nd LIEUT. JACK SEPTIMUS MORRISS, Royal War-wickshire Regiment, son of Mr. H. Morriss, of Stonebridge, Framfield, Uckfield, was born on March 14th, 1897, and was educated at Beaumont and Downside. He was in the School from January, 1912, till February, 1915. He played in the Football Fifteen in 1914, in the Hockey Eleven in 1915, and in the Cricket Eleven in 1913 and 1914, receiving his colours in 1913, owing to his success as a bowler. On various occasions he represented his House (Barlow) at Football, Hockey and Cricket, and was a member of the Barlow Gym. Team in 1913. He won one of the silver medals in the Shooting Competition of 1912. He went to Sandhurst in 1915, and in due course was gazetted to the Royal Warwickshire Regiment. He was killed in action in France on October 5th, 1917, at the age of twenty. One of his fellow-officers wrote of him as follows :—

" He was killed instantaneously by a rifle bullet in the head, leading his men against an enemy strong post. He was a brave officer, and very popular amongst both officers and men in the battalion."

MAJOR EDWARD FRANCIS DALE NICHOLSON, South Lancashire Regiment, only son of the late Major Nicholson and of Mrs. Nicholson, of Thelwall Hall, Cheshire, was born on November 27th, 1883, came to Downside in September, 1895, and left in December, 1899. At School he was held in high regard by both masters and boys. In 1899 he had the best bowling average in the Cricket Eleven, and in one of the matches secured six wickets for twelve runs. In the same year, he won all the swimming races in the First Division in the Aquatic Sports. Soon after leaving Downside he went to Sandhurst, and, on passing out, received a commission in the South Lancashire Regiment. In 1902 he went to South Africa, and received the Queen's medal with two clasps for his services in the war. From South Africa he went to India, where he served until 1916. He was gazetted captain in March, 1914, and was adjutant in 1915, until his appointment as Brigade Major of the 2nd Infantry Brigade at Quetta, in October of that year. In October, 1916, he was called home by the War Office, and went to France with a battalion of his regiment on December 4th. In the following January he was gazetted Major. He was wounded in action on October 12th, 1917, and died on the same day, at the age of thirty-three. He had received absolution from the Catholic Chaplain. He is buried in the Convent cemetery at Locre. All who knew him bear testimony to his excellent qualities as an officer and a soldier, and to the splendid way in which he lived up to his high ideals.

He married, in 1912, Alix Cunningham Robertson, only daughter of the late George Francis Robertson, Dragoon Guards.

MAJOR E. F. D. NICHOLSON
South Lancashire Regiment

Died of Wounds   *October 12th*, 1917

CAPT. C. L. WATERS, M.C.
Royal Berkshire Regiment

Died of Wounds   *October 19th, 1917*

CAPTAIN CHARLES LOUIS WATERS, *M.C.*, Royal Berkshire Regiment (attached Nigeria Regiment), was the son of Mr. George Waters, of Midleton House, Midleton, Co. Cork. He was born on September 5th, 1883, came to Downside in September, 1896, and left in July, 1901. He was a generous and cheerful boy and took a leading part in all school games. He played in the Cricket, Football and Hockey Elevens, and in 1900 became Captain of the School. In the same year he won the School Tennis Tournament. He received a commission in the Royal Berkshire Regiment from the Militia in 1905, and served in Dublin, Egypt and India. Always an ardent sportsman and an excellent shot, he was captain of the Regiment Rifle Team, which won the " Hopton Cup " and the " Brooke Bond Cup " at the All India Rifle Meeting at Meerut in 1910 and 1911. In 1911 he was seconded to the West African Frontier Force, and served with the Nigeria Regiment until his death. He received his captaincy in September, 1914. In 1914-15, the task of maintaining order in Nigeria during the absence of the greater part of the Nigeria Regiment in the Cameroons, fell almost entirely on him and his company. During that time he took part in six punitive patrols and expeditions, and was mentioned in despatches during the Udi Patrol (October, 1914—January, 1915). In October, 1915, he joined the Cameroon campaign, and served till the finish of hostilities. In November, 1916, he went to German East Africa with the " Nigerians," and early in the following year received the M.C. for his gallant services. He was mortally wounded on October 18th, 1917, and died on the following day, at the age of thirty-four, in one of the Mission Houses of the Fathers of the Holy Ghost. At the time of the engagement in which he fell he was second in command of his battalion. He has since been awarded a bar to his Military Cross.

CAPTAIN RICHARD VICTOR AGIUS, 3rd London Regiment, youngest son of the late Mr. E. T. Agius and Mrs. Agius, of 3, Belsize Grove, N.W., was born on September 19th, 1896. After receiving his early education at St. Mary's, St. Leonards-on-Sea, he came to Downside in September, 1907, and left in July, 1914. His was an active and enthusiastic nature, deeply religious, and full of energy and zeal in work and games. He passed the Lower Certificate in 1910 and 1911, and the Higher Certificate in each of the three following years. He played in the Hockey Eleven and in the Cricket Second Eleven, and represented his House (Roberts) on many occasions at Cricket, Hockey, Football and Sports. He was a very keen member of the O.T.C., took part in two House Competitions, and attained the rank of sergeant in 1913, in which year he won a silver medal in the Gregorian Shooting Competition. During his last year at Downside he was one of the School Prefects. Soon after the outbreak of war he obtained a commission in the London Regiment, and in January, 1915, he went to Malta, and thence to Khartoum in the following April. With his battalion he went to Gallipoli in September and took part in the fighting at Suvla Bay. He was caught in the floods at the end of November, and was invalided to Mudros, but soon rejoined his unit in Egypt. They stayed there until May, 1916, when they were transferred to another front. In July he had his first and last leave, during which he paid a visit to Downside. His old sickness still worried him, and he was unfit for service abroad until the spring of 1917. He served with his reserve unit, receiving his permanent rank of lieutenant in June, 1916, and of captain in the following December. On May 24th, 1917, he left for the Western Front, where he served without a break until his death in action at Poelcappelle, near Ypres, on the following October 26th. He was killed instantaneously, shot through the head, leading his company to the assault. From the many tributes to his memory we quote the following :—

"He was only just twenty-one, overflowing with enthusiasm for his job, generous to a fault, beloved by his fellow-officers, and worshipped by his men."

It was his intention to enter to the Noviciate at Downside at the end of the war.

CAPT. R. V. AGIUS

3rd London Regiment

Killed in Action   *October 26th, 1917*

In Memoriam

MAJOR H. I. GREIG

Royal Garrison Artillery

Killed in Action   *November 2nd, 1917*

MAJOR HUGH IRWIN GREIG, Royal Garrison Artillery, younger son of the late Col. P. Greig, Bombay Infantry, was born on July 18th, 1876, came to Downside in April, 1888, and left in March, 1891. He is remembered at Downside as a boy of exceptional ability at study, and well able to hold his own in the various school games, notably at Cricket and Tennis. He adopted a military career, passed through Woolwich, and rendered excellent service before and during the war. He was a most enthusiastic and successful officer, and was appointed an Officer and Knight of the Order of Leopold for distinguished service. As major in the Royal Garrison Artillery he was killed instantaneously by a shell, whilst commanding his battery in action on the Western Front, on November 2nd, 1917. At the time of his death he was forty-one years of age. The following extract is from a letter written by his commanding officer :—

" During the last few months I have had every opportunity of learning his sterling worth as a gunner officer, and the regiment has lost a most capable and practical officer. His whole heart was in his work and, during the last few weeks, he has brought to my notice two of his ideas for improving the shooting of his guns, ideas which when put to a practical test will, I am sure, be of great value to us. Yet again, only last night, he rang me up on the telephone to tell me of another improvement one of his men had invented. To such a conscientious and brave officer his death must have been the most glorious end of all—a great death for the greatest of all causes, the freedom of mankind from an alien domination. . . . His cheerful optimism and joviality impressed all of us, and we feel that we have lost a very great friend besides a first-rate, zealous officer."

MAJOR (TEMP. LIEUT.-COL.) ALFRED DURHAM MURPHY, *D.S.O.*, *M.C.*, 2nd Leinster Regiment, was the younger son of Lieut.-Col. E. W. Murphy, of Ballinamona, Cashel, Co. Tipperary, who had also served in the same regiment. Alfred Murphy was born on April 30th, 1890, came to Downside in April, 1902, and left in December, 1906. He was a quiet and unassuming boy of fine character, and was a keen member of the Cricket League. In 1906 he passed the Lower Certificate and won his form prize and prizes for French and German. He joined the Leinster Regiment from the Special Reserve in 1911, and embarked for France in September, 1914, with part of the original Expeditionary Force. He took part in the Battle of the Aisne and in many other important engagements, and continued at the front, with only short intervals of leave, until his death. He received his captaincy in October, 1915, and his brevet of major in January, 1917. His acting rank of lieut-col. was dated August 22nd, 1916. He commanded his battalion for more than a year, with conspicuous courage and distinction, endearing himself to all by his cheery spirits and great consideration for the welfare of those under his command. He was four times mentioned in despatches, and was awarded the M.C. and D.S.O., as well as Brevet-Major. The award of the D.S.O., in 1917, was accompanied by the following official statement :—

" With great presence of mind he moved up troops to fill a gap, which he had discovered by means of a personal reconnaissance, between his unit and the next division, afterwards handling his battalion with exceptional skill and personally selecting the best positions under heavy fire. His reports were invaluable and accurate, clearing up an obscure situation, and he has on all other occasions set a splendid example of fearlessness and ability."

At the time of his death, near Hargicourt, on November 6th, 1917, he had just brought some men, whom he thought were not in a safe position, into the officers' mess, when the hut was wrecked by a big shell, and all were killed. He was twenty-seven years of age.

The following description of Alfred Murphy at the front is from a letter written by one of the Catholic chaplains :—

LIEUT.-COL. A. D. MURPHY, D.S.O., M.C.

2nd Leinster Regiment

Killed in Action   *November 6th,* 1917

" If Ireland and Downside has produced anything greater in this war, I have not struck it. He was, indeed, quite a unique personality. A young man with a very old head upon a pair of somewhat slender shoulders, in keeping with a figure that could only be described as slim. And he dressed the part : not that he was a bit of a dandy—he was far too big a man for that —but everything that he had on him was adequate to the situation in which he found himself, whether it was a mess dinner dress, or the elaborate, but necessary, array of trench paraphernalia. But behind the external appearance there was the silent, resolute man, who had never been a boy except in years, but who was always a man, since nothing, however human, was foreign to him. And so it was, that whilst holding his place as Colonel of one of the old regular battalions he mixed with each and everyone of his officers as a brother in arms. To many of them he was, indeed, a kind of elder brother, for he had taught them their trade ; and as they had learned from him, so they grew up to love and follow him in the many places where the 2nd Battalion of the Leinsters found itself in tight corners. And as it was with his officers so it was with the men ; they believed in him. ' He'll never ask you to go anywhere he won't go himself ' they told me during my time with them at Affringues."

His services during the war were thus described in *The Times* of November 21st, 1917 :—

" Joining the Leinster Regiment in December, 1911, Lieut.-Col. Murphy embarked for France on September 8, 1914, with the 2nd Battalion, which formed part of the 6th Division of the original Expeditionary Force, as subaltern and transport officer. In this capacity he did sterling work, his coolness, resource, and powers of leadership clearly foreshadowing the ability for command he was subsequently to show. With his battalion he took part in the Battle of the Aisne, and, later, on October 20th, 1914, near Lille, when his battalion had suffered severely, he volunteered for, and performed, invaluable work in reorganising the broken remnants of the 2nd Leinsters. Shortly after he succeeded to the adjutancy, and while holding the appointment succeeded also to the command of the battalion. In this responsible position he did splendid work, winning the golden opinions of his seniors, and the intense devotion of his men. For more than three years Lieut.-Col. Murphy had been fighting continuously and, fearless and careless of himself as he was, his luck had become almost proverbial. Until he met his end he had never received a scratch. All old Leinsters will offer their deep and heartfelt sympathy to their old second-in-command, Major E. W. Murphy, for the loss of his gallant son—a born soldier, cool, clear-headed, and determined, who knew of fear simply as other men know of an obscure word in a dictionary."

LIEUT. LEONARD WILLIAM BUTLER, Royal Irish Fusiliers, third son of Mr. J. P. Butler, of 40, Fitzwilliam Place, Dublin, was born on November 8th, 1897, came to Downside in September, 1909, and left in July, 1915. At School he won for himself the regard and affection of all by his sincerity, earnestness and good temper. He had a high sense of duty and plenty of courage to take the path that seemed to him the right one—qualities which afterwards made him a most successful officer in the Army. During his last year at Downside he played in the Football Fifteen, and in the Second Eleven at Hockey, and on several occasions he played for his House (Roberts) at Football, Hockey and Cricket. He took part with the Roberts' section in the O.T.C. Competitions from 1913 to 1915, and won a medal in the Shooting Competition of 1914. He was also a member of his House Gym. and Sports Teams, and became a House Prefect in 1915. He had long intended to enter the Noviciate at Downside on the conclusion of his time at school, but the call to arms intervened, and postponed without in any way weakening his desire to test his vocation in the monastic life. He obtained a commission in the Royal Irish Fusiliers, and in due course was sent to France, where he rendered excellent service. He proved himself a most keen and capable officer, and, regarding it as his duty to remain in the firing line, refused to avail himself of an opportunity of military work in a less dangerous position.

He was shot through the head by a sniper and killed instantaneously in the action of Fontaine, on November 20th, 1917, having just completed the superintending of the wiring of a position which he had gallantly taken with his platoon. At the time of his death he was twenty years of age. His colonel wrote of him that " he was bravery itself, and loved by all the officers and men. . . . He is indeed a great loss to us as a soldier," and another of his senior officers paid the following tribute to his memory :—

" I have known your son since November, 1915, when we were together in Belfast, and we were very good friends, and I feel his death as a friend as well as the loss of one of my best officers. He has done splendid work for me on patrol on several occasions and had no idea what fear was. It was a great feat of his to put up the wire he had to and get his party back again, and you have good reason to be proud of him."

He was buried in the cemetery at Croisselles, and a cross with his name and regiment painted on it was placed over his grave.

Leonard Butler was the fourth Old Gregorian who intended to join the Downside Community on the conclusion of peace and was killed in action in the war.

LIEUT. L. W. BUTLER

Royal Irish Fusiliers

Killed in Action   *November 20th,* 1917

CAPT. C. W. BRUCE

3rd Gordon Highlanders, attached R.F.C.

Killed in Accident   *November 22nd, 1917*

CAPTAIN CHARLES WILLIAM BRUCE, 3rd Gordon Highlanders (attached Royal Flying Corps), younger son of Mr. and Mrs. Archibald Bruce, and grandson of the late Sir Walter Smythe, Bart., of Acton Burnell Park, Shropshire, was born on September 6th, 1895, received his early education at St. Anthony's, Eastbourne, came to Downside in April, 1910, and left in July, 1914. He had a natural talent for games and sports, was a most useful member of his House (Roberts), and was a House Prefect during his last year at Downside. He also did good work in the choir, in which he sang as alto. On the introduction of Rugby Football into the School in 1912 he became a member of the Fifteen, received his colours in the following year, and continued to play for the School until he left. Meanwhile he rendered good service to his House in the Cricket, Hockey, and Football matches and in the O.T.C., and Gym. Competitions. He was also successful in Aquatic and Athletic Sports, and won the Hurdles in the School Sports of 1914. On leaving Downside he went to Sandhurst, and was gazetted to the Gordon Highlanders in December, 1914. Shortly after he was sent to France, where he was twice wounded, the first occasion being in May, 1915, during the big Festhubert advance. For some time he was attached to the Black Watch and, more recently, to the Royal Flying Corps. After three months' training abroad as an observer his course was temporarily delayed through illness, and he was invalided home. In April, 1917, he was put on light duty and was given the command of a Cadet Corps at Oxford, a position which he held with marked success for three months. In July he resumed his training for the R.F.C., and at the end of six weeks passed first out of sixty officers in his examination. He was then sent to Rochford, in Essex, received his "wings" on October 2nd, and joined the Scouts Squadron. He was killed in an accident, whilst testing a new machine, on November 22nd, 1917. At the time he was only about a hundred and fifty feet from the ground, and the accident seems to have been due to some defect in the machinery. His commanding officer described him as a brilliant pilot, most capable and confident, and he was held in high regard and affection by the entire squadron. He took the deepest interest and a keen delight in his work. " I am so happy," he wrote in one of his letters, " I sing as I fly." At the time of his death he was twenty-two years of age and held the rank of captain.

2nd LIEUT. WILFRID GERVASE CARY-ELWES, 2nd Irish Guards, eldest son of Mr. Charles Cary-Elwes, of Courtlands, Eltham, Kent, and grandson of Sir J. Roper Parkington, was born on October 20th, 1898, came to Downside in September, 1908, and left in December, 1915. He was a bright and affectionate boy, full of energy and courage. As an athlete he had few equals in the School, and distinguished himself in games and sports of every kind. For three years he played regularly in the Hockey Eleven and for two years in the Cricket Eleven and the Football Fifteen. He received his colours for Football and Hockey in 1915. He was a member of the Games Committee and Secretary of the Golf Club. For his House (Barlow) he played many times at Football, Hockey and Cricket, took part in the Inter-House Gymnastic and Sports Competitions, and helped to win the Golf Cup in 1915. He became a House Prefect in 1914 and a School Prefect the following year. On receiving a nomination in the Irish Guards he went to Sandhurst early in 1916, and was gazetted in the following August. He was anxious to go to the front, and made repeated but unsuccessful efforts to be sent there, but only received marching orders on the eve of his nineteenth birthday. After a farewell visit to his old School, to which he was devotedly attached, he left England on October 25th, and fell in the attack on Fontaine, his first engagement, on November 27th, 1917. On the previous evening he advanced with the company to which he was attached and, after considerable delay, caused by hostile shelling, reached Bourlon Wood about midnight. In the early morning, taking up his position on the left of the company line, he advanced to the attack, fearless and cheerful to the end, his only anxiety being for his family, to whom he sent an affectionate message by a fellow-officer. He was shot through the head during the attack, and died in a few seconds without regaining consciousness. Later on a sergeant was sent to the spot to see if he could find any wounded or recover any of the bodies of those who had fallen, but before he had proceeded far, he was himself wounded and taken prisoner.

It is evident from the many letters received by his parents that the death of Wilfrid Cary-Elwes was felt as a great loss by his regiment as well as by his many friends. His colonel described

2nd LIEUT. W. G. CARY-ELWES
2nd Irish Guards

Killed in Action   *November 27th, 1917*

him as " a charming boy whom everybody loved, and such a fine young soldier. I am afraid we shall all miss him dreadfully." His company commander wrote of him : " He gave promise of being such a splendid officer, cool, reliable, self-reliant and capable." Other letters testify to his promise as a soldier and the affectionate esteem in which he was held by his brother officers.

His late commanding officer wrote :—

" We all feel his death most keenly, as your son was loved by everyone who came in contact with him. He was a most promising officer, and should he have been spared I feel sure he had a great career in front of him."

The adjutant, in writing from the front, said :—

" I spent one year with him at Warley, and was adjutant of his battalion since he came out. I was a very great friend of his. I cannot tell you what a loss he is to the regiment. He was liked so much by everyone, and had the makings of a first-class soldier. I am sure he would have got on."

And the Catholic Chaplain wrote of him as follows :—

" Your boy is a great loss to us here where we have so few Catholic officers. It was a great consolation to me to see him bringing his men to Mass whenever we had Battalion Mass. Owing to our movements during the last month or so, it was some time since we had had Mass before his death ; but the evening before his death I gave him Absolution, and he was quite happy and brave ' going over the top.' "

2nd LIEUT. JOHN WILLIAM DAME, 2nd Irish Guards, only son of Mr. J. M. Dame, of 29, Marine Lines, Bombay, India, was born in 1898, came to Downside in May, 1909, and left in July, 1916. In his character there was an excellent blending of gentleness and strength which made him both effective and popular in control of other boys, and he held various positions of authority throughout every stage of his life at School. He played in the Junior Cricket Eleven in 1912, in the Second Eleven in 1913, and in the First Eleven from 1914 to 1916, receiving his colours in 1915. He batted well and fielded well at wickets. He also played in the Second Hockey Eleven, was a member of the Hockey and Cricket Committees in 1916, and represented his House (Roberts) in Cricket, Football, Hockey, Golf, Gym. and Sports from 1914 to 1916. In the O.T.C. he was successively Lance-Corporal, Corporal and Cadet Officer, and was a member of his House Corps Section during his last three years at school. He was appointed a House Prefect in 1914, a School Prefect in 1915, and Head of Roberts House in 1916. On leaving Downside, he went to Sandhurst, and in due course received a commission in the Irish Guards. Whenever an opportunity presented itself, he returned on visits to the School, and he spent part of his last leave with his friends at the Downside Harvest Camp in Norfolk, in August, 1917. Shortly after he was sent to France, and shared in the severe fighting on the Western Front in November. Whilst taking part in an attack he was killed in action on November 27th, 1917, the day on which his friend, Wilfrid Cary-Elwes, also fell on the field of battle. John Dame was nineteen years of age at the time of his death. His colonel wrote of him : " He was a splendid officer, and we were all very fond of him in the regiment."

2nd LIEUT. J. W. DAME

2nd Irish Guards

Killed in Action   *November 27th, 1917*

In

Memoriam

CAPT. J. B. M. BURKE, M.C.

4th Grenadier Guards

Killed in Action   *December 1st,* 1917

CAPTAIN JOHN BERNARD MARY BURKE, *M.C.*, 4th Grenadier Guards, was the only son of Sir Henry Farnham Burke, K.C.V.O., C.B., F.S.A., Garter Principal King of Arms. He was born on November 6th, 1892, and was at Downside from April, 1907, to July, 1909.

At Cricket he was a useful bat and bowler, and played in the First Eleven in 1909. In the previous year he won the Golf Cup in the School Competition. In 1909 he passed the Higher Certificate. On the Downside stage he acted with much success, appearing in widely different characters, and always showing a facile adaptability to his part. He was especially good as Uncle Gregory in " A Pair of Spectacles."

During the war he saw much service with the Grenadier Guards on the Western Front, and was awarded the Military Cross " for conspicuous gallantry and devotion to duty . . . under heavy shell fire," in the fighting near the Yser Canal (July, 1917).

On December 1st, 1917, he was killed in an attack on the village of Gonnelieu, which the Germans had captured and where they were strongly entrenched. He started forward for the attack in the middle of the second wave, making for the left half of the village, through the greater part of which he had already forced his way, when he was wounded in the leg below the knee by a machine-gun bullet. He must have been killed in the subsequent fighting, though at first he was reported " wounded and missing," and was thought to have been taken prisoner. His body was found in Gonnelieu village in August, 1919, and was buried in Gouzeaucourt Cemetery. One of his fellow-officers wrote shortly after the engagement in which Bernard Burke was killed :—

" I cannot tell you how we all miss him . . . the company all but achieved the impossible, and got on much further than anybody else, which is most gratifying. Our losses were extremely heavy—about 60 per cent.—but it undoubtedly broke up a strong German attack."

The following account we owe to a member of the Downside Community who was chaplain to the battalion to which Burke belonged :—

" I first came in contact with him at the front, about August 20th, 1916, when I assumed my duties as chaplain to the 3rd Guards Brigade, and from then onwards till the time of his death I saw a great deal of him, as I was attached to his battalion. Being one of the very few Catholic officers in the battalion, I relied very much on his help, and he never failed me. Promoted to the command of his company—a position which he held with distinction—he gave me every help in ministering to the spiritual needs of the men, and set a fine example in always hearing Mass and approaching the Sacraments when he had the opportunity. His death occurred during the latter and less fortunate stage of the great battle of Cambrai, which had opened with promise of a great victory in the last week of November, 1917, and went very near to closing in disaster to our arms a few days later. The Guards Division, which had already suffered very heavily in the fighting at Bourlon Wood, was thrown in to stem the force of the massed German attacks on the south of our lines, and to recapture, if possible, the positions taken by the enemy on our flank. To the Fourth Battalion of the Grenadier Guards was assigned the hopeless task of recapturing the ruined village of Gonnelieu, where the enemy were strongly entrenched. It was in this attack that Burke fell. He was at first reported missing, and when last seen was using his revolver unsparingly. It was not for some time that his body was found. I heard his confession and gave him Holy Communion a few days before the attack. He never went into the line without preparing himself for death, and more than once he asked me for Absolution in trench or dug-out when there was no time for Confession."

MAJOR A. E. HAWKINS
Royal Field Artillery

Died of Wounds   *December 12th, 1917*

MAJOR ALEXANDER EDWARD HAWKINS, Royal Field Artillery, only son of Mr. A. F. Hawkins, of Clarence Parade, Southsea, was born on December 10th, 1894, came to Downside in September, 1907, and left in April, 1910. He was a very capable and versatile boy, combining in his character much strength and charm. In 1909 he won his Form Prize and prizes in Greek and French, and passed the Lower Certificate with First Classes in four subjects. In other directions he also showed great promise, particularly in the Boxing Competitions and in the Shooting Club, in which he won medals on two occasions. In 1910 he went to Cheltenham, where he became Captain of the Shooting Eight and held the Challenge Cup for a year. He entered the Royal Military Academy, Woolwich, in September, 1913, and received his commission in the Royal Artillery a year later. In January, 1915, he went to the Flanders Front and remained on active service until his death, except for a short interval on sick leave when he was engaged in training others at home. He took part in the second battle of Ypres and many other actions, became adjutant in June, 1916, captain in the following September, and major in May, 1917. About the same time he was mentioned in despatches. He was a born soldier and won golden opinions from officers and men by his courage and enterprise. " He loved his battery and was so proud of it and they of him. One former officer of his wrote to say that out of many subalterns he had under him he was the only one with whom no fault could be found. His battery was always complimented." He was wounded on December 10th, 1917, his twenty-third birthday, by a shell which killed another officer with whom he was talking, and died thirty-six hours later, on December 12th. He was cheerful to the end, and had the consolation of receiving Absolution and Extreme Unction from the Catholic Chaplain at the casualty clearing station at Ytres. He was buried at Rocquigny Cemetery, Manancourt.

His colonel wrote of him as follows :—

" . . . how much we all liked your boy, and how personally glad I was when I was able some time ago, in spite of his youth, to get him posted as major to one of my batteries. He has since done magnificent work, and gained the affection and confidence of his battery . . . His death came as a great blow to us all."

CAPTAIN HON. ROBERT EDMUND NOEL, Royal Fusiliers, was the third and youngest son of the Earl and Countess of Gainsborough, of Exton Park, Oakham, and Campden House, Gloucestershire, and was born in 1888. After receiving his early education at Ladycross he came to Downside in April, 1901, and left in July, 1907. He was a bright and cheerful boy and, throughout his life, was always popular with those with whom he came in contact. At School he was a keen Tennis player and a good forward at Hockey and a very useful member of the choir. He also took a conspicuous part in the School theatricals. After leaving Downside he went to Trinity College, Cambridge, and was secretary of the Fisher Society in 1909. He was gazetted 2nd lieutenant in the Royal Fusiliers in April, 1910, promoted lieutenant in 1912, and captain in 1915. In January, 1914, he was seconded from his regiment to join the Nigerian Police, his headquarters being at Lagos, where he held the position of Assistant Commissioner with the local rank of captain. On the outbreak of war he was appointed Provost-Marshal at Lagos. In 1915, he was attached to the Nigerian Regiment, then operating in the Cameroons, until a bad attack of fever caused him to be sent home on sick leave. In June, 1916, after returning to Lagos, he was ordered up country to put an end to local risings, and carried out this mission with distinction. In July, 1917, he proceeded with a draft to reinforce the Nigerian Regiment in German East Africa, and after helping to clear that country of the enemy, he died at Massassi on February 2nd, 1918, of a fever contracted during the campaign. He was twenty-nine years of age.

His brother, to whom we are indebted for most of the above particulars, concluded his letter as follows :—

" A Requiem was sung for him at Exton on February 12th, and also a Requiem Mass at the Oratory on March 1st. . . . He always said that when he reached the age of thirty he would become a Benedictine monk or Catholic Chaplain to the Forces. He loved the Church and everything to do with its services and ceremonials."

CAPT. THE HON. R. E. NOEL

Royal Fusiliers

Died on Service   *February 2nd,* 1918

2nd LIEUT. T. E. BYRNE

Welsh Guards

Killed in Action   *March 9th, 1918*

2nd. LIEUT. THOMAS EDMUND BYRNE, Welsh Guards, eldest son of the late Mr. Thomas C. Byrne, of Hawthorne Lodge, Wylde Green, Birmingham, was born on August 19th, 1898, came to Downside in April, 1910, and left in April, 1916.

" Teddy " Byrne was a strong, direct, somewhat reserved boy, with plenty of courage and determination. He was fond of reading, and sometimes took part in the debates of the Abingdon Society. During his last year at Downside he was a member of the committee of the Petre Library. He played in the Junior Cricket Eleven in 1911, in the First Hockey Eleven in 1916, and in the Football Fifteen in 1914 and 1915, receiving his cap during the latter season. He was a House Prefect, 1915-1916, played for Caverel at Cricket, Football and Hockey, and took part in the Inter-House O.T.C. and Sports Competitions. He was also a member of the School choir. His contemporaries will probably remember him best as a most plucky and enthusiastic boxer. He won the second division prize in 1915, and subsequently became Captain of the Boxing Club. On leaving school he joined the Artists' Rifles and obtained a commission in the Welsh Guards early in 1917. He went on active service in May, 1917, was invalided home suffering from trench fever in September, returned to the front in the following February, and was killed in action in France on March 9th, 1918. He was nineteen years of age.

The following extract is from a letter written by his colonel :—

" The enemy were shelling us heavily, and a shell burst near the mouth of your son's dug-out, killing him instantaneously. He had only been with us a few days, but was doing very well. He was very cool in action and would have made a most excellent officer. He is a great loss to the battalion, just one of those one would have liked to keep."

The officer in command of his company wrote as follows :—

" He was very keen and had the great gift of making the best of things, which is really everything out here. I had put him in charge of a party of men and had told him to keep them under cover during a heavy bombardment which we were expecting.

He got all his men in, and I think, owing to his keenness, he did not go far enough down the steps of the dug-out himself. A shell burst just in the entrance, and he was killed instantaneously. . . . The R.C. priest attached to our brigade buried him in a little cemetery not far from where he was killed."

LIEUT. O. F. STAPLETON-BRETHERTON

Lancers

Killed in Action   *March 22nd, 1918*

LIEUT. OSMUND FREDERICK STAPLETON-BRETH-
ERTON, Lancers, only son of Major F. B. Stapleton-Bretherton,
was born on August 2nd, 1898, came to Downside in May, 1908,
and left in July, 1915. Both in appearance and character he was
a typically English boy, cheerful and straightforward, and fond of
all games and sport. At Cricket he played successively in the
Junior Eleven, the Second Eleven and the First Eleven (colours),
at Hockey in the Second Eleven and the First Eleven, and at
Football in the Second Fifteen. He was a House Prefect in 1914
and 1915, and on various occasions represented his House (Caverel)
at Cricket, Football and Hockey and in the Inter-House Sports,
Gymnastic and O.T.C. Competitions. He was a member of the
Sacristy from 1910 to 1915. On leaving Downside he went to
Sandhurst, was gazetted to the Lancers in July, 1916, and received
promotion in the following year. He was killed in action on the
Western Front on March 22nd, 1918, at the age of nineteen years.

LIEUT. GEORGE FRANCIS PAULING, *M.C.*, Grenadier Guards, only son of the late Henry Clarke Pauling, C.E., and of Mrs. Hill Kelly, of Llanfoist House, Abergavenny, was born on January 23rd, 1895, came to Downside in September, 1906, and left in December, 1907. Subsequently he went to Beaumont College, Old Windsor, whence he passed into Sandhurst in 1912. At Sandhurst he was known as a keen amateur boxer, and won a cup for athletics. He was gazetted to the 17th Lancers in 1914, and exchanged into the Grenadier Guards in January, 1916, as he wished to take a more prominent part in the fighting. In the following September he won the Military Cross at the Battle of the Somme. He was wounded in the Battle of Messines Ridge in 1917. After his recovery he returned to France on February 17th, 1918, and was killed in action near Arras, on the night of March 25th, by the concussion of a bursting shell, after getting his men into safety. He was twenty-three years of age. His colonel, who described him as " a very brilliant soldier," highly commended his work.

On February 10th, 1920, after a Requiem Mass had been celebrated, a Calvary and Lych-gate, erected to the memory of George Pauling by some of his old colleagues, were solemnly blessed at the Church of our Lady of Sorrows, Effingham.

LIEUT. G. F. PAULING, M.C.

Grenadier Guards

Killed in Action   *March 25th, 1918*

LIEUT. J. H. NASH

1st Irish Guards

Killed in Action   *March 27th, 1918*

LIEUT. JAMES HARAN NASH, 1st Irish Guards, eldest son of Sir Vincent Nash, of Shannon View House, Kilmurry, co. Limerick, was born on March 5th, 1898, came to Downside in September, 1908, and left in July, 1915. He played in the Junior Cricket Eleven in 1911, and won silver medals in the shooting competitions of 1911 and 1912. Later on, he played for the Second Football Fifteen and for his House (Barlow) at Cricket, Football and Hockey. He was also a member of the Barlow Corps Section. He took part in athletic sports and distinguished himself in many boxing contests, in which he displayed an excellent style and much skill in attack and defence. In May, 1916, he was gazetted to the Irish Guards and received promotion in the following year. He was killed in action on the Western Front on March 27th, 1918, at the age of twenty. The following extract from a letter written by his commanding officer describes the circumstances of his death, and sketches his character in terms which all who knew him at Downside will appreciate :—

" ' Boy,' as we used to call him, was one of the brightest and cheeriest fellows that ever breathed ; we all loved him and his men were devoted to him. On March 27th, after a heavy bombardment, the enemy attacked, and were easily repulsed. The boy was quite splendid, and really enjoyed himself throughout the whole show. During the afternoon he was doing a bit of sniping, and must have exposed himself too much. He was shot through the head by a bullet (machine gun, I think), and death was absolutely instantaneous. He died a gallant death, and was happy as anybody could be right up to the moment he died. I don't think he had a single care . . . He was buried by our priest."

2nd LIEUT. JOHN BERNARD MORRALL, Royal Warwick-shire Regiment, youngest son of the late Mr. Edward Morrall, of Nechells, Birmingham, was born on March 9th, 1879, came to Downside in September, 1892, and left in July, 1898. He was a grand-nephew of the late Dom Alphonsus Morrall, of Downside Abbey.

Bernard Morrall was a very able boy and his strong religious feeling and upright character won for him considerable influence over his contemporaries. He was first in his class and won many prizes all the way through the School. He passed the Oxford Junior Locals in 1896, the Senior Locals (with Honours) in 1897, and the Higher Certificate in 1898. He was Librarian of the Petre Library, 1897-8, and took a prominent part in the debates of the Abingdon Society. He also acted with distinction in several plays and farces. After leaving Downside, he spent some months in the Noviciate at Belmont, and afterwards distinguished himself as an artist. In January, 1916, he joined the Artists' Rifles and went to France. In due time he received a commission in the Royal Warwickshire Regiment, fought in five battles, and was wounded at Beaumetz on March 23rd, 1918. He was taken prisoner by the Germans, and died of his wounds about four days later. He was thirty-nine years of age.

The following sketch, which will help to illustrate his character, we owe to his brother, Dom Edward Morrall, of Douai Abbey, Woolhampton :—

" He left Belmont, persuaded that he owed a duty to his parents in their loneliness. When his parents died, although in his heart he still yearned for the Benedictine life, he felt that he had grown too fixed in his habits to face a radical change. Even so late as January, 1918, he said : ' I should have loved to have lived and died at dear Downside.' In actual life he endeavoured to live up to the Benedictine ideal and retained to the last the habit of Benedictine meditation. For twenty years and more, morning and night, he meditated on the chapter in the *Imitation of Christ* on ' The Royal Road of the Cross.' He tore the pages out of a book and carried them in his breast pocket into battle. Suffering and sacrifice were dear to him. ' In the interior and spiritual life,' wrote one who knew him well, ' Bernard moved upward and onward.' With regard to his intellectual attainments, he had a scholarly appreciation of Greek and read with ease Plato, Aristotle and the Greek dramatists. He had a wide and accurate knowledge of English

2nd LIEUT. J. B. MORRALL

Royal Warwickshire Regiment

Died of Wounds   *March 27th, 1918*

Literature and was a keen student of Shakespeare. His knowledge of Newman's works was astonishing, and he would frequently quote from them in his conversation. 'Newman's day has not yet come,' he would say, 'I wonder when Catholics will wake up to the value of Newman.' His real work lay in the world of Art, in which his skill was undoubted and was supported by a knowledge that was wide and minute. Sir Whitworth Wallis wrote of him as 'a brilliant and distinguished student. He gave promise of great things. Death has robbed us of one who might easily have been a shining light.' His best designs are to be found in the Edinburgh home of the Marquis of Bute ; in the Australia Offices in London ; in the church of St. Antoninus, Newark, U.S.A. ; in Holy Trinity Church, Southport, etc. He was offered the position of an official artist for the Imperial War Museum, but he died before the necessary formalities were carried out. Some of his water-colour drawings of places on the Western Front have been purchased by the Imperial War Museum, and the remaining ones have gone to the War Museum at Birmingham. . . . During the War, he passed unscathed through five battles, but was wounded at Beaumetz on March 23rd, 1918. Owing to the loss of officers, he remained to the last to see the men withdraw, displaying complete coolness and deliberation, although the Germans were closing in upon him. When picked up by the enemy, his wounds were not attended to ; he was carried away on a waggon, and thrown with others into a railway truck. He was last seen by an Englishman on March 26th, suffering very much from open wounds, very hungry and thirsty, and with his clothes covered with blood, so the end could not have been far off. Many have testified to his sterling character. Four men of an agnostic type have written to the effect that owing to his influence they have become Catholics. One of his superior officers wrote of him as ' a real influence for good among officers and men,' and a private described him as ' a splendid officer. His men loved him and miss him. He was always considerate and would do anything for the men. Never shall I forget his rescuing three men after the set-back at Cambrai. We all admired his upright character.' Thus did he live up to his ideals of being a Christian scholar and gentleman, ever striving to fulfil his Benedictine motto that God may be honoured in all things."

2nd LIEUT. BERNARD BASIL JOSEPH BUTLER-BOWDON, Lancashire Fusiliers, youngest son of Col. and the late Hon. Mrs. Butler-Bowden, of Pleasington Hall, Lancashire, and Southgate House, Derbyshire, was born in 1899, came to Downside in September, 1908, and left in February, 1915. He was a member of Roberts House. After passing through Sandhurst he received a commission in the Lancashire Fusiliers, and was sent to the Western Front. In March, 1918, after the fighting at Fampoux, near Arras, he was reported missing; later on he was officially presumed to have been killed in action during the engagement, on March, 28th, 1918. He was nineteen years of age.

2nd LIEUT. B. B. J. BUTLER-BOWDON

Lancashire Fusiliers

Killed in Action   *March 28th, 1918*

CAPT. A. B. HOBDELL

Wiltshire Regiment

Died of Wounds   *April 16th, 1918*

CAPTAIN ARTHUR BIRT HOBDELL, Wiltshire Regiment, only son of Mr. A. H. Hobdell, of Southbank, Linkfield Lane, Redhill, was born on April 18th, 1895, came to Downside in April, 1903, and left in July, 1911. He passed the Lower Certificate, with First Classes in Latin, Greek and French, in 1910 and 1911, and in the former year was awarded the Junior Latin and Greek Prose prizes. He played well at Hockey, was a good boxer, and was a keen member of the Natural History Club. After leaving Downside he went to Germany to learn the language. He remained there two years, mixing thoroughly with the people, and returned to England with the firm conviction that a war between the two countries was inevitable, and was looked forward to in Germany. He was preparing for a career in diplomacy, and was on the point of taking his final exams., in which he had every likelihood of success, when the war broke out. Filled with a strong sense of duty and patriotic feeling, he put aside his own personal interests and enlisted in the Honourable Artillery Company on the very day war was declared. Later on he received a commission in the Wiltshire Regiment, and was twice wounded. When the great battle of March, 1918, began, he was home on sick leave, and went back at once before being summoned. Whilst in command of a company of infantry on the Western Front he was severely wounded, and died on April 16th, 1918, two days before his twenty-third birthday. An account of the circumstances under which he was wounded is given in a letter from his commanding officer, who also bore eloquent testimony to the high regard in which he was held :—

" Perhaps I can help you in a small degree by saying how much I and the officers of this battalion—not to mention the N.C.O.'s and men—thought of your son. I have only been with the battalion about three weeks, but, in a very short time, I saw how conscientious and cheerful a worker he was in *very* hard times—and, in the last few days before he was hit, how very gallant he was. . . . The enemy attacked on our right and forced the next unit to us back a bit ; your son, who was in command of the support company, went up towards our first line to warn the front company that their flank was becoming exposed, and of the necessity of forming a defensive flank. In doing so he was forced to go over very exposed ground, and it was when he was about half way to the front line that he was hit in the stomach by a sniper. His company did all they could to get him back quickly, and he was sent on to hospital as soon as possible. . . . Everybody has spoken to me of his cheerfulness and gallantry at all times. I was particularly struck by his loyalty to myself, when, although new to the battalion, I had to take command of it during the fighting. I could trust him more than any of the company commanders ; and now, when we are trying to reorganise the battalion rather hurriedly, I feel how useful he would have been."

The following is from a letter written by the late Lord Alexander Thynne, the colonel commanding the battalion in which Arthur Hobdell was serving. He was in England at the time of Hobdell's death, recovering from a wound :—

" I want to tell you how much we shall all miss your son, especially at the present time, for I had always looked forward to his becoming adjutant ; he was at different times attached to Battalion Headquarters in various capacities, but he was never really happy away from his platoon, for he was devoted to his men, and they returned his affection in full measure. There was not an officer in the battalion more popular with all ranks, and it is not surprising ; his constant cheerfulness in the most depressing and trying circumstances, his high sense of duty, his complete disregard of personal danger, all these primary qualities of leadership he possessed in a high degree.

" I remember the feeling of complete confidence he gave one when he first took over the command of C Company in the Hindenburg line last January ; in feeling that he was putting his very best into the work, one forgot his extreme youth. And if anything can be a consolation to you I hope you will remember that he died a captain, commanding a company of infantry in the battle line. I am sure it is the death he would have wished. Even more than as an officer of the battalion I shall regret him as a personal friend. I cannot tell you what a resource he was during the hard times we went through last winter, always in good spirits and laughing, taking an interest in everything, collecting all the news ; he has left a gap in our little Mess which it will be hard to fill."

LIEUT. G. I. TURNBULL, M.C.

Welch Regiment

Died of Wounds   *April 20th, 1918*

LIEUT. GERARD ILTYD TURNBULL, *M.C.*, Welch Regiment, fourth son of the late Mr. Philip Turnbull, J.P., The Heath, Cardiff, was born on July 11th, 1886, came to Downside in January, 1899, and left in July, 1904. He took a conspicuous part in games and athletics of every kind, being a fair bat and an excellent fielder at Cricket, a good forward in the Hockey team, and at Football the best half-back of his generation at Downside. He was a member of the Cricket Eleven and the Hockey Eleven in 1904, and of the Football Eleven in 1903 and 1904. He won the Boxing Cup, open to the whole School, in 1902, and again in 1904. After leaving Downside he represented Cardiff at Hockey for several seasons, and was a member of the Glamorganshire Golf Club. He was well known at Cardiff Docks, where he was employed as chartering clerk by Messrs. Mann, George & Co. In August, 1914, on the outbreak of war, he offered himself to the Honourable Artillery Company, but was medically rejected. Eventually, he joined the Inns of Court O.T.C. in 1915, obtained a commission in the Welch Regiment, and went to France in October, 1916. On March 21st, 1918, he was wounded, but remained on duty. On April 9th he was again wounded, this time severely, and was taken prisoner. He died in a German field lazarette on April 20th, 1918, at the age of thirty-one. It has been ascertained that, whilst fully conscious, he received the last Sacraments, and that he was buried with the rites of the Catholic Church and full military honours in the cemetery at Ronchin, village near Lille. A number of German officers and men and many of the French inhabitants of the village attended the funeral which took place on April 22nd. Over his grave has been placed a cross bearing his name. The colonel of his battalion wrote to say that Iltyd Turnbull had been recommended for the Military Cross " for fine services rendered during the fighting on March 21st, and subsequent dates." The following is the official statement which appeared a little later :—

" When acting as battalion scout officer, he carried out a series of daring reconnaissances into the enemy lines for six days and nights without rest, bringing back information of the greatest value."

CAPTAIN JOHN ERIC TREVOR-JONES, *M.C.*, 10th Rifle Brigade, younger son of Major E. J. Trevor Cory, R.A.M.C., of 38, Hyde Park Gate, London, S.W., was born on August 19th, 1897, came to Downside in September, 1906, and left in July, 1914. He was a bright and capable boy of exceptional charm, always much liked by all with whom he came in contact. As a small boy he was a conspicuous member of the Junior Football and Cricket Elevens, being Captain of the latter in 1910 and 1911. Later on he played for the Second Eleven at Cricket (1912-1914), rendering good service both with bat and ball, for the First Hockey Eleven (1913, 1914), and for the First Football Fifteen (1914). He also took part in Aquatic and Tennis competitions. He represented his House (Roberts) at Cricket, Football and Hockey from 1912 to 1914, and was a member of the Roberts' Section O.T.C., Gym. Team and Sports Team. On leaving Downside he went to Clare College, Cambridge, and commenced his studies for the medical profession, to which he intended to devote his life. In January, 1916, at the age of eighteen, he joined the Army, and was gazetted to the Rifle Brigade, becoming subsequently captain and adjutant. In July, 1916, he proceeded to France, shortly after the death of his elder brother, who was killed at the Battle of the Somme, whilst assisting a wounded man to safety. In March, 1917, Eric Trevor-Jones was awarded the Military Cross for gallantry in the field. The official statement is as follows :—

" Accompanied by two men he cut a lane through our wire under very heavy fire. Later he organised a bombing party and drove off an enemy attack. On another occasion he established a block under heavy fire, thereby saving a critical situation."

He was killed in action on April 22nd, 1918, at the age of twenty, having for the previous six weeks been attached to the brigade in which his brother was also serving at the time of his death in 1916. The following extract is from a letter from Eric-Trevor Jones' colonel :—

" He was quite one of my best officers and a charming personality ; he, unfortunately, was only with us a short time. I wish he had been longer ; he was just the type of man we can so ill afford to lose and whose place it is quite impossible to fill."

Capt. A. WALSH, M.C.,
South Lancs Regt.

Lt. R. N. PERCIVAL-
MAXWELL, Lancers.

Sec.-Lt. H. T. R. EVANS,
Royal Warwickshire Regt.

Capt. E. BUDD, M.C.,
Irish Guards.

Lt. R. R. PLAISTOWE,
Norfolk Regt.

Sec.-Lt. G. E. LASCELLES,
Rifle Brigade.

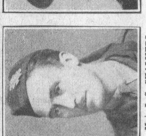

Maj. J. S. CHALMERS,
Highland Light Infantry.

Lt. O. ROBINSON,
R.N.V.R.

Lt. A. W. FORBES, D.S.O.,
R.N.

Capt. J. E. TREVOR-JONES,
M.C., Rifle Brigade.

Lt. M. HUNTER,
Lancers.

Sec.-Lt. P. St. Q. BRAYSHAW,
R.F.A.

Portraits by Elliott & Fry, Brooke Hughes, Lafayette, Bassano, Swaine, Russell, and Claude Harris.

Capt. T. G. D. BURDETT,
M.C., Royal Welsh Fus.

Lt. H. A. CAMERON,
Hampshire Regt.

Lt. W. W. OGILVY,
Hussars.

a stage carpenter, a Tube liftman, and a printer—but a "printer," so he said, of menus—on Atlantic liners.

Our unit, in short, was a miniature replica of that splendid *mélange*, the New British Army. Throughout the hospital's wards the same queer, and altogether pleasant and wholesome medley was, and is, observable. True, the aitchless is—well, commoner in the men's wards than in the officers'. But authentic aitchless-ness is less common universally than facetious littérateurs would have the world believe.

"Independent Means!"

I think that if one wanted to draw the typical British soldier of to-day—though the desire to define the typical is perhaps rather absurd—one would look for a lower middle-class man of the kind which Pett Ridge has immortalised. That subtle artist should, by the way, have something to tell us about the matter, for he is now labouring as honorary librarian in the very hospital of which I write.

This question of the soldier's origin interested me. I remember my inward chuckle when I learned that one of our favourite patients had been—and hoped to be again—a lavatory attendant ; and I frequently questioned the convalescents who helped me in my dish-washing and linen sorting.

One, I recollect, gave a blasé toss of the head, and informed me that he had "independent means." Pursuing my investigations, I found that he was a publican, and owned his pub. He was exceedingly proud of the fact, and "independent means" in his case—as in others' of a higher status—did not spell idleness. I gathered that he worked hard to maintain and improve his property, and in peace time was seldom absent from behind his bar. "It's a small house to look at," he said ; "but we pull more beer than any other in Blanktown."

I believe he was regarded with deference by his fellow-patients, the "independent means" claim being tacitly admitted and endorsed.

Whereas a greengrocer, who overseas to help the Homeland. It appears that in Australia this series of forces which, as the months and years dragged on, were raised and then shipped westward, were called : 1. The Tourists ("the six-bob-a-day tourists") ; 2. The Dinkums (*dinkum*, a common Antipodean word for "good") ; 3. The Super-Dinkums ; 4. The War Babies ; and 5. The Hard Thinkers.

I think it will be admitted that "The Hard Thinkers" is shrewd.

Our hospital, ever since the Gallipoli period, has always housed hosts of Australian patients. Once, in my ward, two of these fine fellows, in adjacent beds, were recovering from the operating-table experience, and, still under the influence of the anaesthetic, were maundering in the manner typical of that state. The first of them kept groaning, "I want to go home! I want to go home!" And at last the second—equally unconscious, but with an odd effect of sudden, clear-headed exasperation—exclaimed, "Then you'd better learn swimming !"

Homesick though he often excusably is, the "Ozzi"—this is our amicable *nom de guerre* for the Australian—is, as a rule, a superb specimen of mankind, and, despite the many jokes anent his some-what casual interpretation of the word Discipline, makes a fierce and fearless fighter.

Cockney Irrepressibles

What, however, has surprised all the military experts is the soldierly courage also exhibited on every field by that comparatively frail and weedy soul the Cockney. This once-scorned genus, in all its grades from costermonger to humble clerk, has won golden opinions from those in command. And if the Cockney is game in battle, we at the hospital can testify that he is an ideal patient when wounded.

The Colonials are cheery giants in the wards, but the little Cockney has an irreverent and irrepressible mischievous-ness peculiarly his own. One rascal, I remember, when we were visited by an august personage, was asked what was

As ill-fortune would have it, the august personage halted opposite this bed, and surveying the bulbous and bandaged compassionately, "Were you hit by a bullet or shrapnel ? " The victim mumbled, "A gnat!" But the timid answer escaped the ears of the august personage, who observed, "I trust it did not knock any of your teeth out," and passed on, followed by the retinue of grave red-tabs and brass hats, with a fringe of anxious hospital officials, each afraid of catching the other's eye.

The mistake was, to be sure, a not unaccountable one, for the hospital has contained countless cases of injuries to the jaw.

temp. On one occasion an orderly of the hospital was bitten on the cheek by a gnat, said gnat having evidently banqueted before-hand on unsavoury meats, for the orderly's blood became poisoned, his face swelled to an alarming size, and he had to be put to bed in a ward alongside the pukka wounded.

To the Victor—Teeth

Our chief dental department is kept busy devising ingenious jaw splints, and thereby saving many a sufferer who, under similar circumstances a few years ago, would have been condemned to life-long subsistence on liquid foods, if, indeed, he had survived at all.

Our chief dental surgeon was waited on the other day by a soldier who produced a "set of fancy teeth," as he called them, said they were fitting badly, and asked to have them adjusted. "But this isn't your own plate," exclaimed the surgeon when he had examined it. Mr. Atkins admitted that.

It was, he confessed, a German plate. The Boche, in a struggle, had knocked out and broken Mr. Atkins' false teeth ; so Mr. Atkins, observing that his foe was similarly supplied, helped himself to Fritz's. "They've never some-how seemed quite right, though, sir," he remarked, more in sorrow than in anger ; "and I begin to think I might have been kinder to take that chap prisoner instead of killing him !"

HUMOURS FROM A WAR HOSPITAL

By Ward Muir

MORE OBSERVATIONS OF AN ORDERLY

Author of the Popular "Observations of an Orderly"

TWO hundred and four men comprised the unit at the war hospital when I enlisted there as an orderly. (The number has since then been reduced, owing to the introduction, in some departments, of women substitutes.)

We were "rather a mixed crowd," as the R.A.M.C. initials are supposed to indicate. I compiled, for a paragraph in our magazine, a list of the avocations from which my comrades had been drawn. The result was curious. Khaki is, in the popular phrase, a perfect camouflage. Until you interrogated him, you seldom knew what any given khaki-wearer had been in civilian life.

It turned out that, amongst our ranks, we had several schoolmasters, two actors, a lexicographer—he had been employed on the learned staff of a great dictionary, and I confess made me for the first time realise that "lexicography" is actually a profession—a cinema pianist, a piano tuner, a fireman, two boxing

was also his own master, and might therefore have been supposed to enjoy the same financially aristocratic position, received no such esteem; he was merely looked askance at because he smoked Egyptians, instead of being content with the usual cheap Virginian cigarette. "Swank," was the verdict; and someone put the story about that the greengrocer's shop was in reality his wife's.

The Australians were less classifiable by English standards; even those who came from cities seemed rather open-air men than clerks or shopkeepers. And most could be summed up in this fragment of ward dialogue:

"What was Dan before the war?"

"Oh, he was a married couple on a sheep station."

From "Tourists" to "Hard Thinkers"

To which, for the benefit of psychologists and future historians, I must take leave to add, as not without significance, the list of nicknames bestowed on the

his trade, and answered unabashed, "A Viennese bandsman, sir." The statement, if audacious, was valid. He had played in one of those orchestras which, before the war, were constrained to call themselves, "Herr So-and-So's White Viennese Band," to please the snobbish people who hired them for evening receptions, although, under their uniforms, the musicians were true-blue Britons. They were mainly Yorkshiremen, in point of fact; but this particular player was Bermondsey born and bred.

The same man, after his discharge from hospital, laconically conveyed to us the news that he had been ordered back to the front by sending a postcard with this grim, yet engaging, inscription: "*Reserve Bed 5 for me, please, Sister.*" And I think Sister treasures that message, both as a testimonial and a memento, for our comrade who penned it will return no more, either to enliven his ward or to make melody behind the palms of West End drawing-rooms.

THE EMPIRE'S ROLL OF HONOUR

MAJOR-GENERAL RICHARD HUTTON DAVIES, C.B., who died on May 9th, had been in the New Zealand forces, held a commission in the Hawere Mounted Rifles, and went to South Africa with the first New Zealand contingent, subsequently commanding three other contingents from the Dominion, the first oversea officer to be given command of a composite column in the Boer War. He was twice mentioned in despatches and awarded the Queen's Medal with five clasps, and the King's Medal with two, and the C.B. In 1905 he was appointed Inspector-General of the New Zealand Forces and a member of the Council of Defence. In 1907 he came to England to the Staff College at Camberley, and was given command of the 6th Infantry Brigade at Aldershot, the first oversea officer to command a British brigade. He commanded it in the early days of the war, and was invalided to England in October, 1914. On recovery he was promoted major-general and given command of the 20th Division, New Armies, in France. Again invalided in 1916, he was appointed to the training centre at Cannock Chase. He was twice mentioned in despatches during the war.

Lieut.-Colonel Hugh Acland Troyte, of Huntsham Court, Bampton. North Devon, was educated at Eton, and served for six years with the 20th Hussars. In 1899 he retired to his estate and devoted himself to public and philanthropic work. At the outbreak of war he commanded a Territorial battalion of the Devonshire Regiment, to which he had belonged for many years, and took it to India and Mesopotamia. After a year at home, invalided, he again volunteered, and was appointed area commandant in Italy and in France, and was killed by a shell while evacuating the civil population of a French village.

Captain Thomas George Deane Burdett, M.C., Royal Welsh Fusiliers, was son of the late Mr. G. Deane Burdett, bank manager at Rhyl. Admitted a solicitor, he was a member of the University of Wales O.T.C. at Aberystwyth, and was given a commission in the Royal Welsh Fusiliers in September, 1914. He saw much service in Gallipoli, Egypt, and Palestine, and was killed in action in the Holy Land. He was mentioned in despatches in March, 1917, and in April, 1918, was awarded the Military Cross.

Captain John Eric Trevor-Jones, M.C., Rifle Brigade, was educated at Downside School and Clare College, Cambridge. He was gazetted to the 6th Rifle Brigade, and went to France in July, 1916, being attached to the 10th Rifle Brigade, of which he became captain and adjutant. He was awarded the M.C. in March, 1917. Six weeks before his death in action he was attached to the brigade in which his brother was serving when killed at the Battle of the Somme on July 1st, 1916.

Maj.-Gen. R. H. DAVIES, C.B. Lt.-Col. P. A. CLIVE, M.C. Lt.-Col. H. A. TROYTE. Maj. H. P. PEDDEROD. Mai. G. R. KENDERDINE, M.C.

CAPT. J. E. TREVOR-JONES, M.C.

10th Rifle Brigade

Killed in Action   *April 22nd, 1918*

2nd LIEUT. E. C. LORD

Irish Guards

Killed in Action   *May 8th, 1918*

2nd LIEUT. EUSTACE CHARLES LORD, Irish Guards, only son of the late Major C. H. Lord, Royal Welch Fusiliers, of 9, Moreton Avenue, Harpenden, and of Mrs. Lord, of 38, Rivers Street, Bath, was born on October 6th, 1898, came to Downside in May, 1908, and left in March, 1917. He was an able and high-spirited boy, bright, cheerful, and witty. He passed the Lower Certificate in 1913, with First Classes in Latin and Greek, and the Higher Certificate in 1914, 1915 and 1916, gaining a History distinction in 1916. He was on the staff of *The Raven* and took a conspicuous part in the debates of the Abingdon Society. He was a member of Caverel House. In the first year of the war, his father, Major C. H. Lord, who although over sixty years of age, had rejoined his old regiment, the Royal Welch Fusiliers, on the outbreak of hostilities, died suddenly whilst training men of the new army ; the son was destined to give his life in the same great cause when it was nearing its final triumph. On leaving Downside, in March, 1917, Eustace Lord at once commenced his military training at Bushey ; four months later he received a commission in the Irish Guards, spent two months at Warley, and proceeded to the Western Front in October, 1917. About five weeks later he wrote : " I am very happy out here and enjoying life thoroughly." After taking part with credit in the fighting against the enemy attack in the following March, he was killed in the early morning of May 8th, 1918, by an explosion caused by a German shell. He was nineteen years of age at the time of his death.

From the many letters received by his mother from those who knew him in the Army, it is evident that he was held in high regard and affection by both officers and men. The following are a few extracts :—

From his commanding officer :—

" He was going round the posts at ' stand to ' with his company commander, Captain Budd, when a trench mortar shell hit the post, killing Captain Budd, your son and seven others. It was simply cruel, bad luck. Your son was such a good, cheery boy, and we all liked him. He was a good soldier and did very well when the Huns attacked us in March last. . . . The battalion has certainly lost one of the nicest, cheeriest little fellows that ever breathed."

From the officer commanding the battalion at the time :—

" I cannot tell you how sorry we all are. The boy was so young and so keen and always had a cheery smile and way with him, and when I saw him so short a time before he seemed so cheerful and happy, that it seems doubly sad. I had him buried with Captain Budd in separate graves in a little military cemetery, in a pretty little ruined village, not far from where he was killed. The place is really an orchard, and all the trees in it are in blossom in spite of the shells that fly over. . . . We are having a cross with his name and regiment erected."

From the Catholic chaplain attached to the Irish Guards :—

" First of all I should like to tell you how fond we all were of your son, and what a gallant, cheerful officer he proved himself to be. He was very brave and always bright and happy, and the men were all devoted to him. His death is a great loss to me, for Catholic officers like him are rare, and he was always an example to the men. He used to serve my Mass on Sundays. He received the General Absolution and Holy Communion only five hours before his death. . . . It is difficult to say how long a time elapsed between the explosion and Eustace's death ; probably only a few seconds—at the utmost a minute. According to the stretcher-bearer's account Eustace just opened and shut his eyes—that is all. When I saw him he looked quite unchanged and was in no way disfigured. . . . I buried him the same day, and his grave is marked with a cross."

From one of his fellow-officers :—

" I knew him quite well, both at Bushey when we were in the same platoon, and out here, when we were in the same brigade. . . . He won golden opinions out here as a boy with charming manners and a soldier with a gallant spirit. Captain Budd, a great friend of mine, always spoke most highly of him. . . . I was present when they were buried, side by side, behind a pretty little French village, on one of the most perfect evenings that May can bring. A brief life like that leaves only good behind it, a sort of golden atmosphere with nothing to spoil the fuller perfection of the Life Beyond."

About three months after his death, his former school friend, Hugh O'Farrell, wrote of him as follows :—

" Lord seems to have been exceptionally popular with everyone here, and I often hear them talking about him. Though not physically very strong, he seems to have been very plucky. He was in this company and was called ' Rosey.' "

LIEUT. H. E. DOLAN, M.C.
Royal Air Force

Killed in Action   *May 12th, 1918*

LIEUT. HENRY ERIC DOLAN, Royal Air Force, elder son of Mr. Alfred A. Dolan, of 11, Horse Fair, Banbury, Oxfordshire, was born on January 20th, 1896, came to Downside in September, 1909, and left in July, 1913, in which month he passed the Higher Certificate. He played Association Football in the First Eleven, 1911-12, and Rugby in the First Fifteen, 1913 ; in this latter year he also played in the Cricket and Hockey Elevens. He was a corporal and bugler in the Officers' Training Corps, and attended camp three times. He was a good shot, and was second in the Shooting Competition in 1913. A most useful member of his House, he represented Roberts at Hockey, Cricket and Sports, and took part in its O.T.C. section in the Inter-House Contest of 1913.

At the time of the outbreak of the war, Eric Dolan was in Canada, and at once joined the First Canadian Contingent, arriving in England in October, 1914. On November 23rd he obtained a commission in the Royal Field Artillery, and went to France in August, 1915. In the following year he took part in the fighting on the Somme, was twice wounded, and was awarded the Military Cross in January, 1917, "for continual good service during the past year in personally superintending the Brigade communications often under heavy shell fire. A very gallant officer—on one occasion he continued at his work under shell fire after he had been wounded."

In April, 1917, he joined the Royal Air Force, but was in hospital a good deal, off and on, with trench fever, and did not get to France with his squadron (No. 74) until April, 1918. He was a brilliant airman, and met with great success. At 5.30 on the evening of May 12th, he went out on an offensive patrol with ten other machines ; they dived on about the same number of German machines, six of which were brought down in the ensuing fight, the remainder escaping. Dolan did not return to the British lines with the patrol, and was at once reported as missing ; later on he was officially reported killed in action on May 12th, 1918. He was twenty-two years of age. About two months afterwards his cousin, who made inquiries concerning him, was able to add the following information :

" It seems that they were scrapping with several Huns over the line and had driven them off when Eric's machine was seen to go down in a spinning nose dive. Either he or the machine was hit, but no one actually saw him crash. I wish you could have heard the way the major spoke of him. He said he was one of the finest pilots they had, and was absolutely without fear. . . . They said he was the heart and soul of the place, and that his mechanics cried when they heard he was done for."

Shortly after the engagement, his commanding officer, Major K. L. Caldwell, wrote to Eric Dolan's father as follows :—

"The squadron is very much upset over it, as he was most popular with officers and men, and his skill and courage as a fighting pilot were exceptional. In the thirteen fights he has had in this squadron he has crashed five German machines and driven down three others absolutely out of control, which is really a marvellous record. A few days ago he was recommended for a further reward, and this is about due to appear in the *Gazette*."

About the same time his Flight Commander wrote in the following terms :—

"Eric, or Bolo, as was his nickname, was in my flight, and he was far and away the most wonderful fighting man it has been my good fortune to meet. Always cheerful and happy, he was the life and soul of the whole squadron, whether at work or play. Always first with me in attack, he showed superb contempt for danger in any form, and his success in air fighting during the short time he was out here, constitutes a record. His loss to the squadron is a very severe blow indeed, and I am afraid he cannot be replaced (which is a very serious thing to say nowadays in the Air Force). It may interest you to know that in the scrap referred to we totally destroyed six of the enemy machines, and Eric's desire to account for the other two or three may be responsible for his disappearance . . . there was a very strong west wind blowing during the day in question, and his engine may have failed him. In any case, I am confident that he would do the right thing under any circumstances, so much faith had I in him. He was my nearest chum, and we always fought together and he was a braver man than I. I cannot pay him a greater tribute than this. You should be a very proud father in having possessed such a man for a son."

Captain E. Mannock, R.A.F., *D.S.O. and Bar*, *M.C. and Bar*, the gallant and brilliant airman who wrote the above, brought down a total of fifty enemy aeroplanes before he was reported missing from July 26th, 1918.

Another of Eric Dolan's fellow-officers added this further tribute:

"I have the honour to serve in the same squadron in which he so greatly distinguished himself . . . I think I may claim to have been an intimate friend of Eric's and flew with him several times in France, and may I say that he was the bravest man I ever met, and his example an inspiration to the squadron."

LIEUT.-COL. E. R. S. PRIOR, D.S.O., M.C.

South Lancashire Regiment

Died of Wounds   *May 27th, 1918*

LIEUT.-COL. EDWARD ROBERT SEYMOUR PRIOR, *D.S.O., M.C.*, South Lancashire Regiment (attached 11th Cheshire Regiment), younger son of Mr. F. H. Prior, of Broadway, Horndean, Hants., was born on May 2nd, 1890, came to Downside in September, 1905, and left in July, 1908. His life at school was happy and uneventful ; he was a good-natured, undemonstrative, entirely friendly boy, who got on well with everybody. By the time of the Great War he had developed into a superb soldier and a brilliant, successful and popular officer ; his career in the Army from the time of his landing in France until his death was marked throughout by the most conspicuous bravery, resource and military skill. He held the rank of captain in 1916, of major early in 1917, and he became Lieut.-Col. later in the same year. He was awarded the M.C., Bar to the M.C., and the D.S.O., and was mentioned several times in despatches. By a happy coincidence, the chaplain attached at one period to his regiment was a member of the Downside Community, and had been a contemporary of his in the school.

To him we are indebted for the following account :—

" He received the M.C. and Bar for work on the Somme in 1916. He was major and second in command of the 8th South Lancs. Regiment at the beginning of 1917. As major he actually led the battalion at Messines on the 7th of June. The same year at Ypres the colonel of that battalion was wounded on the first day of our attack, July 31st, and Major Prior took command. Soon after that date, he became Lieut.-Colonel, and commanded the 8th South Lancs. until the old colonel returned in November. Col. Prior then took command of the 11th Cheshire Regiment. He was awarded his D.S.O. in the New Year's Honours of 1918. He particularly distinguished himself on March 21st and the following days on the Bapaume-Cambrai Road and the defence of Bapaume. He also did most excellent work in resisting the attack on Ploegsteert of April 10th, and more especially that on La Clytte on April 29th. Finally he was seriously wounded on the afternoon of May 27th, and was only taken out of a little village south of the Aisne just in time to avoid capture. It is almost certain, though not official, that he died a few hours later. An officer who saw him being taken out of the village said he was already dead. . . . He was absolutely worshipped by all who knew him, and as a soldier he was hard to beat."

At first there appears to have been much uncertainty as to what actually happened after he was wounded, and conflicting statements were made. He was seen to fall during the engagement, badly wounded in head, stomach and feet, and was heard to say to his men : " Carry on, and don't mind me." One report added that he was seen being carried off by the Germans, and it was hoped for some time that he might be alive as a prisoner. Immense but unavailing efforts were made to ascertain if this was the case. There can be no doubt that he remained for some time lying on the field where he fell. It is possible that the Germans, finding him badly wounded, may have abandoned the attempt to remove him, which explanation would reconcile the well-authenticated reports stated above. In any case it seems certain that this gallant Old Gregorian died of wounds received in action on May 27th, 1918. He was twenty-eight years of age at the time.

The official statement of the award of the D.S.O., gazetted on January 1st, 1918, was as follows :—

" For conspicuous gallantry, able leadership and devotion to duty, whilst commanding his battalion during the fighting at Messines and Ypres from June to September, 1917. In the battle of Messines his battalion captured and consolidated all its objectives and took numerous prisoners and machine guns. At Ypres, after the attack on July 31st, Col. Prior held the Westhoek Ridge for six days under very heavy shell fire and the most adverse weather conditions, and during the period August 7th to August 18th, his battalion was continually in the forward area and did excellent work in consolidating captured positions and carrying up stores. The energy and cheerfulness of this officer have set a very fine example to the officers and men of his battalion."

LIEUT. N. E. J. C. LEAHY
Royal Field Artillery

Killed in Action   *August 9th,* 1918

LIEUT. NOEL EDWARD JOSEPH CARROLL LEAHY, Royal Field Artillery, was the third son of the late Mr. Thomas J. Carroll Leahy, J.P., of Woodfort, Mallow, Co. Cork, and was born on December 23rd, 1898. He was educated at Ladycross and Downside (September, 1912, to July, 1915). He played in the Second Football Fifteen in 1914, and for his House (Barlow) at Hockey in 1915. After passing through Woolwich, he received a commission in the Royal Field Artillery in May, 1916, and went to the Western Front. He was killed in action in France on August 9th, 1918, at the age of nineteen.

LIEUT. LOUIS MARY JOHN BELLOC, Royal Engineers (attached Royal Air Force), was the eldest son of Mr. Hilaire Belloc, of Kingsland, Shipley, near Horsham, and was born on September 23rd, 1897. He came to Downside in September, 1911, and left in June, 1915. He was an able and attractive boy, talented and versatile. He was a member of Caverel House, which he represented at Hockey ; he also played Hockey sometimes for the Second and sometimes for the First School Eleven. In 1913 and 1914 he passed the Higher Certificate, and in the summer of 1915 was placed eighteenth in the entrance examination for the Royal Military Academy, Woolwich, which he entered shortly after. Later on he was gazetted to the Royal Engineers, and went to France, where he was wounded. From the front he wrote a number of interesting letters to Downside, where he had several friends in the Community, on one occasion enclosing a sketch which he had made of the grave of his friend, Philip Koe, who had been killed in action in August, 1916. He also paid us a visit when on leave. Having joined the Royal Air Force he was killed in action before Cambrai, on August 26th, 1918, at the age of twenty.

LIEUT. L. M. J. BELLOC
Royal Engineers, attached R.A.F.

Killed in Action   *August 26th,* 1918

PRIVATE F. LETEUX

Canadian Machine Gun Corps

Killed in Action   *September 2nd, 1918*

PRIVATE FRANCIS LETEUX, Machine Gun Corps, Canadian Army, son of the late Mr. Louis Leteux, and of Mrs. Leteux, of Harrogate, was born at Elbœuf, in France, on June 1st, 1866, and was educated at St. Edmund's College, Douai, and at Downside. He was in the school from December, 1879, till July, 1883, during the Priorship of Cardinal Gasquet. After leaving school, he went with another Downside boy to the United States, where a career of strenuous activity and adventure awaited him, and where most of his subsequent life was spent. On March 4th, 1909, he married Miss Hala Wilson, in Tucumari, New Mexico. They had one son, Louis Leteux. Desirous of serving in the war, although over fifty years of age, he enlisted in the Canadian Army, in May, 1917, before his adopted country entered the great conflict. In the following month, he left Canada for overseas service and arrived in England as a member of a Winnipeg draft of the C.A.M.C. On his first leave, he had the happiness of visiting his brother, Father Charles Leteux, of Hemsworth, Yorkshire. About the same time, Father Prior received a letter from him full of affectionate remembrance of Downside, and asking for prayers. After a period of training at the C.A.M.C. depôt at Westenhanger, Kent, he was graded A1 in health, and was transferred to the Canadian Machine Gun Corps. He sailed for France, his native land, on January 27th, 1918, full of patriotism and religious faith. After experiencing much severe fighting, in which he rendered excellent service as a gunner, he was killed in action on September 2nd, 1918. He was fifty-two years of age. One of his officers wrote of him as follows :—

" He was one of the first boys I have come in contact with out here. In fact many's the time we have chatted together in the trenches about old France and his dear ones at home. Regarding his end, it may be of some comfort to you to know that he died instantly, and that his body received a Catholic burial. His grave has been recorded. . . . Being a Catholic like himself, we used to discuss many Church matters, and his stories about France were very interesting to me. He was always prepared to come into the line, for I used to go to the church with the boys for

Confession and Communion. Never do I remember him complaining about hardships. Always a smile, and doing his duty like a hero."

The following further details have been forwarded to us by his brother :—

" In America he saw every kind of adventurous life, being at one time a cowboy in the Indian Territory ; at another, a gold miner ; at another he worked at lumber-cutting in the Far West, where he built two Catholic churches. On one occasion he shot a ' bad ' man who had threatened him and fixed his revolver on him, but Frank got his shot in first and killed him. He was tried and acquitted, in fact, complimented. I don't think there was any adventurous calling that he did not follow at some time or other. . . . We are French, and in the recent war he could not resist the call of his country when he saw its dire need. I volunteered twice as a chaplain, but was refused, so I raised a battalion of miners here instead in the volunteer days. In his last letter, written on August 23rd, he said he thought the next push would be the final one, and that the war would end in November, which was pretty correct. He also said that the fight out of which he had just come was the Germans' greatest defeat of the war, and that his battalion made a record by going a mile further than any other battalion on the Western Front.

" ' I hope God watches over me as well in the next scrap as He did in the last,' he wrote ; ' one realises how entirely one is in His hands. It was a splendid sight to see the cavalry sweeping across open country. But tanks are worth a regiment of cavalry against machine guns. They certainly saved us many a life.' His officer wrote of him : ' He was killed by machine gun fire while advancing with great bravery and determination. It was through men like him that our very successful advance on that day was made possible.' "

LIEUT. J. M. TIDMARSH

West Riding Regiment, attached R.A.F.

Killed in Flying Accident   *September 3rd, 1918*

LIEUT. JOHN M. TIDMARSH, West Riding Regiment (attached Royal Air Force), was the third son of Mr. David Tidmarsh, of Lota, Limerick, and was born on May 6th, 1893. He came to Downside in September, 1905, and left in April, 1910. At School he took part with success in athletics. After leaving Downside he spent a short time at Wimbledon College, and then proceeded to Sandhurst. He passed into the Regular Army in 1913, being gazetted to the Duke of Wellington's (West Riding) Regiment. After service in Ireland and India he joined the Royal Air Force in September, 1917, and after a few months' training was sent to Suez as Instructor. In July, 1918, he was granted a month's leave, which he spent at his home in Ireland. In August he was appointed Instructor at Doncaster, and whilst occupying that position he was killed in a flying accident on September 3rd, 1918. His mother has supplied us with the following details :—

"He had been about ten days in Doncaster. On Tuesday, September 3rd, about 6.30 in the evening, Jack took up a pupil to teach him the Innerman turn to the left ; they had just turned when an aviator, flying behind Jack and taking photographs of the latter's machine, collided with our dear boy's aeroplane, cutting it in two. As it fell about five thousand feet, both Jack and his pupil were killed. The priest was fetched at once and gave conditional absolution. Jack looked as if asleep, and there were no marks on his face. Both of the boys were seen coming out of the Confessional on the previous Saturday, so I suppose they were at Holy Communion on Sunday. Jack was also at his duties here in August. The poor fellow who caused the accident lived for seven days in great agony ; both his legs were broken and his head was badly injured. His greatest suffering was sorrow that he could not be taken to ask pardon of Jack and his pupil ; he had no idea they were killed.

"Jack loved Downside, and used to say it had a wonderful future before it. He was wonderfully affectionate to his own, and he loved his home. The officer who came over to represent Jack's squadron at the funeral was also a Catholic. He said Jack was very popular with his pupils—he was so cheery with them and so keen on his work. He never allowed a pupil up before he himself had examined every bolt and part of the machine, and, if a pupil looked in the least nervous, he would say, ' Now don't go up to-day—wait until to-morrow.' "

At the time of his death Jack Tidmarsh was twenty-five years of age.

2nd LIEUT. C. E. BELLORD

Royal Air Force

Killed in Action   *September 15th, 1918*

2nd LIEUT. CHARLES EDMUND BELLORD, Royal Air Force, second son of Mr. Edmund Bellord, of 40, Belsize Grove, N.W., was born on January 6th, 1900, came to Downside in September, 1910, and left in July, 1916. He was a boy of a very English type, plucky and straightforward, somewhat shy and reserved, but with much strength of character and quiet humour. He was a member of Caverel House. He went up to Oxford in 1917, and spent one year at Balliol. On attaining the age of eighteen, he volunteered for the Royal Air Force, and after six months' training in England he was sent to France in August, 1918. About three weeks later he took part with six other planes in an air fight over Metz. They were attacked by a superior German force, and compelled to retire to the English lines. Bellord did not return with the others, and was posted as " missing." At first it was thought that he was wounded and a prisoner in the hands of the Germans, and it was reported that he had died of wounds in a military hospital, but the authorities are now fully satisfied that he lost his life in the attack over Metz on September 15th, 1918. It seems certain also that his grave has been located in the neighbourhood. At the time of his death he was eighteen years and eight months old.

In a number of the *Oxford Magazine*, published shortly after, Charles Bellord was described as " very mature in character, yet with plenty of humour and a charm which made him a delightful friend," words which will be appreciated by all who knew him at Downside.

2nd LIEUT. HUGH ARCHIBALD O'FARRELL, Irish Guards, only son of Sir Edward O'Farrell, K.C.B., of Cuil-na-greine, Carrickmines, co. Dublin, was born on April 9th, 1899, came to Downside in September, 1908, and left in July 1917. He was a clever and capable boy, and took a conspicuous part in many school activities. The exercise of authority brought out his natural strength of character, and he made an effective and successful Prefect and Head of the School. He played in the First Football Fifteen in 1915, and in the Second Hockey Eleven in 1916, and at various times for his House (Caverel) at Football, Hockey and Cricket. In the O.T.C., in which he did excellent work, he was successively Lance-Corporal, Sergeant, and Cadet Officer, and he took part with the Caverel Section in the Inter-House competitions of 1915 and 1917. He passed the Lower Certificate in 1912 and 1913 and the Higher Certificate in the four following years, securing a distinction in History in 1916, and in French in 1917. He was appointed a House Prefect in 1916, and a School Prefect, Head of Caverel House, and Head of the School in 1917. He was a member of the choir from 1908 to 1912, and sang in the chorus of " The Gondoliers " in 1911.

He took part with distinction in the debates of the Abingdon Society, and was editor of *The Raven* in 1917. He was awarded an Exhibition at Worcester College, Oxford, in 1917, and on leaving school he was also awarded the Gregorian Scholarship. He spent part of his last summer holidays at the Downside Harvest Camp, in Norfolk. After training at Bushey, he was gazetted to the Irish Guards in February, 1918, and went to the front in the following May. He was killed in action in France, on September 27th, 1918, at the age of nineteen.

The following is from a letter received by Sir Edward O'Farrell from the colonel of his son's battalion :—

" Your son was killed in action on September 27th, when we were attacking the Hindenburg Line and capturing Flesquières. . . . . . Although he only joined my battalion in June last, I had very soon marked him down as a most capable and promising young officer, and I can assure you that your loss is also a very great loss indeed to the battalion. He soon made himself very popular with officers and men, and, in expressing

2nd LIEUT. H. A. O'FARRELL

Irish Guards

Killed in Action   *September 27th, 1918*

my sympathy to you, I am expressing that of the whole battalion. It may be some comfort to you to know that he died at the head of his platoon, while leading them in the attack, and therefore died as gallantly as any gentleman could wish . . . He was buried by Father Scannell in the Guards' Divisional Military Cemetery that has been registered near Flesquières."

Lieut. P. R. Barry, who was in the School with him at Downside, wrote as follows :—

" He was hit by a machine-gun bullet during the advance on the 27th. The first wound was bad, and a sergeant in his platoon tried to bind it up. As he was doing so, another bullet went through the sergeant's fingers and killed Hugh at once. He can have suffered no pain. He had been to Mass and Holy Communion a day or so before. . . . I have known him for years, and I cannot say how much I will miss him and how sorry everyone is about his death. During his time in the battalion he had made a great reputation as an officer, and he will be a terrible loss to the battalion."

Another of his fellow-officers thus described him :—

" I wish to say how magnificently he bore himself all through the day, and how conspicuous he was as he led his company forward, his steel helmet in his hand. I can see him now, walking quietly on, full of keenness and glorying in his responsibility and as I watched him I admired him more than I can say. . . . His company still say of him : ' He was a great lad,' and if you know the Irish soldier, it is the finest thing to be said of him."

And the following is from a letter from Fr. J. Scannell, C.F. :—

" I was always struck by his kindness, sincerity and solid piety. He was, I know, most assiduous in attending Mass and the Sacraments with the battalion . . . He has left an extraordinarily good impression with the officers and men of his battalion. Many have spoken to me about him in the highest terms. . . . I shall remember him as a brave Irish Catholic gentleman who lived a good life and died a heroic death. As priests we have every reason to be proud of our Catholic officers and men, and though, as in this case, our hearts go out in sympathy to the bereaved friends at home, we are happy in the conviction that the soundness of their faith and the heroism of their death go far to procure that respect and admiration for Catholicism which is daily growing out here."

CAPTAIN DEMETRIUS FREDERICK GREEN, 5th Northumberland Fusiliers, youngest son of the late Mr. Charles Martin Green, of Gosforth, Northumberland, was born on May 14th, 1883. He received his early education at Stonyhurst, came to Downside in September, 1897, and left in July, 1900. He was Librarian of the Petre Library and Secretary of the Abingdon Society in 1899 and 1900. In the latter year, he passed the Higher Certificate. During his last year at school he played for the Hockey and Cricket Elevens. He was a useful member of the choir and was always to the front in the School theatrical entertainments. After leaving Downside he held an appointment in the Bank of England until 1906, when he left for India to take up a similar appointment in the Bank of Bengal. He returned to England in 1910, and in the following year married Miss Beatrice Parke, daughter of Mr. Henry Parke, of Scarborough. In 1914, on the outbreak of the war, he obtained a commission in the Northumberland Fusiliers, and saw much active service. In 1917 he received a staff appointment in Italy and was returning thither, after having been on leave in England, when he was taken ill in Paris. He died of influenza, followed by pneumonia, in a military hospital on October 15th, 1918, fortified with the last rites of the Church. He was thirty-five years of age, and held the rank of captain. He was buried in the Parisian Cimetière de Pantin, on October 18th, with full military honours.

Fred Green was a brother of Dom Edward Green, of Downside Abbey, and a nephew of the Somerset Herald.

CAPT. D. F. GREEN
5th Northumberland Fusiliers

Died on Service   *October 15th, 1918*

LIEUT. C. P. FRIEND

Royal Field Artillery

Died on Service   *October 15th, 1918*

LIEUT. CHARLES PHILIP FRIEND, Royal Field Artillery, second son of the late Mr. Charles Friend, of Seville, was born on April 2nd, 1892, came to Downside in October, 1902, and left in July, 1910. He passed the Lower Certificate in 1907, and the Higher Certificate in 1909 and 1910, with distinction in Spanish. He played in the Second Cricket Eleven in 1910. He was a useful member of the choir, first as a treble, and later as a bass. On leaving Downside he went to New College, Oxford, and took Final Schools in the Summer Term of 1913. During the following year he was at Bonn University, where he matriculated. After the outbreak of war he joined the Royal Field Artillery, and was sent to the Western Front. In September, 1916, he was wounded during the fighting near the Somme. The Guards had made several attacks east of Guillemont and Guinchy, which had failed. One company lost its bearings, and a man was sent back to the artillery in support to find out its position. With this man as a guide, Lieut. Friend and two others were told to locate the company during the night, but in trying to do so they lost their way in the dark, and found themselves unexpectedly within a few yards of the German trenches. At the same moment they were noticed by the Germans and fired upon. A bullet passed through Lieut. Friend's right lung, narrowly missing the spine. He fell into a shell-hole and shouted to the men behind him. About half an hour later the guide came to him and helped him back to his own lines.

After recovering from his wound, Charles Friend was appointed to an official position in Madrid, and later on was transferred to Barcelona, where he died of pneumonia on October 15th, 1918. He was twenty-six years of age.

CAPTAIN ARTHUR ERIC McMURROUGH CUMING, *M.C.*, 1st Royal Irish Fusiliers, only son of Lieut.-Col. A. E. Cuming, Laurentinum, co. Cork, was born on June 6th, 1898, came to Downside in January, 1912, and left in June, 1915. He played in the Junior Cricket Eleven and in the Colts Football Fifteen in 1913, in the Second Cricket Eleven and in the First Football Fifteen in 1914, and in the Second Hockey Eleven in 1915. He represented his House (Caverel) at Cricket, Football, Hockey, Tennis and Sports. In 1915, he won the First Division prize and the School Challenge Cup for boxing. He was a House Prefect in 1914 and 1915. After passing through Sandhurst, he received a commission in the Royal Irish Fusiliers and was sent to the Western Front, where he saw much fighting. In the summer of 1918 he was awarded both the Military Cross and bar " in recognition of gallantry and devotion to duty in the field." The following were the official statements accompanying the awards :—

Military Cross :—

" When on patrol with four other ranks he engaged an enemy patrol, killing four and dispersing the remainder in a hand-to-hand struggle. On this and other occasions this officer was the means of rendering valuable information to the brigade."

Bar to the Military Cross :—

" When in charge of a party of scouts raiding an enemy post to obtain an identification he led his men through a gap in the wire, and charged the post. Two of the enemy stood their ground, but he wounded one and dragged him struggling 200 yards back to our lines. In this enterprise he displayed fine courage and determination."

On October 21st he was wounded in action at Courtrai, and died in a British Red Cross Hospital at Wimereux on October 26th, 1918. He was twenty years of age, and held the rank of captain.

CAPT. A. E. McM. CUMING, M.C.

1st Royal Irish Fusiliers

Died of Wounds   *October 26th, 1918*

CAPT. J. C. WOOLLETT

Royal Air Force

Died on Service   *November 16th, 1918*

CAPTAIN JOHN CHARLES WOOLLETT, Royal Air Force, son of Dr. C. J. Woollett, F.R.C.S., of Ambleside, Streatham, S.W., was born on May 20th, 1891, came to Downside in September, 1901, and left in July, 1905. In October, 1914, he joined the 6th London Brigade of the Royal Field Artillery as 2nd lieutenant. Later on he transferred to the Royal Air Force, in which he held the rank of captain at the time of his death, at Hythe, from pneumonia, on November 16th, 1918. He was twenty-seven years of age.

We received the following further details in a letter from his father :—

" My son joined the Army at the beginning of the war, and obtained a commission in the Territorial Artillery, with whom he went to France, and served there for about two years. He then volunteered for the R.A.F. and, after a period of training, was made pilot ; he returned to the Western Front and carried out a great deal of observation work for the artillery. In the summer of 1918 he was appointed to the School of Aerial Gunnery at Hythe, he married in October, and was made captain. In November he was attacked with influenza, but nevertheless played in a football match for his team, as he had promised to do. Pneumonia developed and he died at Hythe, and was buried with military honours at Seabrook Cemetery. He was a great favourite everywhere, being upright, kind, and a good sportsman. He was very fond of his old School."

CORPORAL CLEMENT CHAMBERLAIN CAFFERATA,
Canadian Forestry Corps, son of Mr. R. P. C. Cafferata, of
Staunton Hall, Orston, Notts, was born in September, 1885,
came to Downside in April, 1896, and left in July, 1905.

At school "he excelled in Natural History studies. He was also
looked upon by his companions as an authority on angling. He
was a very keen long-distance runner, and would often get a set
together for a run" (*The Raven*, December, 1905).

During the war he served in the Canadian Forestry Corps,
and was in France for over two years. He died in a military
hospital at Eastbourne, on February 8th, 1919, aged thirty-three.

In Memoriam

CORPORAL C. C. CAFFERATA

Canadian Forestry Corps

Died of Illness   *February 8th, 1919*

PRIVATE L. J. S. WELD-BLUNDELL

Queen's Westminster Rifles

Died on Service   *February 8th, 1919*

PRIVATE LOUIS JOSEPH S. WELD-BLUNDELL, Queen's Westminster Rifles, was the younger and only surviving son of Mr. C. J. Weld-Blundell, of Ince Blundell Hall, Lancashire, and was the heir to the Ince Blundell estates, and heir-presumptive to the Lulworth estates in Dorsetshire. He was born on March 16th, 1889, and was educated at Downside and Beaumont. He was in the School at Downside from September, 1902 to April, 1905, and was a very promising football player, taking part in the Second Eleven matches in 1904. He had a fine voice, and after leaving school studied singing at Paris and Milan. When war broke out, he enlisted in the King's Liverpool Regiment on August 7th, 1914, and afterwards transferred to the Queen's Westminster Rifles. A fine sportsman, who never minded roughing it, he proved a most efficient and successful soldier, liked by one and all. He survived almost continual active service, two years in France and nearly two years in Salonika and Palestine, and he was with the first regiment that marched into Jerusalem. From time to time he had been urged by his general in Palestine, and others, to take a commission, and would have done so, in the Irish Guards, if the war had continued. In October, 1918, he arrived in England on a month's leave, returning to his regiment on the day before the Armistice was concluded. Whilst on his way home to be demobilised he was taken ill with influenza, which developed into pneumonia, and he died in the Eighth Canadian Hospital at Dunkirk on February 8th, 1919, at the age of twenty-nine. He had received the last Sacraments from the chaplain who visited him during his illness. He was buried in the cemetery at Dunkirk, and, shortly after, a Requiem Mass was celebrated at Farm Street Church, in the presence of a detachment of the Queen's Westminster Rifles. His elder brother, 2nd Lieut. Richard S. Weld-Blundell, Liverpool Regiment, had died as the result of an accident whilst on active service, on January 1st, 1916.

LIEUT. EUSTACE JOSEPH McGEE, Royal Air Force, son of the late Mr. McGee, of Melbourne, Australia, was born on October 24th, 1898, came to Downside in September, 1907, and left in July, 1910, to join his relatives who had gone to Canada, where he continued his education. During the war, though under age for military service at the time, he joined the Canadian Field Artillery, along with a number of older boys from his school, and was sent to England. During his stay in this country he paid a visit to Downside. Later on he joined the Royal Air Force, and was killed in an aeroplane accident at Ampthill, Bedford, on the 12th of February, 1919. He was twenty years of age.

LIEUT. E. J. McGEE

Royal Air Force

Killed in Flying Accident   *February 12th, 1919*

LIEUT. T. J. McMANUS

2nd Middlesex Regiment

Died of Wounds   *December 23rd, 1919*

LIEUT. TERENCE JOSEPH McMANUS, 2nd Middlesex Regiment, second son of Mr. John McManus, of 237, Hammersmith Road, London, W., was born on May 4th, 1897, came to Downside in September, 1910, and left in April, 1915. He was a member of Roberts House during the latter part of his time at school. His natural charm, unselfishness and pluck, together with a delightful gift of humour, made him a universal favourite here, as was the case wherever he went. When he visited Downside shortly before his death, it was very evident that, in spite of many trying experiences and years of suffering, his character had simply developed along its natural lines ; he was quite unspoiled and as bright and joyous as ever.

At school he played Rugby successively for the Colts, the Second and First Fifteens and also for his House ; he was likewise in the Roberts Gym. and Sports Teams and Corps Section. For two years he sang in the choir as a tenor. In 1915 he left to receive his military training at Sandhurst. For the rest, we quote from an excellent account of Terence McManus, written with full knowledge and insight, and sent to us after his death, which occurred at Brighton on December 23rd, 1919, as the result of an operation for the wounds received on the Somme, July 1st, 1916. He was buried at Eastbourne.

" Terence McManus was very proud of and devoted to his school, and always spoke of it with great affection. Even in those days he was full of the sense of humour and gaiety and *joie de vivre* which all his life made him so popular with young and old, and from his own reminiscences his school life was a very happy one. On leaving Sandhurst in 1915 he was gazetted to the Middlesex Regiment, and after some months in England was sent to France in May, 1916, where he joined the 2nd Battalion. He was wounded in the fighting on the Somme on July 1st in that year. He fell near the German lines, and as our men had been driven back, no stretcher-bearers could be sent out on that shell-and-bullet-swept region. Very seriously wounded (his right thigh was fractured by a large piece of shell, and he had several other wounds as well), it was eight days before he was picked up, and during all that time, in the blazing July weather, he had no food, and very little water. He afterwards described his sufferings during those dreadful days. He had to lie very still during the daytime, for if he made the slightest movement the Germans fired at him. Twice parties of our own wounded, trying to find their way back to our line, came across him, and some of them gave him a little water. He gave his revolver to one man who promised to send him help if he himself got back alive. To relieve his thirst, which was the most dreadful part of his sufferings, he crawled painfully on his back, dragging the broken leg, to the bodies lying around him in order to get any water remaining in their water-bottles. After that gave out, he sucked a spoon he had in his pocket, which helped to check his thirst. Once or twice it rained, and then he sucked the moisture from his drenched tunic. When he moved at all, it had to be at night, or he was fired at. One night he managed to drag himself into a shell-hole, which afforded a little shelter. All that time he never lost hope, and said his rosary as he lay there. He had a strong feeling that his life would be saved in the end. Some of the time he must have been delirious, but he seemed to have been conscious most of the time. He suffered a great deal of pain from his wounds ; luckily the mud and blood must have congealed, or he would have bled to death. At last, on the 8th of July, he saw a party of English soldiers. It was a burial party, sent to bury the bodies lying round —it was not thought possible that anyone was alive after all that time. Terence tried to shout, and felt despair for the first time when he realised he was too weak to make a sound. He was just able to wave his arm feebly, and that mercifully attracted their attention. They put him on a stretcher and ran with him to a dressing station.

" The surgeon could hardly believe he had been lying out for eight days, but the state of his wound convinced him, and corroboration came later from the remnant of his battalion, which had been nearly wiped out. Terence's family, in the meantime, had suffered the greatest anxiety, as he had been posted as ' Wounded and missing,' and they could get no news of him. Then they heard he was alive and was on his way home. He was taken on a barge to the coast, and brought over in a hospital ship to England, and finally sent to the 3rd London General Hospital, Wandsworth. His wound was septic, and in a very bad condition, and for some time it was doubtful whether he could survive. But the wound healed, although the fractured bones did not unite, and after a time he was able to get about on crutches, which he used until the time of his death. From this hospital he was sent to the Great Central Hotel Hospital, and a few months later to Staveley Court Hospital, Eastbourne, where he received great kindness, and was very happy. His family were at Eastbourne, and he was able to spend a good deal of his time with them. Later he was sent to the orthopædic ward of Guy's Hospital, and from there to Shepherd's Bush. On April 18th, 1918, he was transferred to a section hospital of the last-named, the American Red Cross Hospital, Baroda House, in Kensington Palace Gardens, and, with brief intervals for leave, he remained there until the hospital closed in July, 1919. He was then transferred with the other patients to the Central Military Hospital for Officers, Brighton, where he died, after a very serious operation, on December 23rd, 1919, fortified by the rites of the Church. It had been decided after a consultation to operate, to unite the fractured ends of the femur. This operation had been deferred until more than three years after he had been wounded, so that the septic germs in the wound should quite die down, but the sepsis was still dormant in the bone, and the wound became infected.

" Terence's pluck and endurance and indomitable cheerfulness were the constant admiration of the surgeons and nurses as well as of his fellow-patients, with whom he was a very great favourite. He was operated upon on Friday, December 19th. He must have suffered great pain and discomfort—both legs were in plaster of Paris, which came to his chest, and he could not move, but he never complained or murmured. He realised that his wound might become septic again, and knew what that meant. He had talked of the possibility of his death, and was prepared for it. He received Holy Communion two days before his operation, and he was saying his rosary quietly to himself the evening before he died. His mother and sister, who were staying in Brighton to be near him, were with him when he died, and the priest anointed him and gave him absolution. He is buried at Eastbourne.

"'Terence made friends all his life, quite effortlessly and unconsciously, in a way unusual for a boy of his age. His high spirits and pluck, his constant cheerfulness, his kindness and thought for others, endeared him to a remarkable degree to people of widely varying characters and ages. He possessed the rare gift of a creative as well as an appreciative sense of humour, and a very quick brain. He was a clever mimic, and extraordinarily observant, and used to amuse his fellow-patients for hours with impersonations of hospital and other celebrities. His death was felt as a personal loss by these fellow patients—men accustomed to the idea of death, and to the quickly-made, and often quickly-forgotten friendships of hospital life; they spoke of him as of someone exceptional, and have never forgotten him. He radiated happiness, and it was enough for him to go into a ward, for all the faces to brighten at once. He was full of life, and had a power possessed by few, of stimulating and cheering others. At the casualty clearing station, where he was first brought in, almost dying, he still managed to say cheering words to the other wounded, and to make jokes to the surgeon. He made such an impression on this surgeon that he remembered him during all the intervening years, and on seeing his death in the paper, he wrote to Mrs. McManus saying that out of all the thousands that had passed through his hands, and though his acquaintance with him had been so brief, he had never forgotten this particular patient—had even remembered his name out of legions forgotten, and the pluck, endurance and heroic cheerfulness shown by her son had made a lasting impression on his mind. And this is the impression that will last in the minds and hearts of all who knew and loved Terence McManus."

Lightning Source UK Ltd.
Milton Keynes UK
UKOW06f1513020114

223838UK00002B/64/A